Outdoor Recreation In Canada

Outdoor Recreation In Canada

GEOFFREY WALL

EDITOR, THE UNIVERSITY OF WATERLOO

JOHN WILEY & SONS
Toronto New York Chichester Brisbane Singapore

Canadian Cataloguing in Publication Data

Main entry under title:

Outdoor recreation in Canada

Includes index.
ISBN 0-471-79605-0

1. Outdoor recreation - Canada.   I. Wall, Geoffrey.

GV191.44.088 1989   796.5'0971   C89-093440-1

Printed and bound in Canada by Gagne Printing Ltd.

10 9 8 7 6 5 4 3 2 1

Table of Contents

Preface

Canada is blessed with rich and varied opportunities for people to participate in outdoor recreation. There is also a substantial and growing literature on many aspects of outdoor recreation in Canada. However, although a limited number of books have been written on related topics, such as national parks, a comprehensive text has not been available on the subject. The editor of this volume has been teaching courses on outdoor recreation at the University of Waterloo since 1974, and frustration with the lack of suitable teaching resources and the encouragement of colleagues, particularly Geoff McBoyle, soon prompted the preparation of a volume on outdoor recreation in southern Ontario (Wall 1979). The book was produced specifically for an undergraduate course taught in the Department of Geography at the University of Waterloo and was published by that department. The book served its purpose well and was used as a class text by a number of other instructors, both inside and outside of Ontario, thereby confirming the need for a book of this type. The success of that volume and the length of time which has elapsed since it was first published suggest that the preparation of a new text is now overdue.

The present text retains the broad structure of the early volume but differs from it in a number of ways. The change from an emphasis on southern Ontario to a consideration of the whole of Canada should make this work less parochial than its predecessor and, therefore, of use to a larger number of readers. Each section of the earlier volume consisted of a collection of short papers, some of which were reproduced from other sources, while others were prepared specifically by the editor for the book. In this publication each major section is written in its entirety by a single author with an established reputation for his research and writing on the subject.

Authors were invited to contribute to the volume based primarily upon their previous scholarly writings but, to ensure that adequate regional coverage would be achieved, chapters were solicited from authors living in many parts of the country. All contributors teach at Canadian universities and all have training in geography, although not all currently teach in geography departments. Although authors have reached beyond disciplinary boundaries in preparing their contributions, similarity in disciplinary background has assisted in forging a common perspective.

Like its predecessor, this is an edited volume but it differs from many edited volumes in that, while no attempt has been made to impose a common writing style, a serious effort has been made to make this something more than a collection of individual papers. This was done in several ways. First, a logical structure for the book was prepared by the editor so that each author was aware of the context of his chapter. Secondly, all authors were aware of the contents of the publication on southern Ontario. Thirdly, draft chapters were circulated to contributors for comment. Finally, and perhaps most importantly, authors met for several days at the University of Waterloo, where synopses of chapters were presented orally and suggestions for improvements made. The frank but friendly discussion was a pleasant learning experience for all participants. I wish to thank all authors for their willingness to listen to suggestions from colleagues, for making modifications to their chapters where appropriate, for the chapters themselves, and for their patience during the long period when progress was slow, frustrating, and uncertain.

Of course, the book would not have been produced without help from a variety of sources. In particular, financial support was provided by the Canadian Studies Program of the Secretary of State, and the Ontario Research Council on Leisure. In the absence of this assistance it would not have been possible for authors to gather in one place to share their ideas. Marie Puddister prepared the maps and diagrams with her usual skill and promptness, and Lisa Weber's text-processing abilities turned the manuscripts into a book. Jayati Ghosh assisted with the compilation of the index. A special thanks is extended to Hilda Gowans: her interest is greatly appreciated and I trust that her support is deserved.

Any bouquets will be shared with the friends who wrote the chapters; any brickbats should be directed at the editor.

Geoffrey Wall
Waterloo, Ontario
January 1989

Chapter 1

The Nature of Recreation

Geoffrey Wall
Department of Geography
University of Waterloo

The Nature of Recreation

TERMINOLOGY

Studies of leisure and recreation are plagued by imprecise terminology. In spite of the existence of a considerable body of literature devoted to explaining the differences between the meanings of these two concepts, common acceptable definitions have not yet been reached. The problem is compounded by the indiscriminate use of words such as pleasure, fun, spare time and enjoyment, which are often used as synonyms for leisure and recreation and as substitutes for each other. In the interests of clear thinking it is desirable to make a distinction between the meanings of leisure and recreation. Leisure is often considered to be a measure of time. It is the time remaining after work, sleep, and necessary personal and household chores have been completed. It is the time available for doing as one chooses. Leisure may thus be defined as "discretionary time."

Recreation embraces a wide variety of activities which are undertaken in leisure. The majority of these activities require skills, knowledge, and effort, and participation is usually the result of a conscious choice. From this perspective, all recreation takes place in leisure but leisure, because of lack of skills, knowledge, opportunity, or other reasons, need not be filled by recreation in its entirety. In summary, recreation encompasses activities which are selected to occupy leisure.

The definitions which have been presented may appear to be old-fashioned to many recreation researchers, particularly those with a psychological bent. Furthermore, the simple distinction between leisure as time and recreation as activity is difficult to implement, for many activities include both obligatory and discretionary components. For instance, without food we would die and eating is a necessity; it is also a popular form of recreation from which many people derive great pleasure. Similarly, gardening can be both enjoyable and a chore. Such difficulties have prompted some authors to argue that leisure and recreation are states of mind and that they are best defined in psychological terms (Driver and Tocher 1974). While one can be sympathetic to this viewpoint and can acknowledge that individuals recreate for a wide variety of reasons and may even derive different satisfactions from the same activity, the psychological definitions have their own inherent difficulties. The designation of areas for excitement, stress-reduction, socialization, catharsis, or relaxation is uncommon among recreational planners and site managers, who tend to operate on the basis of activities, designating areas for wilderness camping, skiing, or hunting. However, the psychological definitions do serve to remind us that we are not providing opportunities to recreate in and for themselves; rather we are making available the chance to achieve a wide range of satisfactions, which vary from individual to individual, from activity to activity, and from place to place.

Occasional reference is made in this volume to tourism. Again a multitude of different definitions can be found in the literature (Leiper 1979, Smith 1988) and there is debate concerning the relationship between tourism and recreation (Britton 1979, Chadwick 1981, Mieczkowski 1981). This author considers tourism to be a part of recreation and therefore relevant to this volume. It is often, though not necessarily, an extreme form of recreation in that it tends to be associated with relatively long distances travelled and relatively long lengths of stay. For some purposes, such as the calculation of economic impacts, it may be crucial to distinguish tourists from local residents but, on the other hand, they can often be found at the same sites participating in identical activities. Thus, although this book is not devoted primarily to tourism, readers should not be surprised to find the occasional discussion of tourism topics. Those interested in more specific information on tourism in Canada are referred to Murphy's (1983) book on the topic.

Recreation is a phenomenon which does not respect traditional disciplinary boundaries and is best understood by those who are willing to transgress the artificial barriers constructed by those who wish to segment knowledge into academic compartments. Leisure and recreation in the home are probably best studied by sociologists and psychologists. While it is recognized that these and other disciplines will continue to play an important role, it is suggested that the geographer is in a position to make a distinct and significant contribution with respect to the understanding of outdoor recreation. Outdoor recreation is a land use. It is in competition with agriculture, forestry, mining, housing, industry, and a variety of other activities for the same scarce resources of land and water. Recreation facilities such as ski areas, resorts, parks, and swimming pools have service areas comparable to those of stores or ports, and the participation of large numbers of people in outdoor recreation creates patterns of movement analogous to those associated with commuting or migration and susceptible to analysis by similar methods. From these examples alone it is evident that the concepts and methods of the geographer are appropriate to analyses of recreation and have the potential to further understanding of recreational phenomena.

Outdoor recreation cannot be readily isolated from other ways of spending leisure. Indoor and outdoor recreations are alternative ways of being at leisure and the decision to partake of one automatically reduces the time available for the other. To consider the one without the other is to investigate only part of the problem. Some recreational activities, such as swimming, skating, and concerts, take place in both indoor and outdoor settings, and domed stadiums with retractable roofs complicate the distinction further. In the final analysis, the decision to concentrate on outdoor recreation must be justified pragmatically, and the occasional departure, for instance to discuss accommodation for travellers, must be tolerated.

RELATIONSHIPS BETWEEN WORK AND LEISURE

Recreation cannot be fully understood in isolation from the requirements of work (Parker 1983, Clarke and Critcher 1985, Herbert 1988). Relationships between work and leisure, and hence outdoor recreation, can be viewed at at least two scales. At a general philosophical level one can recognize a continuum of perspectives with the Protestant work ethic at one end. The Protestant work ethic views work as the main purpose of life, and the role of recreation is literally to re-create the individual so that work can be better performed. From this perspective, many forms of recreation are regarded as being both a waste of time and, as in the case of dancing, gambling, and cards, may be associated with evil. This can be termed "the devil makes work for idle hands" philosophy.

At the other end of the spectrum are those who may have a hedonistic lifestyle, live for leisure, and who regard work as a necessary evil which must be endured if they are to accumulate sufficient resources to recreate to the full. It is not uncommon for people to refer to their "life's work." This can be viewed as a throwback to the Protestant work ethic. "Life's leisure" is a less common term, but it is not unusual to hear people say about others that they "live for the weekend" or "live for football," these statements reflecting views towards the opposite end of the spectrum.

At another scale, work and recreation are closely interrelated if only because the time required for work eats into that available for recreation. Furthermore, the nature of one's work influences the amount of money and energy available for recreation. Thus, for instance, as labour-saving devices have reduced the energy requirements of many types of work, interest in active outdoor recreation has increased. The need to burn up excess energy and maintain physical fitness has now become a societal problem resulting in the development of such government-sponsored schemes as "participaction," which is designed to promote public health.

The time at our disposal can be divided up into at least five segments. Each segment is associated with greater freedom of choice than its predecessor in the list. The five categories of time are for work itself; for work obligations such as preparing for or journeying to work; for physiological needs such as sleeping, eating, and personal maintenance; for non-work obligations or semi-leisure such as gardening, attending church, or doing odd jobs around the home; and for leisure, a small part of which is occupied with outdoor recreation. Once again, this seemingly simple categorization is difficult to use, for the relationships between each segment are not always clear. Furthermore, this perspective tends to depreciate the responsibilities of home-makers and ignores the fact that women are often expected to look after the children and take care of the food while participating in such activities as camping and picnicking.

Parker (1973) has suggested that it is possible to recognize three relationships between work and leisure. For people in absorbing and creative jobs work may be a more central interest in their lives than either leisure or family life. Parker has termed this situation in which there is a fusion of work and leisure "extension." The professional sportsman, the academic reading textbooks for pleasure, and the businessman playing golf and, at the same time, discussing policies and contracts are examples of the "extension" pattern. In contrast, others have jobs from which they derive little or no satisfaction and in which they use a narrow range of their abilities. They may wish to forget anything even remotely connected with their work during their leisure. For example, an unskilled factory worker or a distant water fisherman may seek "explosive compensation" for work in wild and exaggerated leisure activities. In this situation, there is a polarity between work and leisure and the relationship is one of "opposition". Thirdly, there are neutral jobs which bring neither fulfilment nor oppression, and work and leisure activities are usually different, rather than intentionally different. Parker stresses that the neutrality pattern is not intermediate between those of extension and opposition. Rather, the crucial difference between extension and opposition on the one hand, and neutrality on the other, is that the first two denote, respectively, a positive and negative affective attachment to work, while neutrality denotes a detachment from work. These notions are intuitively sensible, but it is worth noting that recreational choices and constraints on those choices are extremely complex, individuals have different needs at different times, and a single individual may exhibit aspects of each relationship from time to time as his or her decisions on what to do varies.

THE SIGNIFICANCE OF RECREATION

We spend only a small proportion of our lives as active participants in outdoor recreation. Sleep, work, and personal and household chores take up most of our time leaving relatively little leisure. Furthermore, only a small minority of leisure is spent in outdoor recreation. When measured by the time which it occupies, outdoor recreation does not appear to be particularly important. However, time is a poor indicator of the value we ascribe to outdoor recreation. The physical and psychological benefits to be derived from outdoor recreation are out of all proportion to the time which it consumes. Furthermore, outdoor recreation is a voracious consumer of resources. The recreational equipment industry produces a wide variety of products including boats, cameras, cottages, fishing and hiking equipment, skis, tents, and trailers, and large areas of land and water are assigned to outdoor recreation. Thus, outdoor recreation is big business, and it has a much greater impact on people, resources, and the economy than is indicated by the relatively small amount of time which it consumes.

It is appropriate to ask why people participate in outdoor recreation. Partial answers can be found in theories of play, many of which have evolved to explain the play behaviour of children but can also be applied to outdoor recreation. For instance, Spencer's surplus energy theory (Kraus 1971, 230-40) suggests that play occurs to burn up surplus energy; relaxation theory suggests that play provides a harmless outlet for the stresses which build up in living in a complex urban, industrial society; proponents of catharsis suggest that play permits the acceptable expression of bottled-up emotions which might otherwise lead to anti-social behaviour; and proponents of play as arousal-seeking suggest that humans have a need for exciting stimuli and that we seek arousal in play. A wide variety of theories on play has been summarized by Ellis (1971). No single theory satisfactorily explains all play and outdoor recreation behaviour, and some appear to be contradictory. Together they help to indicate why people play and suggest a variety of underlying motives which prompt individuals to participate in play and outdoor recreation.

At a more fundamental level, one may wonder if outdoor recreation is a genuine human need, or whether it is something which is merely desirable (Chappelle 1973). Many recreation professionals subscribe to the view that recreation is a human need, as illustrated in the following quotation from Revelle (1967): "Recreation becomes a human need and must be recognized as a human right in the same sense that we have recognized needs and rights to health, education and welfare." However, Maslow (1954) only indirectly mentions leisure or recreation in his hierarchy of human needs, and many individuals choose to commute leisure for increased work and more pay. Perhaps outdoor recreation is just one among a long list of desirables. That this may be the case is suggested by the fact that, in times of economic stress, recreation budgets are often cut, and governments spend additional money on job creation. Recreation is competing with other potential uses for restricted budgets. The magnitude of resources allocated to recreation will reflect the degree to which its proponents can persuade others of its significance when compared with other highly desirable claimants such as economic development, public health, housing, education, and a wide variety of social services.

THEORETICAL FRAMEWORK

A large number of variables play a part in influencing how people spend their leisure. In an attempt to see some of these variables in greater perspective, a theoretical framework, or conceptual model, was devised by Wall (1979) in the form of a linkage diagram. A simplified version of this linkage diagram constitutes the organizational structure of this book (Figure 1). The remainder of this chapter describes the components of the linkage diagram.

Outdoor recreation may be considered to have two basic aspects: the supply of recreational facilities and the demand for participation. Supply and demand interact through intervening decision-making processes to give rise to patterns of outdoor recreation. These patterns of outdoor recreation have associated economic, environmental, and social impacts.

Supply of Facilities

The supply of recreation facilities is the recreation resources which are available to potential participants. Supply has been defined as "the natural and man-made features which provide or could reasonably be expected to provide in the future opportunities for outdoor recreation" (Phillips 1970, 4). At least six major attributes can be considered with respect to the supply of recreation facilities. These are types, numbers, qualities, capacities, accessibility, and climate and weather.

(i) Type of facility refers to the activities for which a facility has been designed or is suitable, be it a national park or a hockey arena. Facilities may also be classified in other ways. For instance, they may be distinguished by ownership, as in the case of private and public facilities, or by administrative jurisdiction, as illustrated by national, provincial, and municipal parks. In addition, they may be grouped according to location as urban or rural, or, to use the terminology of Clawson and Knetsch (1971, 36-40), user-oriented, intermediate, and resource-oriented. The usefulness of each of the categorizations of types of facility will vary with the purposes at hand.

Figure 1: Conceptual Framework

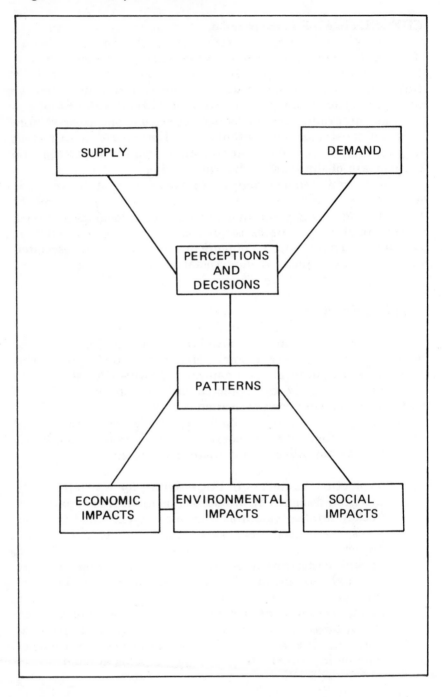

(ii)   Number is a measure of the quantity of recreation
        facilities of each type; for instance, the number of picnic
        sites or the number of swimming pools in an area.

(iii)   Quality is concerned with the suitability of a facility for
        an activity when compared with other facilities of the
        same type. Quality is compounded from those factors
        which enhance an activity at a site, minus those factors
        which detract from the activity at that site. One of the
        more obvious and intractable examples of variations in
        quality is scenic beauty.

(iv)   Capacity is a measure of the maximum level of use which
        can be accommodated at a recreation site. This
        seemingly simple concept is in fact very complex.
        Tanner (1969, 47-8) suggested that capacity can be
        measured in three distinct ways:

    a) physical capacity, which is controlled by the
       area of land and water available for
       recreational activities and for associated
       facilities. For example, the capacity of an area
       for sailing may be determined by reference to
       the area of water and the number of moorings
       that can be made available;

    b) environmental capacity, which is a measure of
       the maximum levels of use which can be
       sustained without an unacceptable
       deterioration in the quality of the
       environment. It will reflect such factors as the
       vulnerability of natural habitats, landscape
       values, and the interests of local inhabitants;

    c) the capacities of ancillary facilities, such as
       access roads, parking and accommodations.

To Tanner's measures may be added perceptual capacity,
which reflects the degree of tolerance by participants of
recreational pressures, and is sometimes defined as the
maximum number of users who can participate in an
activity at a site without an unacceptable deterioration in
the quality of the recreation experience. The most

valuable definition of capacity will vary with the nature of the problem under consideration and the goals of management for a site.

(v)   Accessibility is the ease or difficulty which potential participants experience in making use of a facility as a result of the characteristics of that facility. Accessibility may itself be considered under five headings:

a) Distance from the source of demand of the recreation facility may put constraints upon its use. The friction of distance may be measured in units of length, travel time, travel cost, or fatigue.

b) The means of transportation which may be used to reach the recreation facility.

c) Opening times, or the times at which a facility is available for use. Thus, for instance, there may be seasonal restrictions on the use of a facility which may limit use even though the facility may be easily reached. Such is often the case with hunting and fishing where open and closed seasons are prescribed.

d) Charges for the use of a facility (admission fees) may also act to reduce the ability of potential users to take advantage of a resource.

e) Given that the four preceding constraints on accessibility can be overcome, accessibility may still be hampered due to other restrictions on the availability of a resource. Thus, the recreation facility may be in the possession of an individual or a club, access being confined to members or friends.

Thus accessibility, as used in this context, includes a variety of constraints upon the use of a facility, distance between the potential user and the resource being only one of these constraints.

(vi)   Climate and weather are viewed as recreation resources and are, therefore, included under the supply of recreation facilities. In some cases it may be more appropriate to consider weather as an influence upon the decision-making process.

The various aspects of the supply of recreation facilities are not all independent variables and not all can be readily quantified. Types, numbers, qualities, capacities, and accessibility can all be influenced by the injection of capital. Resources utilized by such sports as golf are quantifiable and finite items -- it is not difficult to count the number of courses and holes -- but in the case of pleasure motoring and other informal activities, the problem of identifying the resource becomes formidable. It is extremely difficult to quantify a resource like landscape, even if it is possible to develop some consistency in the exercise of subjective judgement.

Demand for Outdoor Recreation

The demand for outdoor recreation may be defined as "the number of persons (or units of participation) requiring to take part in a particular recreation activity, and hence is manifested as a demand for facilities" (Phillips 1970, 2). A distinction should be drawn between effective demand or consumption, and latent demand. Effective demand, use, and consumption all refer to a demand which currently exists. Latent demand is a demand which, for some reason, is not effective, but which would be so in other circumstances. It is a demand which is frustrated by such factors as the lack of facilities or socio-economic constraints on participation.

Five major factors have been isolated as being of potential significance in influencing the demand for outdoor recreation. These factors are available leisure, income, education, mobility, and individual and household attributes. The last factor may be further subdivided to include sex, age, marital status, household size and structure, and health. Unfortunately, socio-economic variables provide an incomplete explanation for variations in the demand for outdoor recreation and, in consequence, there has been increased interest in the influence of psychological variables which should probably be added as a sixth factor.

Just as the aspects of the supply of recreation facilities are not independent of one another, so the factors influencing the demand for outdoor recreation are interrelated. For instance, marital status is likely to influence available leisure time, and disposable income varies with marital status and household size. Income also tends to vary in association with education. Consequently, considerable care must be exercised in evaluating the role of any single variable.

Supply and Demand Relationships

The supply of recreation facilities and the demand for outdoor recreation both influence the decisions which are made concerning outdoor recreation. Individuals make decisions regarding outdoor recreation on the basis of their information fields, which incorporate both knowledge of outdoor recreation activities and an awareness of the supply of facilities potentially available to them. The information field, of individuals reflects such things as their education, their length of residence in an area, and their level of interest in outdoor recreation. It may also be manipulated by advertising.

The relationships between the supply of facilities, the demand for outdoor recreation, the information field, and recreation decisions are extremely complex. The supply of recreation facilities is not independent of the demand for outdoor recreation and the demand for recreation is partly a function of supply, the creation of new facilities in itself stimulating demands. The supply of facilities can turn latent demand into effective demand and can also create changes within the pattern of effective demand, switching demand from one type of activity to another, or from one location to another. A decision to take part in any form, and particularly a new form, of outdoor recreation will change an individual's accumulated recreation experience and thus enlarge his information field, thereby influencing future recreation decisions. Thus, there is feedback between recreation decisions and the information field. In addition, recreation decisions themselves influence the supply of facilities, the decision to participate influencing the quantity of resources available to others. The whole area of decision-making in recreation is one which is incompletely understood and which requires further investigation. Jackson considers many of the issues in chapter 4, "Perceptions and Decisions."

Patterns of Recreation

The aggregate of multifarious individual decisions comprises the pattern of outdoor recreation, which may be defined as the spatial and temporal incidence of outdoor recreation phenomena. For each recreation activity it is convenient to consider the pattern of recreation as comprising a number of components:

(i)   Number and frequency are measures of the quantity of individual decisions to take part in an activity. If the study is of a moment in time, the number of participants is likely to be the appropriate measure. If the investigation aims to consider a long period of time, frequency of participation may be more suitable.

(ii) Location is an indication of the distance of the place of recreation from the residence of the participant and whether or not single or multiple destinations are involved. It may also embrace the attributes of the recreation site, such as whether the site is coastal or inland, or whether it is in an urban or rural area.

(iii) Duration is the length of time spent in participating in an activity. In some cases it may be appropriate or convenient to include travel time in duration.

iv)   Timing refers to the temporal distribution of participation. It includes the daily, weekly, and seasonal incidence of participation.

(v)   It may be important to consider if temporary accommodation is required, and, if so, the types of accommodation that are used.

(vi) The size and composition of groups taking part in an activity or visiting a site may also be worthy of consideration. It may also be useful to know whether or not people are participating for the first time and whether activities are spontaneous or planned.

IMPACTS

The distribution of people and recreation equipment across the land results in a variety of impacts. For convenience, three types of impact can be distinguished: economic, environmental, and socio-cultural (Mathieson and Wall 1982). Environmental impact encompasses alterations to air, water, landforms, soils, and biota (Wall and Wright 1977). Economic impacts include the monetary costs and benefits resulting from the construction, maintenance, and use of recreational facilities. Socio-cultural impacts are the changes in the way of life of both "hosts and guests" (Smith 1977) which result from outdoor recreation and tourism. Again, the categories are not distinct. For instance, environmental impacts may be modified by site management, but this costs money. Similarly, increased recreation may generate jobs and hence additional income for employees, but working hours may be such that family life is affected. However, the three-fold division is useful for descriptive purposes.

The nature of impacts will have repercussions for future participation decisions and for the supply, demand, and patterns of outdoor recreation.

COMMENTARY

The theoretical framework which has been presented is by no means the only possible one (see, for example, Wolfe 1964, Burton 1967), nor is it exhaustive in its content. Nevertheless, it can accommodate the recreation patterns of both individuals and groups, and is of wide applicability. It is an attempt to create a logical structure as a basis for studies of the major elements of outdoor recreation. Each box in the diagram has been discussed briefly to draw attention to some of the factors that underpin it, and the items identified in the text constitute a checklist incorporating most of the major components of outdoor recreation.

The linkage diagram also constitutes an organizing framework for the remainder of the volume. Following this introduction, the book comprises seven sections reflecting the components of the diagram: supply, demand, perceptions and decisions, patterns, economic impacts, environmental impacts, and social impacts. A final chapter examines the future of outdoor recreation. Selection of materials has been necessary and not all topics and areas of the country are covered in equal depth. However, together the chapters provide a good indication of the range of patterns and problems in outdoor recreation in Canada.

Chapter 2

Supply

Reid Kreutzwiser
Department of Geography
University of Guelph

Supply

Supply refers to the recreational resources, both natural and man-made, which provide opportunities for recreation. It is a complex concept influenced by numerous factors and subject to changing interpretations. It is also a concept which has prompted much thought in terms of classification and evaluation.

This chapter aims to discuss the concept of supply, with emphasis on biophysical resources rather than man-made facilities, to review several approaches to the classification and evaluation of recreational resources, and to describe selected recreational resources in a Canadian context. This will afford an opportunity to discuss several issues surrounding the concept of supply.

DEFINING A RECREATIONAL RESOURCE

Traditional conceptions have considered recreational resources as physical and often static elements of the environment such as land, forests, water, or wildlife or as physical facilities such as playing fields or swimming pools. This stress on the physical attributes of recreational resources ignores numerous important human influences. As Zimmerman (1951) noted, resources are culturally defined, expanding and contracting in response to changing human wants and abilities. While the biophysical environment represents a source of "potential" resources, elements of that environment become "actual" resources only when numerous human conditions are met.

Contemporary interpretations, on the other hand, recognize the dynamic and functional nature of resources and stress human as well as physical attributes. A recreational resource can be defined as an element of the natural or man-modified environment which provides an opportunity to satisfy recreational wants. Implicit is a continuum ranging from biophysical resources to man-made facilities.

Also implicit is a range of ownership patterns from private personal and commercial resources and facilities to public ownership and management at all governmental levels. The quality, capacity, and accessibility of resources and facilities are other important characteristics.

This definition of recreational resource recognizes the significance of both the environment and human wants. It also acknowledges other human influences. The environment is only an opportunity for the satisfaction of recreational desires if we possess the ability or technology to utilize or gain access to that environment. We must also perceive that environment to be capable of satisfying specific wants. Institutional factors such as ownership patterns and regulations may also be important influences on whether or not a particular environment provides an opportunity to recreate. These are just several of the many factors influencing the supply of recreational resources and serve to illustrate the complexity of the supply concept.

CLASSIFYING AND EVALUATING RECREATIONAL RESOURCES

Numerous schemes have been developed to classify or distinguish types of recreational resources and to evaluate these resources in terms of quality or quantity. These schemes employ a variety of resource attributes or criteria and provide a basis for inventorying, evaluating, planning, or managing recreational resources. Generally, these schemes emphasize one of the following: the physical attributes of the resource or area, the suitability of the biophysical environment for specific activities, the use capacity of the resource, or the type of recreational experience afforded.

Physical Attributes

One approach to distinguishing recreational resources utilizes the physical characteristics of the resource. A basic distinction, for example, can be made between land and water resources for outdoor recreation, or more complex classifications of water resources are possible. Other attributes of the resource or area, its level of development or accessibility to urban populations, for example, can be incorporated to recognize the functional nature of recreational resources.

An early classification scheme developed by the Bureau of Outdoor Recreation (BOR) in the United States (Outdoor Recreation Resources Review Commission 1962) distinguished six types of outdoor recreation areas. High Density Recreation Areas (Class I) are intensively developed, often located in or adjacent to urban areas and managed for heavy use. General Outdoor Recreation Areas (Class II) are larger areas, accommodating diverse resource and facility-based recreational activities. Natural Environment Areas (Class III) are large, less developed areas accommodating activities compatible with a natural setting. Unique Natural Areas (Class IV) and Historic and Cultural Sites (Class VI) are areas of outstanding scenic splendour, scientific importance, or historic or cultural significance. Primitive Areas (Class V) are large, undisturbed, roadless areas accommodating dispersed, non-mechanized recreational activities.

The BOR and related schemes are descriptive and reveal little about an area's recreational suitability or capacity. The criteria for assigning any particular recreational resource or area to a class are general and largely subjective.

Suitability

Other schemes distinguish recreational resources by evaluating the biophysical environment in terms of its suitability for specific activities. Specific environmental elements, such as weather and climate, have been so evaluated (Crowe *et al.* 1975). The environment, more broadly, also has been evaluated in terms of its recreational potential. A plethora of methodology, for example, has been developed to assess land as a visual or scenic resource (see reviews by Dearden 1980 and Zube 1982).

An often referenced scheme which evaluates land in terms of its suitability for a number of recreational activities is the Canada Land Inventory (CLI) capability classification. The classification assumes a common level of demand and accessibility and assigns an area of land to one of seven classes on the basis of the number of recreationists that can be attracted and accommodated (Department of Regional Economic

Expansion 1970). Classes 1 and 2 land have a high capability, while Class 7 land has a very low capability to attract and sustain recreational use. Subclass designations are used to indicate up to three of twenty-five activities suitable in that environment. Only biophysical attributes of land are considered in the evaluation. For example, criteria for classifying shoreland for beach activities include size of water body, length, gradient and material composition of the beach, water temperature, clarity and freedom from hazards and aquatic nuisances, and backshore available for parking and other support facilities. Many of these criteria require assumptions about recreationists' preferences for particular biophysical attributes.

Approximately 2.6 million square-kilometres of southern Canada have been evaluated and mapped using the CLI scheme. The CLI provides a useful indication of relative suitability of land for particular recreational activities based on the biophysical characteristics only of that land.

Use Capacity

Numerous attempts have been made to assess the capacity of land (or water) to accommodate use. This carrying capacity, or maximum level of use, of a recreational resource can be defined in several ways.

Physical capacity refers to the space requirements of recreational activities; it is controlled by the amount of land or water available for the activity and involves the application of arbitrary space standards, for example, five hectares of lake surface per boat. Physical capacity may also be defined by the capacity of ancillary facilities such as parking or boat mooring spaces. Environmental capacity is the maximum level of use which a recreational resource can sustain without unacceptable degradation of the biophysical environment. Behavioural capacity refers to the maximum use which can be accommodated by a recreational resource without an unacceptable deterioration in the quality of the recreational experience. Much of the work on behavioural capacity has emphasized the effects of crowding on the recreational experience. There is a very rich literature on these various interpretations of use capacity, including some useful reviews (for example, Liddle 1975, Heberlein 1977, Stankey 1982, Vaske *et al.* 1983).

The Ontario Recreation Supply Inventory (ORSI) is an attempt to inventory a range of recreational resources in Ontario and develop a methodology to calculate the supply of various recreational opportunities (Tourism and Outdoor Recreation Planning Study Committee 1975). As such, it represents an ambitious effort to inventory the physical capacity of Ontario recreational resources. This computer-based inventory provides information on the nature, size, location, and ownership of public and private recreational sites for a number of resource-oriented activities (swimming at a beach, boating, canoeing, hunting, and fishing) and facility-oriented activities (picnicking, camping, trail activities, fairs and special events, nature exhibits and viewing, golf, and alpine skiing). Commercial tourist accommodation, vacation camps, and outfitters' camps are also inventoried.

The ORSI also provides methodologies for calculating opportunities (user-days) of recreation afforded by inventoried sites. Opportunities are determined by applying a number of factors or standards to the quantity of the resource (number of picnic tables or length and width of beach). A space standard or access capacity must be applied. A space standard is the assumed space required for one opportunity of recreation, for example, four-hundred metres per person for hiking trails. Access capacity refers to the accessibility of a resource, for example, in terms of car parking spaces. Turnover rate is the number of times per day that a resource or facility can provide an opportunity. Season length is the average number of days per year during which the activity can be enjoyed, and recognizes the important influence of weather and climate. The institutional factor accommodates peaking in use due to institutional constraints such as opening hours and the aggregate weekly distribution of leisure time. A portion of supply will go unused because of these institutional constraints.

These adjustments can be applied to the inventory data to yield estimates of instantaneous, daily, and yearly capacity. For example, the number of picnic tables multiplied by the space standard would yield instantaneous capacity. Instantaneous capacity multiplied by turnover rate constitutes daily capacity, and daily capacity multiplied by season length is yearly capacity. A distinction can be made between accessible supply, that available at the present level of development and existing level of physical accessibility, and actual supply, which is accessible supply multiplied by the institutional factor.

The ORSI is an interesting attempt to develop a quantitative, managerially useful measure of supply. It recognizes a range of physical and behavioural factors important in defining a recreational resource. A weakness, however, is its reliance on space standards which may lack a sufficient empirical base.

Experience Afforded

The above described approaches to classifying and evaluating recreational resources tend to emphasize physical attributes of the resource or the recreational activity itself. They fail to recognize fully the growing attention being given to recreation as a behavioural experience (for example, Driver and Tocher 1970, Driver and Brown 1978). This interpretation of recreation stresses the importance of the "experiences" obtained from specific activities in particular settings. These experiences might include solitude, physical exertion, skill development, or family togetherness. Utilization of recreational resources, per se, is simply the means through which participants obtain these experiences.

The Recreation Opportunity Spectrum (ROS) developed by the United States Forest Service represents a resource classification scheme which explicitly incorporates a behavioural perspective. The ROS conceptualizes a recreational resource or setting as a combination of biophysical, social, and managerial conditions that give value to a place (Clark and Stankey 1979). Various combinations produce a diversity of opportunities for the attainment of recreational experiences. By providing users with information on the nature of these opportunities, the ROS can serve to facilitate a closer matching of user expectations and recreational settings.

The biophysical environment is acknowledged as a basic factor. In addition, six resource attributes, capable of being manipulated by managers, are used to define various opportunities along a continuum from primitive to modern. These factors are access, non-recreational resource uses such as logging, on-site management (for example, facilities and landscaping), social interaction or contact among users, acceptability of visitor impacts, and acceptable regimentation or control over recreational use. Figure 1 demonstrates how these manageable factors interact to define a semi-modern opportunity along the spectrum. All opportunity types are

Figure 1: Factors Defining Outdoor Recreation Opportunity Settings

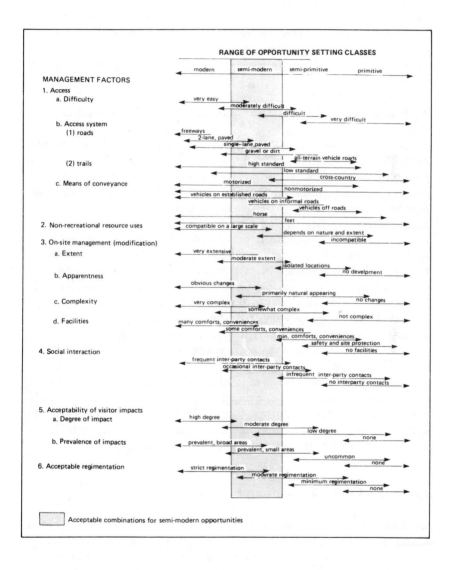

Source: Clark and Stankey 1979.

possible within any biophysical environment or setting, for example, alpine, lake, forest, or desert.

By adopting a behavioural perspective, the ROS represents a potentially useful aid to achieving efficient allocation of supply to meet recreational demands. A disturbing aspect of the ROS, however, is the assertion that there is nothing intrinsic in the biophysical environment that suggests an appropriate opportunity type for that setting (Clark and Stankey 1979, 16-17). Certainly, the environmental sensitivity of settings varies enormously, with implications for managing human impacts.

THE RECREATIONAL RESOURCE BASE OF CANADA

Canada possesses a diverse, complex, and extensive recreational resource base. This is reflected in part in a wide range of biophysical settings. It is also reflected in a myriad of ownership and management patterns. While a basic distinction can be made between private and public ownership of resources and facilities, further distinctions can be drawn. Private resources can be personal or commercial in nature; cottages and commercial resorts, which may include rental cottages, typify this distinction. Governments at all levels are also involved in the provision of recreational opportunities, as the existence of urban, provincial, and federal park systems illustrates. Indeed, very few government agencies are not involved, in some way, directly or indirectly, in the ownership or management of recreational resources and facilities.

While it is far beyond the scope of this chapter to attempt a comprehensive overview of Canada's recreational resources, some insights can be gained by examining, selectively, elements of this resource base. Reference is made to the influence of climate and weather, recreational capability of shorelines, and national and provincial parks.

Canada's Climatic Landscape

Climate is of fundamental importance to outdoor recreation in Canada, although it is often either ignored in studies of Canada's recreational resource base or considered negatively as a nuisance factor or constraint to recreational and tourist development. Despite images of Canada's harsh climate, a pronounced seasonality across most of the country creates diverse recreational opportunities.

Climate and weather influence recreation in several ways. Weather conditions can impair access to recreational resources. While this is particularly so for more remote, and often northern, fly-in fishing or hunting areas, winter driving conditions in urbanized southern Canada occasionally limit accessibility of skiing or snowmobiling sites. Climate itself is also a recreational resource, as it defines the nature and length of summer and winter seasons and, consequently, creates opportunities for activities such as swimming and cross-country skiing. Finally, weather conditions influence our enjoyment of many recreational activities with some more sensitive to weather conditions than others, for example, swimming as distinct from landscape touring.

A functional interpretation of recreational resource recognizes the important influence of technology. While our ability to modify weather and climate presently is extremely limited, technology's influence on climate as a recreational resource is not inconsequential. Snow-making equipment, for example, is used to increase the number of suitable activity days at many downhill ski resorts. Improvements in clothing and camping equipment have made cross-country skiing, snowshoeing, and winter camping more popular and enjoyable activities. Indeed, the development of the snowmobile as a recreational machine has transformed snow into a resource for many Canadians who previously viewed it only as a nuisance.

Canada's climate is diverse, reflecting the country's size and range of latitude. Mean January and July temperatures of 1.8 and 13.6°C in Victoria, -3.2 and 18.3°C in Halifax, -4.3 and 22.3°C in Windsor, and -14.7 and 17.5°C in Edmonton hint at the range of seasonal fluctuation across a large part of the country. Within smaller regions, climatic variability also can be considerable. Even subtle micro-climatic variations, for example, within particular parks, can influence recreational satisfaction.

Variations in temperature and other elements of climate define season lengths and create opportunities for various recreational activities. On a national scale, for example, high summer or the time period during which mean daily maximum temperature is 18°C or greater is 153 days long in Windsor but only 102 days in Edmonton (Masterton *et al.* 1976, Crowe *et al.* 1977). On the other hand, the period of reliable snow cover,

defined by the first and last dates snow remains on the ground
for at least seven consecutive days is 0 days in Windsor and 129
days in Edmonton. This provides a measure of meaningful
winter season for activities such as snowmobiling and cross-
country skiing. Regional variations in these season lengths,
however, can be considerable. Locations in southern Ontario
less than two hundred kilometres from Windsor experience
forty or more days of reliable snow cover. Similarly, the length
of the swimming season in southern Ontario ranges from 66
days in Algonquin Park to 134 days at Point Pelee along the
north shore of Lake Erie.

Climatic and weather conditions also influence how
satisfying particular recreational outings will be. Air
temperature, humidity, precipitation, cloudiness, amount of
daylight, visibility, wind, water temperature, and snow and ice
cover are among the parameters deemed to be important. These
factors have important interactive effects. In summer, air
temperature and humidity can combine to create uncomfortable
conditions for vigorous activities, while wind and temperature
in winter can create a wind chill hazardous to outdoor
recreationists.

Table 1 represents an attempt to develop criteria for
designation of suitable activity-days for specific activities or
groups of activities. While subjective and general, these criteria
can be applied to historical weather data to estimate the mean
number of suitable activity-days per year for particular
locations. At a broad scale, this information is useful to
planners and managers of both public and private recreational
resources, for example, in making locational and investment
decisions concerning specific facilities. Indeed, climatic
parameters are incorporated into both the Canada Land
Inventory and Ontario Recreation Supply Inventory previously
described. At the scale of the recreational site, micro-climatic
information can be useful in the layout and design of trails,
campsites, and other facilities to minimize discomfort due to
local conditions.

Climate and weather are important elements of the
recreational resource base with economic, social, and even
environmental implications. The length of the tourist season
affects rate of return on capital investments in accommodation
and other tourist-related enterprises as well as employment
patterns. Seasonality is an often-referred-to limitation to
development of tourism in many parts of the country.
Seasonality also creates peaking in utilization of recreational

Table 1

Suitable Days for Outdoor Activity

	Humidex**	Visibility	Sky Condition	Wind	Precipitation
Landscape touring	-12 to 89	over 3 miles	--	below 25 mph	none
Passive activity (lounging)	over 54	over 1 mile	not overcast	below 20 mph	none
Vigorous activity (games, etc.)	55 to 89	over 2 miles	not overcast	below 20 mph	none
Beaching	over 64	over 1 mile	not overcast	below 15 mph	none
Skiing *	over 6	over 1/2 mile	--	below 15 mph	little or none
Snowmobiling *	over -6	over 1/2 mile	--	below 15 mph	little or none

*   one inch or more of snow cover is needed
**   composite of air temperature and humidity

Source: Gates, 1975.

resources, which often contributes to overcrowding, a decline in user satisfaction, and deterioration of the biophysical environment. Further implications arise when periods of peak use coincide with the vegetative growing season.

Shorter-term fluctuations in weather also can be economically and socially disruptive. For example, the timing and duration of the downhill ski season in southern Ontario can affect resort operators and communities dependent on these resorts.

Canada's climatic landscape is also significant in that it is changing. The precise nature of this change is uncertain, although global climate models generally suggest a warming in Canada in response to increased carbon dioxide levels in the atmosphere (Canadian Climate Centre 1986). Regional effects over the next fifty years are even more tenuous to postulate. Possible effects identified by the Canadian Climate Centre include a lowering of Great Lakes water levels by twenty centimetres through reduced water supplies, with implications for beach activities and recreational boating. Lakeshore marshes, such as that in Point Pelee National Park, could disappear. Mean winter snowfall over southern Ontario could decrease by sixty centimetres, and much more in the snow-belt areas, resulting in a loss of reliable snow cover in the Georgian Bay downhill ski region. On the other hand, the summer recreational season across most of Canada would increase. The positive and negative socio-economic and environmental implications of such changes have not been fully explored, but are likely to be considerable.

Canada's Recreational Shoreland

Canada is truly a coastal nation, with 243,800 kilometres of marine coast, including 58,500 kilometres of mainland coastline, and several times this in fresh-water shore. In a recreational context, however, this extensive coast only becomes significant when one considers the popularity of water-based recreation. In Ontario, over 66% of the population twelve years of age and older swims, while participation rates for power boating and fishing are 33% and 38% respectively (Tourism and Outdoor Recreation Planning Study 1977). The enjoyment of many other popular activities, including landscape touring, picnicking, and camping, is enhanced by the presence of water.

In keeping with a functional definition of resource, only a portion of Canada's extensive marine and fresh-water shoreland can be considered a recreational resource. Quality of beach and water conditions and accessibility in a locational and public-ownership sense influence the extent of the shoreland resource.

The Canada Land Inventory, previously described, provides an assessment of the inherent or natural capability of over 571,000 kilometres of marine and fresh-water shoreland in southern Canada (Environment Canada 1978). Table 2 shows the distribution of the 85,000 kilometres of high-capability shore (Class 1-3) among the provinces. This high-capability shore is a relatively small proportion, 15%, of the inventoried shore, and the 1,600 kilometres of Class 1 shore represents only .003% of the shore inventoried.

Considerable provincial variation in the distribution of high-capability shore is also evident in Table 2. Over 60% of the Class 1-3 shore is found in just two provinces, Quebec and Ontario, where numerous Canadian Shield lakes contribute substantially to the resource base. Less than 2% of high-capability shore is found in Prince Edward Island, although over half of the inventoried shore is of high-capability. The Prairie provinces are generally deficient in high capability shore, with only 11% of the Canadian total despite the fact that over 26% of the inventoried shoreland in Canada is found in these three provinces (Environment Canada 1978). Water temperature of more northerly lakes is obviously an important limitation.

The Canada Land Inventory does not address accessibility in a locational sense. Proximity to urban centres is a critical element influencing the extent to which shoreland represents a recreational resource. If a day-use radius of 121 kilometres around each of Canada's twenty-two Census Metropolitan Areas (CMAs) is delimited, "accessible" high-capability shore can be determined. Accessible here refers only to location; ownership and road systems may limit access but are not considered. Pollution of swimming beaches, occasionally a problem in highly urbanized areas, is also a limitation not considered by the Canada Land Inventory.

Less than 24% of the inventoried shore in Canada is found within the 121 kilometres day-use zone. Of this accessible shore, 22,700 kilometres or over 16% is Class 1-3 (Environment Canada 1978). Over 3,600 kilometres of this shore has a high capability for swimming. Sudbury, Ottawa-Hull, Montreal, and

Table 2

CLI Shore Capability for Recreation

	Class 1	Km of Shore Class 2	Class 3	Total 1-3	Class 1-3 as a Percent of Inventoried Shore	Class 1-3 as a Percent of Canadian Total
Newfoundland	90	887	5,422	6,399	9.6	7.5
Prince Edward Island	313	178	812	1,303	51.6	1.5
Nova Scotia	32	265	1,140	1,437	6.0	1.7
New Brunswick	24	149	1,673	1,846	16.8	2.2
Quebec	258	2,220	24,649	27,127	24.6	31.8
Ontario	333	1,896	22,371	24,600	18.5	28.9
Manitoba	54	484	3,293	3,831	6.4	4.5
Saskatchewan	81	210	3,708	3,999	9.9	4.7
Alberta	76	220	1,518	1,814	3.7	2.1
British Columbia	347	1,782	10,698	12,827	17.0	15.1
Canada	1,608	8,291	75,284	85,183	14.9	100.0

Source: Environment Canada, 1978.

Quebec City are the CMAs with the most extensive accessible shore, while Saskatoon, Calgary, and St. Catharines have the least.

Despite geographic variations in the shoreland resource and acknowledging problems of access and water pollution not addressed by the Canada Land Inventory, Canada's recreational shoreland is extensive and significant. One reflection of this is a preference for vacation homes or cottages that is characteristically Canadian. In only a few other parts of the world does enthusiasm for the cottaging experience equal that found in Canada, especially in Ontario, Quebec, and the Atlantic provinces.

In 1987, 551,000, or 6% of Canadian households owned a vacation home (Statistics Canada 1988). The rate of ownership ranged from 2% in British Columbia to 8% in Newfoundland. The cottaging phenomenon, however, is perhaps best illustrated by Ontario, with its 9,600 kilometres of Great Lakes shore and countless Canadian Shield lakes. Although only 6% of Ontario households actually own a vacation home, the Ontario Recreation Survey suggests that rental or use of a friend's or relative's cottage increases utilization to almost half the population (Tourism and Ontario Recreation Planning Study 1977). The extensive and attractive shore, relatively high level of urbanization and affluence, and the proximity to a large American market for cottage properties has contributed to the rapid growth of cottaging in Ontario. Presently, there are over 300,000 cottages in the province, up from an estimated 29,000 in 1941 (Kreutzwiser 1986).

Much of this growth occurred in the 1960s when adequate planning controls were not yet in place in many rural municipalities, and overdevelopment of some lakes has contributed to water quality, municipal servicing, and other environmental and social problems. Cottage development in some areas also restricts public recreational access to shoreland. The commitment to the cottaging experience remains strong, however, and numerous cottager associations have emerged recently in an effort to resolve problems and preserve the quality of this experience (Kreutzwiser 1986).

Canada's National and Provincial Parks

In some respects, national and provincial parks are Canada's most "typically-Canadian" recreational resources. For a

century, parks like Banff and Algonquin have symbolized
Canada to Americans, Europeans, and others. They have been
featured in numerous tourist promotions, countless photographs
and postcards, and have inspired some of this country's most
famous artists. They have provided a pleasant setting for
outdoor activities such as canoeing and camping, which have a
rich history and tradition in Canada (Wall 1982).

Canada's immensity and geographic diversity have
created opportunities for the development of extensive park
systems nationally and in most of the provinces (Figure 2). At
185,000 square-kilometres, Canada's national park system is
the largest in the world (Table 3). Extensive park systems are
also found in Quebec, Ontario, and British Columbia. In total,
Canada's national and provincial parks occupy 420,000 square-
kilometres. In absolute terms, this represents a substantial
allocation of land for park purposes. In a relative sense,
however, this area represents 4.2% of the country's land and
water area, or .016 square-kilometres per capita. In these
relative terms, Canada falls far behind New Zealand and
several African countries in parkland allocation.

The nature of park systems that have evolved in Canada
differs markedly. The national park system is composed
principally of two types of units, national parks and national
historic parks and sites. These parks are expected to protect
significant and representative examples of Canada's natural
and cultural heritage (Parks Canada 1979). Consequently, a
single unit, the national park, must accommodate varied and
sometimes conflicting objectives of nature preservation,
interpretation of natural features and processes, and provision
of diverse outdoor recreational opportunities. Rationalizing
these objectives is presumably accomplished through use of a
zoning system to allocate land and resources within parks to
particular uses.

In contrast, Ontario attempts to satisfy objectives of nature
preservation, interpretation, outdoor recreation, and tourism
development through both a classification of park units and a
zoning system geared to each class (Ontario Ministry of
Natural Resources 1978). Six units -- wilderness parks, nature
reserves, historic parks, natural environment parks, waterway
parks, and recreation parks -- comprise the Ontario provincial
park system.

Regardless of the approach used, several important issues
continue to surround the management of park resources and
provision of recreational opportunities through national and

Figure 2: Major Parks in Canada

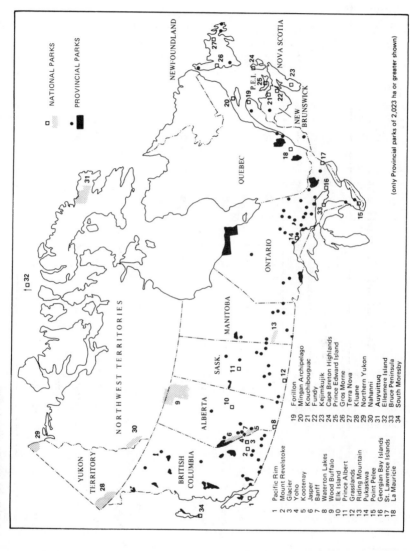

1 Pacific Rim
2 Mount Revelstoke
3 Glacier
4 Yoho
5 Kootenay
6 Jasper
7 Banff
8 Waterton Lakes
9 Wood Buffalo
10 Elk Island
11 Prince Albert
12 Grasslands
13 Riding Mountain
14 Pukaskwa
15 Point Pelee
16 Georgian Bay Islands
17 St. Lawrence Islands
18 La Mauricie
19 Forillon
20 Mingan Archipelago
21 Kouchibouguac
22 Fundy
23 Kejimkujik
24 Cape Breton Highlands
25 Prince Edward Island
26 Gros Morne
27 Terra Nova
28 Kluane
29 Northern Yukon
30 Nahanni
31 Auyuittuq
32 Ellesmere Island
33 Bruce Peninsula
34 South Moresby

(only Provincial parks of 2,023 ha or greater shown)

Source: Adapted from Simpson-Lewis *et al.* 1979.

Table 3

National and Provincial Parks

	Land and Water Area (km²)	National Parks* Number	National Parks* Area (km²)	Provincial Parks Number	Provincial Parks Area (km²)	National and Provincial Parks as a Percent of Total Area
Newfoundland	405,720	2	2,339	75	3,337	1.4
Prince Edward Island	5,660	1	26	31	15	0.7
Nova Scotia	55,490	2	1,332	113	198	2.8
New Brunswick	73,440	2	445	48	233	0.9
Quebec	1,540,680	3	935	91	92,241	6.1
Ontario	1,068,580	5	2,178	219	56,592	5.5
Manitoba	649,950	1	2,976	164	14,316	2.7
Saskatchewan	652,330	2	4,781	31	9,080	2.1
Alberta	661,190	5	53,207	141	12,514	9.9
British Columbia	947,800	6	9,220	367	46,681	5.9
Yukon and NWT	3,909,770	5	107,759			
Canada	9,970,610	34	185,198	1,280	235,207	4.2

* excludes National Historic Parks

Source: Statistics Canada, 1987 and Environment Canada, Parks, 1988.

provincial parks in Canada. Contributing to these problems has been the rapid growth of both the number of parks and utilization of these parks over the past several decades. The number of parks in Ontario, for example, increased from 8 in 1954 to 219 in 1987. In 1986, national parks accommodated 20,300,000 visitor-days of use (Environment Canada, Parks, 1988), while provincial park visitation across Canada in 1985 totalled 38,610,000 (Statistics Canada 1986). A lack of attention, until recently, to planning of both individual parks (master or site planning) and park systems also has been a contributing factor. Among the important issues confronting park managers are the interconnected concerns of providing accessible opportunities, meeting conflicting park objectives, and preserving the quality of both the biophysical environment and recreational experience.

A functional interpretation of recreational resource recognizes the importance of locational accessibility. While Canada's national and provincial park acreage is extensive, a major portion is physically removed from centres of demand. Over 70% of Canada's population resides in Ontario, Quebec, and the Atlantic provinces, while less than 4% of the national park acreage, or 38% of national and provincial park acreage, is in eastern Canada. A more pronounced spatial imbalance exists in Ontario, with over 92% of the population and only 15% of the provincial park acreage in southern Ontario. Accessibility to wilderness recreational opportunities is even more limited than these aggregate figures suggest.

Any realistic assessment of the supply of parkland opportunities clearly must recognize accessibility. It must also be acknowledged that other park systems, principally at the municipal and regional level, contribute to the provision of accessible outdoor recreational opportunities. In southern Ontario, for example, many regional conservation authorities have added recreation to their traditional riverine water management function and provide readily accessible opportunities for a range of outdoor activities. Much of this focus at the municipal level has been on man-made recreational facilities, rather than development and utilization of biophysical resources, although urban forests and other natural areas within and adjacent to urban municipalities have taken on added significance in recent years (Eagles 1984).

Managers of national and provincial parks work with a set of objectives that, at times, appear to conflict sharply. There is a commitment within national parks, for example, to the preservation of significant Canadian landscapes for future generations as well as the provision of recreational opportunities for the enjoyment of present generations. The task of balancing or rationalizing these objectives is perhaps most difficult in smaller parks, more accessible parks, or those with features that attract large numbers of visitors. In Banff National Park, the potential for expansion of alpine skiing with its attendant facilities has fuelled a long-standing and at times bitter debate on a national level of parks policy and implementation of that policy. In 1986, following five years of study and public consultation, Parks Canada released a management framework for Banff and three other Rocky Mountain parks (Parks Canada 1986). The framework sets policies which attempt to balance use and preservation. While emphasizing protection of natural features and processes, the framework permits increased visitor services and accommodation, primarily through redevelopment, upgrading, and more effective use of existing facilities.

The struggle to balance preservation and use is also well illustrated, albeit on a more local scale, in Point Pelee National Park. Point Pelee, in southwestern Ontario, is one of Canada's smallest national parks. Its size, accessibility, and dynamic and fragile environment complicate the implementation of national park objectives. Pelee is a sand spit formation characterized by beaches and dunes which enclose a marsh occupying two-thirds of the park's fifteen square-kilometre area. Prior to 1970, the park's beach and land area was devoted almost exclusively to swimming, camping, picnicking, and other recreational use. Implementation of a master plan in the early 1970s eliminated family camping, restricted vehicular access and reduced beach use (Parks Canada 1972, Battin and Nelson 1982). This shift toward greater attention to preservation of significant park features has reduced visitation from 700,000 annually in the 1960s to 420,000 in the 1970s and 1980s. The master plan was superseded by a 1982 management plan which continues, aggressively, the commitment to preservation in the park (Parks Canada 1982).

A final issue, preserving the quality of the biophysical environment and the recreational experience, is one that is core not only to parks but to the management of all outdoor recreational resources. It often involves a consideration of the carrying capacity concept briefly described earlier and is typically associated with accessible, highly utilized parks or other resources, or where special features or dispersed wilderness activities are involved.

Numerous empirical investigations, many in a park setting, have established qualitative and quantitative relationships between use and environmental quality. Type, duration, and seasonal timing of use as well as characteristics of the environment are among the important parameters in these relationships. The variability of these parameters and differences in methodology employed make it difficult to draw generalizations useful for park or other recreational resource management, and have even brought confusion and discredit to the capacity concept. Similarly, a determination of social carrying capacity involves more than a consideration of density of use or number of encounters; the behaviour of users and experiences sought are also important. These and other problems with the carrying capacity concept as a managerial tool have been addressed effectively by Stankey (1982).

While precise identification of appropriate levels of use for any park environment or recreational resource may be elusive, managers must be cognizant of the complexities and subtleties of supply and work toward meaningful measures of the quantity of recreational opportunities afforded by the resource base. Such measures must more fully acknowledge the significance of accessibility and quality, and due consideration must be given to the experiences sought by recreationists.

Chapter 3

Demand

Stephen Smith
Department of Recreation and Leisure Studies
University of Waterloo

Demand

Definition

Demand is an ambiguous word. Recreation geographers use the word in at least four different ways (Wennergren and Johnston 1977). The most traditional sense is the neoclassical economic definition: demand is a schedule of the quantities of some commodity that will be consumed at various prices. Generally, higher prices are associated with lower consumption; lower prices are associated with higher consumption. Neoclassical demand can be simply pictured as the downward sloping line, on a graph relating price and quantity consumed, as DD' in Figure 1. It should be noted that the word *consumption* in recreation may refer to participation in an activity as well as the actual consumption of a good or service. Generally, you may treat the words *consumption* and *participation* as synonymous in this chapter.

A second definition of demand is that of current consumption. This type of demand is actually represented by a single point, X, on the demand curve DD' in Figure 1. If the price of some recreation commodity, perhaps the cost of a lift ticket at a ski slope, is P_1, the current consumption is Q_1. The pairing of price and consumption, represented by the point X, reflects the demand for lift tickets in terms of current consumption. This particular definition of demand is of limited utility to recreation planners because it tells nothing about trends in participation or about current levels of unmet need. It is, however, one of the most common empirical

Figure 1: Hypothetical Demand Curves

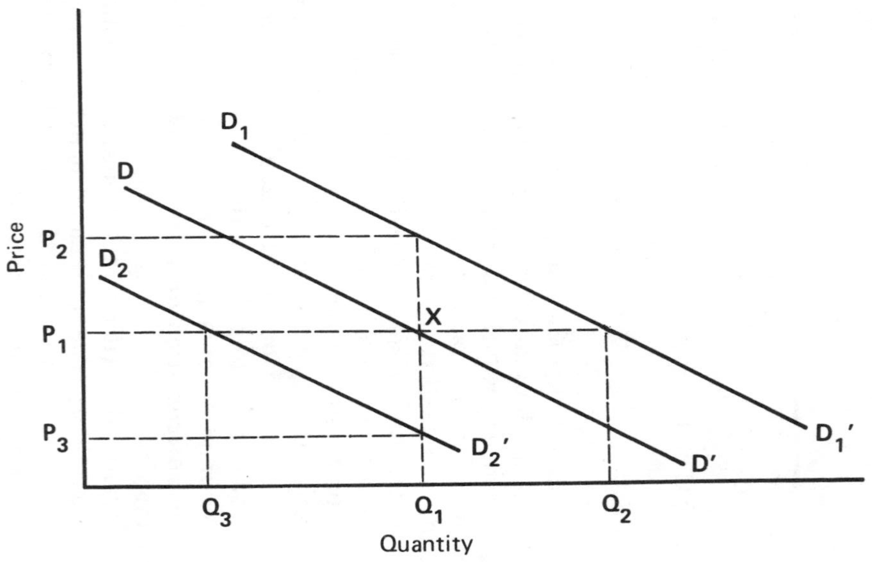

measures of demand because the data are relatively easy to obtain.

Demand is also used to refer to unmet need. This is sometimes referred to as latent demand. Latent demand is a measure of the difference between the potential level of consumption and the current level. Differences exist because of a lack of supply or time, cost limits, or other barriers. If these barriers were eliminated or supply increased, participation would be expected to rise to a higher level. Latent demand is also linked to the concept of option value or option demand. Option value refers to the value of the *opportunity* to use a recreation resource at some point in the distant future, rather than immediately or in the near future. For example, many Canadians value the existence of Banff National Park because, like Heaven, they hope to go there some day but not just yet. Similarly, option demand refers to the number of people who hold this desire.

Researchers may also use demand to refer to a forecast of future consumption. These changes may be due to changes in supply or accessibility, reflecting the meeting of latent demand, or to the creation of new demand through growth in income or population. Demand in this sense is related to the neoclassical concept of demand, but there are certain important differences. In the sense of future participation, the concept of demand is tied to a wide range of variables, not just price, that can influence the levels of participation. Although this perspective is broader in one sense than that of neoclassical demand, which is expressed in terms of price and quantity alone, it is also narrower. Neoclassical demand indicates levels of consumption over a wide range of price conditions, whereas the future participation perspective is focused on only one future time period. It is not possible to generalize from the future participation forecast for one year to any other year without re-doing the entire forecast.

Finally, demand is used to describe the desire for a psychological experience. In this sense, demand is more of a behavioural or social-psychological concept than an economic planning concept (Driver and Tocher 1974). The behavioural conception of demand is beyond the scope of this chapter, but is discussed in the context of perceptions and decision-making in chapter 4.

Demand Shifters

Although neoclassical demand is defined in terms of a price-quantity relationship, the neoclassical concept can be broadened to reflect the effects of other variables. Changes in social attitudes or tastes, the use of promotional techniques, the long-term effects of shifts in occupation, age, and education, and the introduction of new products and recreation opportunities can all influence the demand for any particular recreation activity. The availability of supply, in particular, can influence the level of expressed demand as much as or more than the socio-economic characteristics of the local population (Beaman, Kim, and Smith 1974, Smith and Stewart 1980). These types of variables are referred to as demand shifters. The term refers to their effect on a plot of the demand curve under specified conditions. Consider the total demand for camping in private campgrounds in some province. Under current conditions the demand might be represented by the curve DD' in Figure 1. If private campgrounds begin to add pools, tennis courts, indoor recreation centres, and generally develop into more complete resort campgrounds, the demand curve is likely to shift to the right, reflecting the willingness of people to pay more for the same level of consumption (curve $D_1 D_1'$). Before the shift, campers were willing to pay P_1 for Q_1 days of camping; with the improved campgrounds, they are now willing to pay P_2. Alternatively, they are also willing to purchase more days of camping, increasing from Q_1 to Q_2 if the price remains unchanged at P_1.

On the other hand, if the quality of the campgrounds begins to deteriorate, perhaps due to lower levels of maintenance, one would expect the demand curve to shift to the left, reflecting lowered overall demand. Campers would be willing to purchase campsite space at the original level, Q_1, only if the prices were dropped to P_3. Alternatively, they would decrease the total number of campsite rentals from Q_1 to Q_3 if the price remained unchanged from P_1.

Level of Analysis

Demand may be measured for either individuals or for groups. The patterns of demand tend to be more complex and less predictable when the unit of analysis is the individual. As more and more individuals are aggregated into groups, the stability of demand patterns and analysis tends to increase. Much of the reason for this is the tendency of large numbers of individuals to cause an averaging out of individual idiosyncratic behaviour so that only stable, typical, or mean demand patterns are left. Cyrus Young and Richard Smith (1979) describe the effects of the level of aggregation on the reliability of the analysis. They confirm the experience of many other researchers who have noted that more reliable models are obtained as the level of analysis increases. Unfortunately, the most reliable models come about from the most generalized and highly aggregated analyses -- analyses so aggregated that they are of limited usefulness to any practical recreation forecasting or planning problem. For example, the demand for visits by all Canadians to all national parks can be very accurately and reliably modelled. Such a model is of less use than a model relating the demand for national park visits by specific social or geographic groups. The more specific and useful models, however, are generally less accurate.

USES OF THE DEMAND CONCEPT

The different concepts of demand have different potential applications. The concept with the most limited utility is that of demand as a measure of current consumption or participation. The perspective can indicate the relative levels of popularity for certain activities or the level of consumption of certain commodities, and, with a certain degree of error, the likely level of participation or consumption in the very near future. This concept, however, is not useful for forecasting beyond the immediate future, nor does it have any special utility in recreation planning or policy analysis.

Concepts of demand related to unmet desires or needs or as a forecast of probable future consumption have a greater utility for recreation planning. They can be used to assess the ability of the existing resource and facility base to meet anticipated demands, indicating either a potential shortage or a potential over-supply. Estimation of regional variations in the supply/demand relationship can thus be used to guide locational decisions about future recreation developments (Smith 1977, Cicchetti 1971).

Estimation of Values

An important but perhaps unexpected use of demand is to estimate the value of resources used for different recreation purposes. A basic principle in economics is that resources should be allocated in such a way as to maximize overall returns to society (Brown 1984). This general principle can be stated more precisely: resources ideally should be allocated so that the marginal utility of a resource in any particular use is equal to the marginal utility of that same resource when put to other uses. For example, under the principles of economic efficiency, if a decision-maker is examining whether a certain hectare of land should be put into agriculture, housing, or reserved for recreation, he would allocate that hectare to the use which would return to society the highest value on that hectare. Land is optimally allocated when the value on that hectare of land would be the same regardless of the purpose to which the hectare was put. If the value to society were greatest when the land is allocated to recreation, one would conclude that there is insufficient land available for recreation -- and thus the demand for recreation land has caused the value to rise above that for other purposes.

The problem, of course, is how to determine the value of land for recreation or any other non-market purpose. The concept of demand provides one method for estimating economic value of non-market goods; this procedure produces a measure traditionally known as shadow price. Consider Figure 2, a demand curve for a recreation area with an admission fee of $2.50. At that charge, the site received 500,000 user-days per year. We can see from the curve that many people would have been willing to pay more than $2.50 for a visit. In fact, at least one individual would have paid as much as $6.00 for a visit. This individual receives a consumer surplus of $3.50: he receives a commodity which he values at $6.00 for only $2.50. Every other individual who would have been willing to pay something in excess of $2.50 also receives a consumer surplus equivalent to the difference between his maximum acceptable price and the actual cost. Only the individuals who were willing to pay a maximum of $2.50 do not enjoy a surplus. When the consumer surpluses for all users are aggregated, the total is represented by the area under the demand curve and above the cost curve, area A. It can be seen that as the admission fee drops, the consumer surplus for all users, area A, becomes larger. Eventually, at zero admission fee, the consumer surplus

Figure 2: Consumer Surplus Model

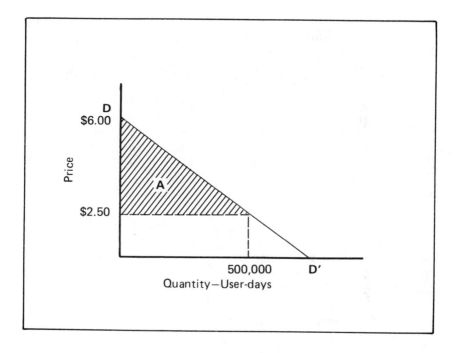

is the entire area under the demand curve. Under this condition, we can apply the following reasoning. Since area A reflects the surplus value all users receive from the site over the cost they paid to enter, and since the cost is zero, the entire area under the demand curve actually represents the economic value of a site. The same reasoning can be applied, of course, when there is a subsidized admission fee, as is the case in provincial and national parks and conservation authorities. The area under the demand curve and above the admission cost line represents the economic value of the site above that implied by any admission charge (Wennergren and Johnston 1977).

Given this model, the problem now becomes one of how to estimate the demand curve. Experimenting with a range of admission fees to determine user levels is normally impractical. Surveys could be employed to estimate the willingness of potential users to pay fees for admission, but such surveys can prompt gaming responses from those surveyed. The respondents will tend to give low estimates if they believe the results will actually be used to set fees. If, on the other hand, they believe that no fees will be set and that their answers will be used to justify preservation of the site, they will tend to give exaggerated answers about their willingness to pay.

A more reliable method is to base the demand curve on actual human behaviour: travel patterns (Clawson and Knetsch 1966). Even if the admission fee to a site is zero, users must still spend money on travel to reach the site. A researcher can identify the origins of visitors, from a user survey or from registration forms if they are available. An estimate of the distance from each origin to the site can thus be made and an estimate of typical travel costs for varying distance zones determined. If the researcher then plots the travel costs associated with different distance zones against the number of people coming from each distance zone, he produces a statistically estimated demand curve. By assuming that the average visitor from all distance zones has the same willingness to pay, the researcher can calculate the area under the derived demand curve and interpret it as a measure of consumer surplus or as a measure of the economic value of the site as described previously.

The best procedures to be used for calculating travel costs are still a matter of some debate. Out-of-pocket costs for fuel are generally considered as a basic cost, of course. The debate concerns whether (or how) to include costs for food and accommodation en route, prorated costs of equipment used on a trip, the value of travel time, and other variable costs. Walsh (1977) summarizes this debate and makes recommendations about what variables he feels are legitimate for cost estimation.

Once the value of a site has been obtained, it can be used to compare the current use of the site with alternative, competing uses to see if a reallocation of that site is warranted. The estimated demand curve for one site can be applied to similar sites to estimate their values. If some of these sites are merely proposed, the estimated value can be used as a basis for deciding whether development of the site is warranted, before funds are actually committed to that project.

Forecasting

Demand curves can be readily applied to make forecasts of potential consumption or use. In the case of a traditional demand curve, one merely needs to know the price that is to be charged for a recreation commodity to be able to anticipate the probable volume of business. The demand curve based on travel patterns, described in the previous section, can also be easily adapted to forecasting. One notes the distribution of population around a proposed site, or the forecast population for some future time period around an existing site, and then calculates the expected travel costs from various distance zones to the site. These costs are then related to the estimated demand curve and the associate use levels are calculated. Total probable use levels can then be obtained by summing over each distance zone.

Forecasts of use levels are also desired, however, when an estimated demand curve does not exist. The challenge is usually to develop directly a model that will give an estimate of future use without the intermediate step of deriving a traditional demand curve (Clawson 1985). Although many models have been developed for this problem, most are variations on two basic approaches: trend extrapolation and structural models (Smith 1983).

Trend Extrapolation

Trend extrapolation is based on the assumption that historical patterns are likely to continue for at least a short period of time into the future. A simple example of this logic can be seen in Figure 3, a graph showing the growth in the percentage of

Figure 3: Percent of Ontario Households Owning Tents

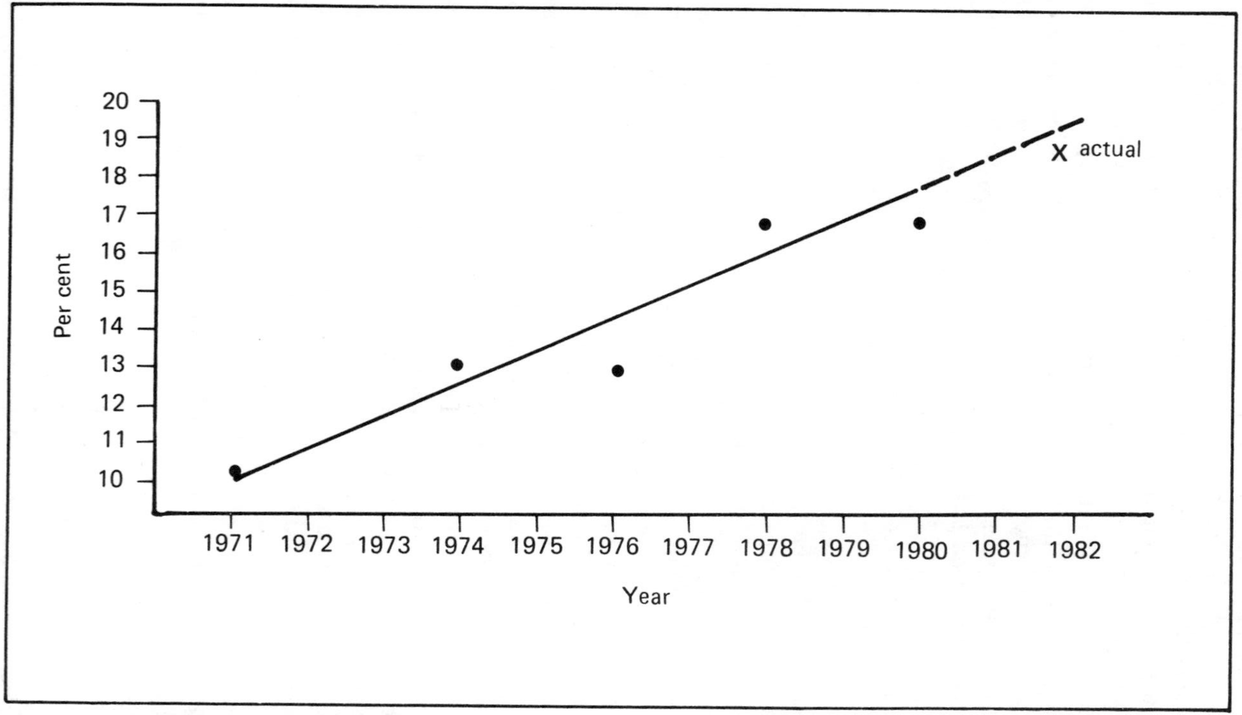

Source: Statistics Canada 1976 and 1984.

Ontario households owning tents. The percentage rose from 10% to 17% in 1980. Extending this trend, either graphically as in Figure 3, or statistically using least squares regression, would yield a prediction of between 19 and 20% for 1982. The actual percentage ownership for 1982 was 19%. Clearly, this method, as simplistic as it is, can yield valid predictions for many types of problems.

Many more trends, however, are not linear but rather curvilinear. Figure 4 is a plot of the percentage of Ontario households owning one or more types of overnight camping equipment. The historical pattern here is one of declining growth, reflected in the concave curve. Extrapolation of the curve from the period 1971 through 1980 to 1982 also produces a fairly accurate prediction of ownership levels.

Increasingly complex curves and time series relationships can be developed, including quadratic, logistic, and harmonic curves. In all cases, however, the basic logic is the same: a historical pattern is described and then extrapolated for a limited period of time into the future. Forecasts using these procedures should normally not be extended beyond either five years or a period that is half that of the historical record, whichever is less.

This forecasting approach works best for recreation consumption patterns for which there is a long history of data, which are not influenced by fads or minor economic fluctuations, and which may involve a significant investment in time or money to begin. This latter requirement implies that once an individual or household has made the initial investment in a particular activity or commodity, they are likely to stay with it for some time. Trend extrapolation is less useful for very new activities, fads, or activities that are highly vulnerable to outside forces such as changes in prices, fuel availability, or advertising efforts.

Structural Analysis

Trend extrapolation uses the passage of time as the basic independent variable for making a forecast. Changes in consumption are seen primarily as a function of time. In fact, of course, other variables influence consumption levels, such as price, income, availability of supply, and education of the general population from which participants arise.

Figure 4: Percent of Ontario Households Owning One or More Items of Overnight Camping Equipment

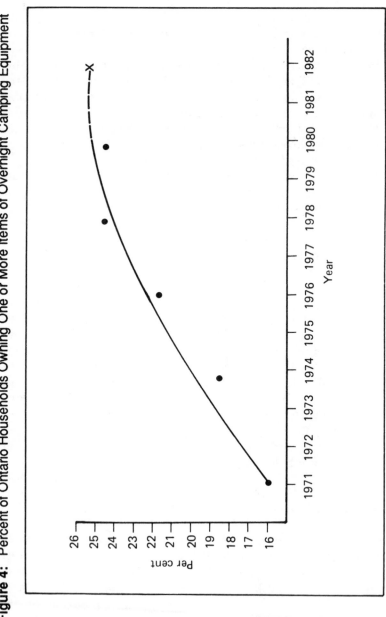

Source: Statistics Canada 1976 and 1984.

The primary statistical tools used for structural analysis are multiple regression or analysis of variance. Another common tool, the general linear model (GLM) is actually a generalized form of multiple regression and analysis of variance. Although the statistical issues associated with calibrating a general linear model are beyond the scope of this book, the logic for forecasting is not complicated.

Data related to historic levels of participation in some recreation activity are obtained. Data related to either personal characteristics of the participants or to general social conditions relevant at the time of participation are also collected. A model is then calibrated relating these characteristics or independent variables to the level of participation, the dependent variable. A typical model might resemble the following:

Probability of participating   =   General participation rate +
in hunting   effect of age + effect of
                                    income + effect of community
                                    size

Serge Rousseau *et al.* (1976) developed a model with this structure for Quebec hunters. They calibrated separate models for men and women using 1972 data; then by applying forecasts for changes in the age structure, income level, and population distribution by municipality, derived forecasts for probable numbers of male, female, and total hunters. Table 1 is a summary of their calculations. The following example may assist in the interpretation of the data in that table. The column entitled Total Population under Male or Female indicates the total predicted number of individuals for each category. The next column, Effect, represents the change in the general or mean probability of being a hunter associated with being in any particular category. For example, being a male between eighteen and nineteen years of age lowers the individual's odds of being a hunter by 0.033 percentage points, while being between eighteen and nineteen raises the odds for females by 0.126 percentage points. This change is multiplied by the estimated sub-population for each category to get a Total Effect in terms of the number of potential hunters to be added to or subtracted from the total number predicted for the province.

Table 1 is designed as an aggregate model; the effects coefficients can also be used as a predictive model for

Table 1

Hunters in Quebec in 1980
Projected by Sex, Age, Income and Urbanization in That Year

Variables	MALE			FEMALE		
	Total Population	General Participation Rate	General Mean	Total Population	General Participation Rate	General Mean
	2,150,782	0.274	599,314	2,274,707	0.033	77,502
	Persons	Effect	Total Effects	Persons	Effect	Total Effects
AGE						
18-19	94,626	-0.033	-3,123	89,788	0.126	11,313
20-24	346,550	0.135	46,784	341,821	0.078	26,662
25-29	293,233	-0.045	-13,195	269,524	0.055	14,824
30-34	189,092	0.181	34,226	255,290	-0.029	-7,403
35-39	219,706	0.012	2,636	214,098	-0.038	-8,136
40-44	198,264	-0.025	-4,957	195,646	-0.037	-7,239
45-49	168,657	-0.024	-4,048	167,411	-0.054	-9,040
50-64	414,605	-0.175	-72,556	441,189	-0.048	-21,177
65	226,049	-0.024	-5,425	299,940	-0.053	-15,897
Subtotal			-19,658			-16,093
INCOME						
0-2999	346,547	-0.143	-49,556	366,514	-0.004	-1,466
3000-4499	11,537	-0.067	-773	12,202	-0.017	-207
4500-5999	44,394	-0.022	-977	46,982	-0.019	-892
6000-7499	321,276	0.043	13,815	339,787	0.015	5,097
7500-8999	387,713	0.061	23,650	410,053	-0.006	-2,460
9000-10499	331,777	0.138	45,785	350,894	0.015	5,263
10500	707,538	-0.011	7,783	748,305	0.016	11,973
Subtotal			24,161			19,522

Table 1 Continued

	MALE			FEMALE		
	Total Population	General Participation Rate	General Mean	Total Population	General Participation Rate	General Mean
Variables	2,150,782	0.274	589,314	2,274,707	0.033	77,502
	Persons	Effect	Total Effects	Persons	Effect	Total Effects
URBANIZATION						
1000-9999	244,701	-0.114	-27,896	253,379	-0.021	-5,321
10000-29999	191,021	0.162	30,945	198,139	0.016	-3,170
30000-99999	198,309	-0.036	-7,139	214,330	-0.017	-3,644
100000-	1,196,204	-0.156	-186,920	1,309,365	-0.012	-15,712
Rural	318,547	0.072	22,935	299,494	0.034	10,183
Subtotal			-168,075			-17,664
Total			425,742			63,267
Total Hunters (Total Males and Females Participating)						489,009

Source   S. Rousseau, et al., 1976.

individuals. In this case, one would begin with the general participation rate of 0.274 for males or 0.033 for females and add or subtract the relevant age, income, and urbanization coefficients that apply to the hypothetical individual being modelled.

One of the key steps in the use of any structural model for forecasting recreation participation is the ability to develop reliable and independent forecasts of future values of the independent variables. Demographic models can provide fairly accurate forecasts of the numbers of people expected in each age cohort for short and medium-term forecasts, but there are few reliable models for forecasting changes in city populations, income levels, educational levels, and other variables often used in the development of structural models. Another problem with structural models is the implicit assumption that the relationship between the dependent and independent variables, as measured by the effects coefficients, will be stable over the time period of the forecast. The example given here includes a coefficient of -0.143 for incomes between 0 and 2,999 dollars. Although this coefficient is empirically based on actual hunting participation, there is no assurance that this coefficient will necessarily remain stable over the eight years between 1972 and 1980. If the actual relationship between this income level and the propensity to hunt changes, the forecast is likely to be in error. A third problem is the adequacy of the model. This refers to the question of whether all relevant variables have been included and whether the structure of the model (additive, multiplicative, exponential) is appropriate.

Researchers rarely go back to verify the accuracy of their forecasts in an attempt to improve future predictions. For example, the actual number of hunters in Quebec in 1980 was 615,112, not 489,009 as predicted. No attempt has yet been made to identify the sources of the error in the hunting model to improve its future performance. The failure of this model is typical of many recreation forecasting models. The primary problems with them include those mentioned previously as well as inadequate model structures. Significant improvement in our ability to make forecasts will not be possible without the honest and critical evaluation of the success or failure of former predictions.

CURRENT LEVELS OF DEMAND

Existing Patterns of Participation

As noted previously, one of the most common uses of the term *demand* is to describe actual levels of participation in activities. Most of our information about national and provincial participation patterns come from independent, specialized participation surveys. There is no nationally organized, regularly scheduled survey of participation in outdoor recreation activities -- or any other type of leisure activities. Among the special difficulties this lack of systematic data-gathering for recreation participation causes is the lack of consistency in: the type of samples drawn, the list of activities included in the questionnaire, the time of year and the context of the survey, and the definitions and coding categories used for summarizing the data. It is obviously difficult to compare the results of different surveys if one was conducted in the summer and the other in the winter or if one asked the respondent to report on what activities, if any, he had engaged in during the day of the survey and the other asked the respondent to recall all activities he engaged in during the twelve months preceding the survey.

Despite such problems, it is still possible to find relatively recent surveys that describe levels of participation in selected outdoor activities. Occasionally, it is even possible to find two roughly comparable surveys conducted several years apart that suggest changes in participation patterns over time.

Table 2 is a summary of participation in selected activities based on two similar surveys conducted in 1971 and 1981. In this list of activities, walking is the single most popular activity in both years. Over half of all Canadians reported walking for pleasure in 1981; over one-third went bicycling and swimming in the same year. In all cases the participation levels increased over the decade between 1971 and 1981. In some cases, such as bicycling or skiing, the increase was at least threefold in terms of per cent of population participating. The increases were even greater in terms of total numbers of participation because of population increase as well as the increase in the participation rate of individuals.

Even though these two surveys are reasonably comparable so that comparisons are possible, they illustrate other types of limitations or problems in data collection. For example, walking is undefined. Some respondents may have taken this

Table 2

Participation in Selected Outdoor Recreation Activities
1971 and 1981

	No. (000s)	%	No. (000s)	%
Walking	6,166	41.9	11,910	57.5
Bicycling	1,736	11.8	7,857	37.9
Swimming	4,194	28.5	7,582	36.6
Jogging	1,045	7.1	4,337	20.9
Cross-country skiing Downhill skiing	1,001	6.8	3,645	17.6
Tennis	739	5.0	3,078	14.8
Golf	1,104	7.5	1,972	9.5

Source: Statistics Canada, 1976 and 1984.

to include an evening stroll around the block while others may have interpreted it to be synonymous only with hiking. Swimming in these surveys was limited to swimming in pools, not at beaches -- thus missing a significant percentage of the total activity. Cross-country and downhill skiing were combined in 1971 but separated in 1981. And more fundamentally, numerous important outdoor recreation activities are totally missing, such as camping, fishing, hunting, and snowmobiling.

There is significant variation among the provinces in participation rates in outdoor activities (see Table 3). Generally, the western provinces have higher rates of participation than the eastern provinces. This is especially noticeable for those activities dependent on certain climate and physiographic conditions, such as downhill skiing. These patterns clearly illustrate the importance of supply as a demand shifter -- a factor referred to earlier. Participation in downhill skiing in the four Atlantic provinces is so low that the data related to participation in that activity, as measured in the 1981 Canada Fitness Survey, were too low to be released, due to high sampling variability. This pattern is consistent with findings by McPherson and Curtis (1986) who found that overall physical activity levels -- recreation and exercise -- were greater for westerners than easterners. McPherson and Curtis also examined the correlations between general activity levels and a variety of personal and social characteristics, such as income, education, sex, marital status, occupation, and language. Their findings suggest that, with the major exception of education, the east-west variations still held when their analysis controlled for the socio-economic characteristics of respondents. In the case of education, individuals with higher levels of education are significantly more likely to report participation in exercise and physical recreation activities; further, there is a significantly higher proportion of highly educated individuals in the west than in the east.

Although the 1981 Canada Fitness Survey did not collect information on the availability of recreation facilities and opportunities, the survey did include questions about the perceptions of the respondents concerning opportunities for participation. Generally, respondents living in the Atlantic provinces and Quebec were more likely to cite lack of opportunity as a reason for not participating than those respondents living in the western provinces. However, McPherson and Curtis found that even after controlling for such

Table 3

Participation in Selected Activities by Province - Per Cent of Population
10 Years and Over

	Canada	Nfld	PEI	NS	NB	Que	Ont	Man	Sask	Alta	BC
Walking	57.5	57.0	54.4	67.2	50.8	59.9	55.8	53.7	51.5	56.4	62.5
Bicycling	37.9	27.1	25.2	26.9	28.9	41.5	37.7	42.4	37.2	42.8	33.1
Swimming	36.6	19.1	10.7	25.0	21.2	33.2	40.3	31.6	32.3	42.7	43.3
Jogging	20.9	17.4	15.5	18.7	17.1	17.4	22.2	22.3	19.9	25.3	24.0
Cross-country skiing	17.6	6.3	9.7	10.8	14.0	26.8	16.1	19.4	13.8	16.2	7.6
Tennis	14.8	*	*	9.6	8.6	13.2	17.5	12.2	12.1	15.6	17.1
Alpine skiing	10.8	*	*	*	*	9.4	9.2	6.0	8.0	26.0	15.5
Golf	9.5	*	*	6.2	*	6.1	10.8	12.8	15.2	13.6	11.2

* Sampling variability too high to permit release

Source: Fitness Canada, 1981.

perceptions, there appeared to be an east-west split in overall activity levels.

Another way of examining the demand for different types of activities is to look at the ownership level of different types of recreation equipment (Table 4). Statistics Canada publishes approximately biannual reports on household facilities and equipment surveys. Many of the items included in those surveys include outdoor recreation equipment. Although not every household that owns a particular piece of equipment will participate in the activity for which the equipment was purchased, such surveys do give an indication of the relative popularity of certain activities. The discrepancy between ownership and participation levels may also give an estimate of latent demand. The difference between potential but inactive participants and former or drop-out participants, however, needs to be kept clearly in mind. This distinction, unfortunately, cannot normally be made from the data available.

Although the data in Table 3 and Table 4 are not for the same years, some general comparisons are possible. In 1981, 37.9% of all Canadians over the age of 10 years went bicycling; between 44% and 48% of all households had adult-sized bicycles. Approximately 24% of Canadian households had at least one pair of cross-country skis, whereas only 17.6% went skiing in 1981. A similar pattern exists in downhill skiing: approximately 16% ownership versus 10.8% participation.

These comparisons must be made with caution because, as noted, the data are not from the same years nor from the same type of survey. Further, the participation data are for individuals, whereas ownership figures apply to households. In any event, it would appear that there is a rather large inventory of outdoor recreation equipment gathering dust in garages and basements across the country.

Trends in Participation

Variations in the levels of participation in activities over time can be of greater practical and theoretical value than synoptic regional variations. A high level of participation in skiing in Alberta, for example, needs to be interpreted in terms of whether further increases are to be expected or if the demand is likely to begin decreasing. Such trend information is of greater usefulness for recreation planners than static data because it permits plans to be made for future developments. Further, an

Table 4

Ownership of Selected Outdoor Recreation Equipment: Per Cent of Canadian Households

Item	1972	1974	1976	1978	1980	1982
Snowmobiles	9	9	10	10	10	8
Adult-sized bicycles	29	30	39	42	44	28
One or more types of camping equipment	18	21	24	27	27	28
Outboard boats	8	8	8	8	8	8
Sailboats	1	1	1	1	1	2
Canoes	2	3	3	3	3	3
Cross-country skis	n/a	n/a	n/a	17	23	25
Downhill skis	n/a	n/a	n/a	14	15	17

Source: Statistics Canada, 1976 and 1984.

analyst can examine some of the population characteristics that appear to be correlated with changes in levels of participation. As was discussed earlier, trend data are relatively difficult to obtain because of the lack of consistency between participation surveys. If the data in Table 2 can be assumed to reflect reasonable consistency between the two surveys that were used to collect the data, then a tentative analysis can be conducted to identify some of the forces that affect changes in participation levels in different activities.

Data pertinent to some major demand shifters were obtained from Statistics Canada sources: age, structure, education, income, employment, occupation in selected industry sectors, and expenditures related to the construction of new recreation facilities (Table 5). These variables were then regressed against the change in percentage participation from 1971 to 1981 for each of the activities listed in Table 2. The results of the multiple regressions are shown in Table 6. The results show dramatic variation in the ability of demand shifters to account for change in participation. At one extreme is participation change in walking. This was not significantly correlated with any of the independent variables selected. The models of changes in participation in swimming and golf were at the other extreme, with 96% and 97% of the total variance explained by a few demand shifters.

Variables related to changes in the age structure were the most common significant demand shifters; five of the six significant models included age-related variables: bicycling, swimming, jogging, golf, and camping. Only the model for tennis did not include an age-related variable. An education variable, the percentage of the provincial population enrolled in university, was a significant variable for tennis -- the only model not based on age variables, and also for camping.

Participation increases in bicycling are positively associated with changes in the percentage of the provincial residents 65 and over and inversely associated with changes in the percentage of residents between 35 and 44 years of age. This negative association with the 35-44 age group can also be noted for swimming and golf. On the other hand, increases in this age group are positively associated with increases in the demand for jogging. Increases in the under-25 age group are positively associated with increases in the demand for swimming and camping.

Tennis, the one activity not connected with age variables in these models, is closely correlated with social status: higher

Table 5

Independent Variables for Multiple Regression Analysis Demonstrating Demand Shifters

Acronym	Variable
DeltaPDI	Per cent change in per capita personal disposable income between 1971 and 1981
PDI	1981 per capita personal disposable income
Unemp	1981 unemployment rate
Mfg	Per cent of 1981 labour force employed in manufacturing
Forest	Per cent of 1981 labour force employed in forestry
FIRE	Per cent of 1981 labour force employed in finance, insurance, or real estate
Univ	Per cent of 1981 population enrolled in university
Under25	Per cent of 1981 population under 25 years of age
Delta25	Per cent change in proportion of population under age 25 between 1971 and 1981
Delta35	Per cent change in proportion of population between 35 and 44 between 1971 and 1981
Over65	Per cent of 1981 population 65 years of age or older
Delta65	Per cent change in proportion of population 65 years of age or older between 1971 and 1981

Table 6

Multiple Regression Results
Effects of Demand Shifters by Activity

Walking

no significant relationships

Bicycling $R^2 = 0.72$, F = 8.91, Prob = 0.01

Variable	Beta	Prob
Delta65	0.77	0.02
Delta35	-0.71	0.00

Swimming $R^2 = 0.96$, F = 30.70, Prob = 0.00

Variable	Beta	Prob
Mfg	9.87	0.01
Forest	2.34	0.05
Under25	5.43	0.00
Delta35	-0.65	0.01

Jogging $R^2 = 0.61$, F = 12.54, Prob = 0.01

Variable	Beta	Prob
Unemp	-0.69	0.01
Delta35	0.17	0.10

Tennis $R^2 = 0.81$, F = 14.99, Prob = 0.00

Variable	Beta	Prob
PDI	0.01	0.00
Univ	3.03	0.14

Golf $R^2 = 0.97$, F = 23.71, Prob = 0.00

Variable	Beta	Prob
Unemp	-0.54	0.00
Conexp	0.04	0.00
Delta35	-0.22	0.00

Camp $R^2 = 0.57$, F = 4.66, Prob = 0.05

Variable	Beta	Prob
Univ	-81.59	0.04
Under25	14.81	0.13

levels of increased demand for tennis are directly related to higher levels of per capita personal disposable income and university enrolments. University enrolments, in contrast, are inversely associated with the increase in demand for camping: higher levels of university enrolments, lower increases in camping demand.

Unemployment levels exercise a dampening effect on demand for many forms of recreation. In these models, the inverse relationship between employment and increased demand for participation was significant for jogging and for golf.

The results of this analysis should be interpreted with caution. Many other variables could have been included in the multiple regression equations, some of which might well have been more significant than those used. For example, there was no recognition of variations in the level of supply of facilities for the different activities by province, nor was there any attempt to control for the costs (if any) associated with participation in any activity in any particular region. The results do, however, suggest the potential significance of demographic and social variables for explaining variations in the demand for some outdoor recreation activities.

Latent Demand

Measurement of latent demand, the potential for additional consumption or participation in recreation activities is difficult. It is possible, of course, to adopt a historical perspective and to examine growth in demand over time and then to infer the existence of a latent demand that has been met. Such a retrospective, of course, is not especially useful for planning. One of the few alternatives for measuring currently unmet demand is to ask people about what activities they would like to start participating in, but currently do not. One can ask, as well, the perceived barriers to such participation (Searle and Jackson 1985).

The 1981 Canada Fitness Survey includes this type of question in the survey instrument. Over one hundred activities were mentioned, but many received responses from less than 0.1% of the respondents. Some of the more popular activities -- those with relatively high latent demand -- are listed in Table 7. Several traditional outdoor recreation activities are also included in the list although they have a lower latent demand.

Table 7

Activities Desired By Canadians
But Not Currently Participated in
(Age 10 and over)

ACTIVITY	PER CENT CITING
Swimming	34.2
Tennis	22.6
Jogging	20.2
Bicycling	18.7
Walking	9.6
Downhill skiing	8.5
Cross-country skiing	7.5
Hiking	3.1
Horseback riding	3.0
Water skiing	1.8
Sailing	1.6
Scuba	1.6
Canoeing	1.4
Camping	1.2
Wind surfing	1.1
Fishing	1.0
Hunting	0.7
Kayaking	0.5

Sources: Fitness Canada, 1981, and author's calculations.

Swimming is the single most desired new activity. Over one-third of all Canadians surveyed indicated they would like to begin swimming but had not yet started because of certain constraints. Tennis, jogging, and bicycling were also frequently cited as activities people would like to begin. With the major exception of skiing, most outdoor activities were named by less than 2% of the respondents as desired activities. The low response may reflect low latent demand for such activities, or it may reflect an unintentional bias inherent in the Canada Fitness Survey. This particular survey was explicitly lined with fitness, lifestyle, and health issues; a sub-sample of all respondents were even given fitness tests in conjunction with the written survey. The emphasis on physical fitness may have tended to cause most people to think more about exercise activities such as jogging than about more recreational activities such as hiking or canoeing.

Another potential problem with any survey intended to measure latent demand is the lack of a strong and reliable link between expressed opinions and attitudes, on one hand, and actual behaviour, on the other. Some respondents will doubtless begin new activities if they can overcome the constraints, but many others will never act on their expressed desires regardless of the actual opportunities afforded them.

The Canada Fitness Survey also included a question about the barriers that kept people from participating in the activities they desired. Table 8 is a summary of the major barriers cited. The single most important barrier is lack of time, due either to other leisure activities or to job and home commitments. This may reflect a genuine lack of time, or it may indicate problems with the management of the time the respondents have available. Those citing lack of time may also use this reason as an excuse for a simple lack of sufficient interest to make the effort to schedule time for an activity.

Lack of facilities was the second most common reason given for the failure to begin a new activity. This reason may have special relevance to many outdoor activities. Access to clean water, public open space, campgrounds, and other specialized outdoor facilities is quite important to the provision of outdoor recreation opportunities. The cost of participating was ranked relatively low, fourth on the list. Although cost can be a significant barrier for specific activities, such as downhillskiing, snowmobiling, or sailing, many other activities involve relatively modest expenditures for equipment and/or admission fees and travel costs. It might be noted,

Table 8

Reasons Given for Not Beginning New Activities
(Age 10 and over)

REASON	PER CENT CITING
Lack of time	38.9
Lack of facilities	28.0
Lack of self-discipline	19.7
Cost	12.8
Lack of equipment	8.8
Weather	8.3
Injury	5.5
No partner	4.3

Sources: Fitness Canada, 1981, and author's calculations.

though, that lack of equipment was cited as a separate reason by almost 9% of the respondents. It is likely that lack of equipment is closely related to the inability to afford it. If this is indeed the case, finances keep over 20% of the respondents from participating in activities they would like to start.

SUMMARY

The term, *demand* is used by recreation researchers to mean many different things. This diversity of meaning reflects the many uses of the general concepts covered by the term. Demand is used to assess the current popularity of activities, trends in participation, the need for new services and resources, the value of resources in competing uses, and probability levels of participation at specific future dates.

The level of demand for some recreation activity is influenced by the cost of participating in that activity as well as by a wide variety of external or social factors such as the age structure of society, income and education levels, availability of supply, previous experience with this activity, tastes, and attitudes. The factors are sometimes known as demand shifters. They can be used to develop forecasting models to predict future levels of participation or to analyse why participation rates have changed despite stability in the cost of participation.

One special conception of demand is latent demand. This is a measure of the potential for participation that is unmet due to barriers of supply, cost, time, or other factors. Latent demand is difficult to measure accurately, but some data related to the phenomenon can be obtained from surveys describing perceived barriers.

Current patterns of participation and participation trends often display significant regional variations. In Canada, one of the most pronounced regional variations appears to be a greater participation in most forms of recreation in the west than in the east. This may be due, in part, to variations in education as well as in lifestyle.

Chapter 4

Perceptions and Decisions

Edgar Jackson
Department of Geography
University of Alberta

Perceptions and Decisions

INTRODUCTION

Geography and Outdoor Recreation

In his review of Canadian recreation research, planning, and management, Wall (1981) has described two reasons why geographers study outdoor recreation. First, the spatial organization of land uses and conflicts, such as those associated with recreation, has traditionally been of interest to geographers. Secondly, recreational resources and facilities attract people, thus creating patterns of movement that are analogous to other forms of spatial behaviour, like commuting and migration. Thus, the same geographical perspectives developed for the study of these behaviours are equally applicable in recreation research.

There are at least two other reasons why outdoor recreation attracts the attention of geographers, and why, in turn, the understanding of outdoor recreation may benefit from their insights. Both demonstrate the value of thinking about recreation, not just as the activities that people do in their free time, but as a set of choices, or decisions, based on perceptions.

First, we can think of recreational resources and facilities, which vary in quantity, location, and quality, as a vast set of opportunities from which people may choose. But opportunities do not *determine* recreational choices: they are *perceived* and *evaluated* by different people in different ways, based on incomplete and imperfect information about the opportunities that are available and how they might satisfy the needs that people wish to fulfil by recreating.

The same can be said of recreational activities: no one
forces a person to spend a weekend downhill skiing, to go
fishing, hunting, or canoeing, or to participate in team sports
such as ice hockey, curling, or football. Like recreationists
everywhere, Canadians *choose* to do these things, and they
choose from the enormous array of recreational opportunities
available in our present-day society, not always knowing if the
chosen activity will be the most fulfilling, enjoyable, or
satisfying one. From this perspective, recreation is inherently a
choice process, in which perceptions of various kinds are
fundamentally important. Geographers, particularly those in
the branch of the discipline loosely described as "resources
geography," have devoted a great deal of effort over the past three
decades to understanding people's perceptions of the
environment and their associated behaviour. Thus, the insights
and perspectives of behavioural geographers can lend much to
the understanding of outdoor recreation choices.

The second reason has to do with the setting for outdoor
recreation. Precisely because outdoor recreation takes place
outdoors, the quality of recreational resources and
environments exerts a profound influence on recreationists'
enjoyment -- although, of course, the level and type of enjoyment
sought and gained vary markedly within and between different
types of activity. An important component of environmental
quality is the extent to which the land and its resources have
been modified, perhaps even degraded, by other types of
recreational use or entirely different resource uses. But, in
exactly the same way that opportunities do not determine
recreational choices, neither does the quality of recreational
environments determine enjoyment. Instead, it is perceptions
of environmental quality and environmental impacts that will
ultimately affect whether or not a person enjoys the activity in
the chosen setting. Since many geographers have concerned
themselves with matters such as *perceptions* of environmental
quality, environmental impacts, and other aspects of human-
environment relations, the study of these issues in a
recreational context is also a legitimate geographic concern.

Recreation as an Activity and as an Experience

Two main approaches to recreation have been common in the
research literature: recreation as an activity, and recreation as
an experience (Driver and Tocher 1970). Both approaches are

useful and important in a theoretical context, which can be defined as the enhancement of our understanding of recreation behaviour. They are also useful in a practical context -- applying the results of recreation research to improve the delivery of recreation services to the public. Recreation planners are generally viewed as having two main objectives to address. They must provide recreation services in the form of resources, facilities, and programs, in such a way that the number, mix, location, and timing of these meet the public's demand for recreation. And they must ensure that the people who take advantage of these recreation services derive the maximum level of enjoyment or satisfaction from them. Recreation planners and managers can only do this by identifying and understanding the influence of factors that enhance or detract from the quality of the recreational experience. On this basis they can, within limits, take steps to modify them.

The Activity Approach

In essence, the activity approach focuses on the recreational activities in which people participate, and uses numerical measures in a head-counting manner, to answer questions such as: What are the activities in which people participate? Which activities are most and least popular? Who participates in different forms of recreation? When and where does participation occur? Many different indicators can be used to measure the concept *recreation participation*: they include participation rates (the percentages of the public who take part in a particular activity), the frequency of participation (how often people take part), and the number, type, and combinations of recreational activities in which individuals and groups of people participate. As we shall see later in this chapter, however, the choice of indicators can strongly affect the interpretation of research results, and therefore their theoretical and practical implications.

Regardless of how it is measured, some indicator of recreation participation can be used as a dependent variable against which to assess the influence of the explanatory factors which will be reviewed later, such as socio-economic variables, motivations, and values and environmental attitudes. Measures of participation can also be used as independent variables to examine activity-based variations in recreational satisfaction, perceived conflict, and the other outcomes of recreation behaviour also to be discussed later in this chapter.

The Experience Approach

The activity approach can contribute much towards achieving the first objective of recreation management noted above, but little, if anything, to the second. Recreation researchers, like practitioners, have also increasingly come to realize the limitations of the activity approach. They now recognize that the activities which people choose are based on motivations, needs, and perceptions of recreational opportunities and environments. These kinds of factors influence recreational choices, as well as enhance or detract from the level and type of enjoyment achieved. Consequently, for both theoretical and practical reasons, another approach to the study of recreation has been developed, in which recreation is not viewed just as an activity, but also as an experience.

In this approach, the focus shifts away from numerical indicators of recreation participation, towards a more qualitative evaluation of the satisfaction or enjoyment that people achieve by participating, and the factors that influence satisfaction and other outcomes. In this sense, recreation is not viewed as an end in itself, but rather as a means to an end. The focus of research is on questions such as why people participate (their motivations), and variations in satisfaction within and between activities.

The Behavioural Approach

The two aforementioned approaches to recreation involve rather different conceptual frameworks, emphasize different types of questions, may imply different methods of data collection, and are directed towards different practical applications. For practical purposes, the fulfillment of both basic goals in recreation management rests upon information describing aspects of participation in recreational activities as well as the quality of recreation experiences. Similarly, recreation researchers, in seeking to achieve the in-depth understanding afforded by the experience approach, cannot neglect the important insights, concepts, and measures contributed in the activity approach. Thus, the two approaches do not conflict with each other, but are complementary. Indeed, an effort to combine them is what defines the essence of the behavioural approach to recreation.

In this approach, recreation behaviour is viewed as a decision-making process. Each stage in recreation behaviour, including the initial decision to recreate, the selection of the most appropriate activity, where and when the activity will take place, and so on, is seen as a choice. In turn, each choice is influenced by a host of perceptions, including imperfect knowledge of opportunities, evaluations of their appropriateness, past experience, expectations of likely enjoyment, and many other factors to be explored later in this chapter.

In the behavioural approach to recreation, the central variables are no different from those investigated in the other two approaches. It is still important to define and distinguish between different forms of outdoor recreation and to examine the quality of recreational engagements. The main contribution of the behavioural approach is to synthesize the activity and experience approaches into a holistic model and conceptual framework. The focus is simultaneously on the entire complex behavioural system made up of the antecedents of recreational behaviours, their outcomes, and the behaviours themselves (Figure 1).

Outline of the Chapter

The main body of this chapter is divided into three sections. First, aspects of outdoor recreation behaviour among Canadians are described. Then, in the second section, some of the factors related to these choices are reviewed, including socio-economic variables, motivations, and values and environmental attitudes. Finally, attention turns to the outcomes of recreational choices, expressed in terms of recreational satisfaction, the capacity of recreational resources, and perceived conflicts between incompatible recreational activities. In the conclusions, the value of the behavioural approach to recreation is recapitulated, as is one of the most important themes of this chapter -- the paradox that, while the results of recreation research may improve our understanding of recreation, they may simultaneously increase the difficulty of recreation management.

Before proceeding to the main body of the chapter, the reader should recognize that other perceptions besides those of the

Figure 1: Elements of the Behavioural Approach to Outdoor Recreation

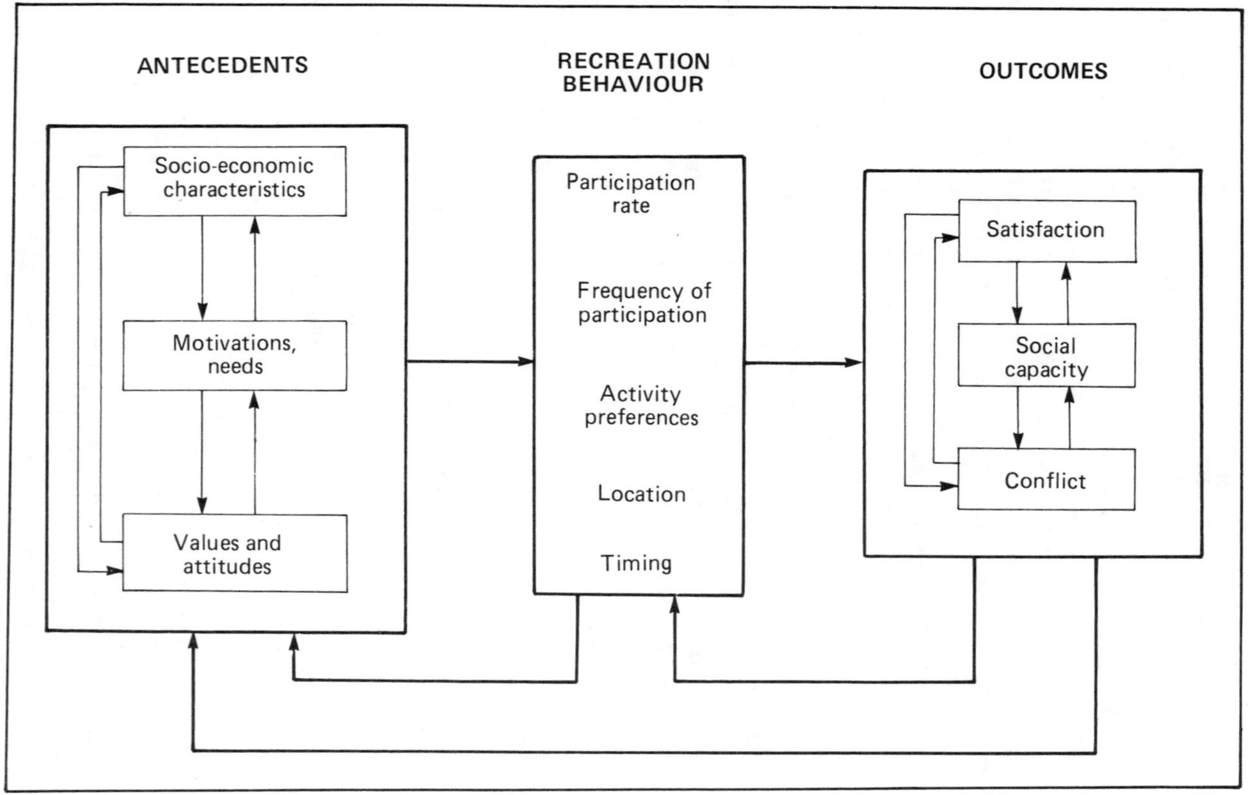

recreationist affect recreational decisions, namely the perceptions and decisions of politicians and the planners and managers of recreational resources, facilities, and programs, both public and private. Obviously such persons base their decisions on their own perceptions of such matters as what the public desires and what they believe the public should desire (White 1966), on their knowledge of resources, on their preferences about desirable levels of environmental quality and acceptable levels of environmental impact, and a complex array of similar factors. The inherent importance of these perceptions and decisions cannot be denied, nor how they directly and indirectly affect the perceptions, choices, and enjoyment of recreationists. This chapter, however, concentrates almost entirely on the perceptions and decisions of the recreationist.

THE CHOICE OF RECREATIONAL ACTIVITIES

Participation in recreation by Canadians might initially appear to be most appropriately dealt with in the chapter on demand, but there are several reasons why recreation participation must also be discussed from a behavioural perspective. First, if recreation is to be viewed as a decision-making process, then it is necessary to know what those decisions are, if only as a base line against which to measure the effects of the various factors which explain people's recreational choices.

Second, some valuable lessons about recreation research can be learned by briefly discussing the conceptualization, measurement, and classification of recreational activities and how our knowledge of people's recreational choices is thus affected. At this stage, it is vital to recognize that the collection and interpretation of data about recreation participation, and therefore about its antecedents and outcomes, are inevitably shaped by the way in which recreation behaviour is defined and measured. All of our information about people's recreation decisions comes from empirical studies: in the research process, researchers must decide how to define, and then measure, the phenomenon of recreation participation. Recreation participation, however, is not an objectively defined phenomenon. Rather, it is an abstract concept for which no single or best indicator or measure exists. Researchers can choose from several options.

Third, simply by comparing the meanings and implications of different measures of recreation, we can actually infer a great deal about recreational decisions, without any elaborate statistical analysis of related variables. Comparisons of different measures show, for example, that the activities in which people participate are not always the same as the ones they most enjoy or would choose most frequently if all barriers to participation were removed. This implies that, while recreation participation is a relatively free choice, it is not an entirely unconstrained one. Also, because the inferences to be drawn from different measures of recreation behaviour can vary significantly, it will become obvious that recreation planners, when collecting information about the public's recreational behaviour, must take great care in choosing appropriate measures.

Canadians' Recreational Choices

From time to time, Statistics Canada conducts nationwide surveys of the public's recreation participation, their activity preferences, and some of the socio-economic and demographic variables related to these aspects of recreation behaviour. In chapter 3 on demand, Smith identifies several limitations of these surveys; in the present context, the major limitation is that the surveys provide data only about a restricted range of activities. Nevertheless, the statistics summarized in Table 1 convey useful information, not only about some of the recreational activities in which Canadians participate and which they prefer, but also about the conceptualization and measurement of recreation behaviour.

The percentages of Canadians who participated in eight selected recreational activities in the year prior to the survey are shown in Table 1. The numbers are further broken down by province, and the row of statistics in parentheses shows the proportions of participants in each activity who described it as being the one in which they most prefer to participate.

The most obvious and superficial item of information conveyed by the table is that participation rates vary among activities: for instance, roughly six times as many Canadians participate in swimming as in curling, while roughly equal proportions participate in cross-country and downhill skiing. The regional differences that can be seen in the lower half of the table are much more important. For some activities, provincial

Table 1

National and Provincial Participation Rates* in
Eight Selected Recreational Activities

	Swimming	Ice-Skating	Tennis	Golf	Ice Hockey	Cross-Country Skiing	Downhill Skiing	Curling
	%	%	%	%	%	%	%	%
CANADA								
Participation rates	31.8	16.8	12.5	11.0	8.4	7.7	6.9	4.7
(Percentage of participants indicating activity as their favourite)	(25.6)	(9.3)	(18.2)	(27.3)	(42.7)	(27.5)	(40.3)	(33.8)
Preference rate	8.1	1.6	2.3	3.0	3.6	2.1	2.8	1.6
PROVINCES (participation rates)								
Newfoundland	21.8	15.5	3.6	**	9.6	**	**	**
P.E.I.	29.5	22.7	8.0	14.8	10.2	**	**	**
Nova Scotia	19.1	17.3	8.0	6.9	9.0	2.3	1.6	2.3
New Brunswick	24.2	16.3	6.9	6.3	8.7	2.6	2.4	3.0
Quebec	27.5	14.6	9.5	6.8	7.7	14.3	6.4	1.5
Ontario	36.4	17.5	15.1	13.3	9.1	5.7	6.7	3.7
Manitoba	31.7	17.9	12.4	12.8	8.0	7.9	5.0	13.1
Saskatchewan	29.3	17.8	8.4	13.9	9.4	6.8	5.2	17.8
Alberta	32.4	20.7	13.4	12.8	8.3	6.3	11.7	11.6
B.C.	33.5	16.4	17.1	14.6	6.7	2.9	11.0	5.8

*   Percentage participating at least once in the year preceding the survey.
**   Inadequate data precluded accurate reporting.

variations are relatively minor: in the case of ice-skating, which had the second highest Canadian participation rate among these eight selected activities, there is only a seven percentage point difference between the province with the highest participation rate (Prince Edward Island, at 22.7%) and the one with the lowest (Newfoundland, at 15.5%). More or less the same is true of ice hockey, with only a 3.5 percentage point spread between British Columbia (6.7%) and Prince Edward Island (10.2%).

On the other hand, distinct provincial and regional differences may be discerned for some other activities. With the exception of Prince Edward Island, participation rates in golf in the provinces east of Ontario are about half of those in Ontario and further west. Curling, also, has a distinct regional character; while by no means confined to the Prairies, substantially larger proportions of people in Alberta, Saskatchewan, and Manitoba choose this activity than residents of the other provinces. Finally, as one would expect, based on regionally varying resource opportunities, the highest participation rates in downhill skiing occur in the mountain provinces of Alberta and British Columbia; also, with the exception of Ontario, it is only in these provinces that downhill skiing is more popular than cross-country skiing.

Regional variations in participation obviously reflect comparable regional differences in recreational opportunities, which in turn partly reflect the physiographic, climatic, and other characteristics of resources and the physical environment (see chapter 2 on supply, by Kreutzwiser). However, it is preferable from a behavioural perspective to view recreation as based on perceptions of, and choices among, opportunities, rather than as determined by them: not everyone goes downhill skiing even where the resource base provides the most outstanding facilities, for example. Thus, knowledge about the supply of recreational resources and facilities, while obviously important, does not contribute much to the understanding and explanation of recreation demand and participation in Canada. For this purpose it is necessary to investigate other explanatory variables, which will be discussed later in the chapter.

Returning to Table 1, the row of statistics in parentheses for the nation as a whole offers a somewhat different perspective on Canadians' recreational patterns. These figures show the proportions of participants who described each activity as their favourite, and again there are some striking inter-activity differences. At one extreme, only about 9% of participants in ice-skating describe this as their most preferred activity, while at the other end of the spectrum, the figures for hockey players and downhill skiers are around 40%. What inferences can be drawn from these data? It may well be that the degree of commitment varies between activities. Those for which the ratio of preference to participation is high, such as ice hockey and downhill skiing, may be attracting the more committed or intense type of recreationist; those for which the ratio is low, like ice-skating, may be attracting a larger proportion of casual participants. Clearly, differences in the nature and intensity of the motivations associated with these types of activities deserve some attention.

Inferences of this kind should probably not be over-emphasized, largely because the data do not tell us what proportions of Canadians *as a whole* most prefer these selected activities. A crude estimation is possible, however, if some simple arithmetic is performed (accepting, at the same time, that a certain amount of error is introduced). Thus, if the percentage of participants in an activity is multiplied by the percentage describing it as their favourite, then the proportions of Canadians who identify these activities as their preference can be estimated: this new variable may be defined as the preference rate. For example, multiplying the 31.8% participation rate in swimming by the 25.6% of participants for whom this was the favourite activity yields roughly 8.1% of Canadians who prefer swimming above all other recreational pursuits.

Less attention should be paid here to the actual numbers derived, and more to the inferences that can be drawn about the relative importance, or ranking, of certain kinds of recreation to Canadians. Among the eight activities shown in Table 1, swimming ranks first on the basis of both participation and preference rates. Beyond this activity, however, the rank-order changes quite markedly. Ice hockey, for which the participation rate of 8.4% ranks it fifth, jumps to second on the basis of preference rate, at 3.6% (8.4% x 42.7%). In contrast, ice-skating, second by participation at 16.8%, drops to joint last with curling, by preference rate, at 1.6% (16.8% x 9.3%).

From these national statistics, we have not only identified some of the activities with which Canadians most frequently fill their leisure hours and most frequently enjoy, but we have also learned two valuable lessons about the study of recreation. Inferences about the relative importance of recreational activities depend, in part, on how the concept *recreation participation* is defined and measured: some activities rank highly on the basis of preference even if they do not appeal to large segments of the Canadian public; others, perhaps more widely participated in, are not necessarily the activities which Canadians most enjoy. From this, it follows that constraints on or barriers to recreation may prevent people from participating, or participating as frequently as they might wish, in the activities which they most prefer (Jackson 1988, Romsa and Hoffman 1980, Searle and Jackson 1985a 1985b).

Recreation in Alberta

Similar conclusions about recreation emerge from data collected in the Recreation, Energy and Environment survey conducted in Alberta in 1984 (Jackson 1985), in which some seven hundred adults replied to questions about their patterns of recreation participation and associated matters (Table 2). There are three main differences between these figures and the national statistics presented earlier (apart from the different geographical scales to which the data refer): the array of activities is much wider; the data for participation rates (columns 1 and 2) are complemented with a second measure of recreation participation, namely frequent participation, defined as the proportion of the sample who participated in each activity at least once a week (columns 3 and 4); and a direct measure of preferences is included (columns 5 and 6), derived from a question asking people to identify the leisure activity that they most enjoy. Only the activities which ranked in the top twenty are shown for each measure.

Striking differences in the apparent relative importance of activities can be discerned depending on the measure of recreation behaviour used to rank them. Some, like reading and walking for pleasure, rank at a comparably high level by all three measures, but these are exceptions. Watching television, for example, with the highest participation rate (nearly 95%) and frequency of participation (78%), ranks only eleventh by preference; it is the most preferred activity of less than 3% of the sample. Downhill skiing, in contrast, which ranks only twentieth by participation rate and does not even appear in the list of the twenty most frequent activities, is seventh by preference.

Several important inferences about recreation are possible from comparisons of this kind. Clearly, activities which rank higher by participation rate than by frequent participation are

Table 2

Albertans' Recreational Activities: Participation Rates, Frequency of Participation, and Recreational Activity Preferences The "Top Twenty" Activities

Activity	Participation Rate		Frequent Participation		Single Most Preferred Activity	
	%	Rank	%	Rank	%	Rank
Watching TV	94.5	1	78.0	1	2.7	11
Reading	94.1	2	75.7	2	10.6	1
Walking for pleasure	87.1	3	47.6	3	5.6	3
Driving for pleasure	78.8	4	32.2	5	-	-
Picnicking	73.1	5	8.0	13	-	-
Gardening	69.0	6	40.4	4	2.9	10
Attending sports events	69.0	6	9.3	11	-	-
Photography	60.1	8	13.4	9	-	-
Indoor swimming	55.1	9	10.9	10	-	-
Bicycling	54.0	10	19.9	7	4.4	5
Aerobics	44.1	11	22.5	6	1.4	19
Outdoor swimming	43.2	12	5.8	16	-	-
Fishing	42.2	13	-	-	3.9	6
Jogging	42.2	13	14.6	8	2.0	14
Ice-skating	40.5	15	-	-	-	-
Hiking	40.2	16	5.2	19	3.3	8
Tent camping	34.7	17	-	-	-	-
Nature study	34.3	18	5.6	17	-	-
Golf	30.5	19	8.3	12	5.1	4
Downhill skiing	29.7	20	-	-	3.6	7
Squash/racquetball/ handball	-	-	6.4	14	2.0	14
Slowpitch/softball/ baseball	-	-	6.4	15	1.4	19
Trailer camping	-	-	5.3	18	-	-
Bowling	-	-	5.0	20	-	-
Camping*	-	-	-	-	8.9	2
Swimming**	-	-	-	-	3.0	9
Hunting	-	-	-	-	2.1	12
Ice hockey	-	-	-	-	2.1	12
Sailing	-	-	-	-	1.7	16
Dancing	-	-	-	-	1.5	17
Tennis	-	-	-	-	1.5	17

*   Includes all forms of camping.
** Includes indoor and outdoor swimming.

those which attract a greater than average proportion of casual participants: they include picnicking, attending sports events, and outdoor swimming. The proportion of more committed, or at least more frequent, recreationists is higher in bicycling, aerobics, jogging, and golf, which are examples of activities that rank higher by frequency of participation than by participation rate.

Turning to the preference data, several activities rank much lower by preference than by the other two measures, including watching television, gardening, and aerobics. More important, especially from an applied standpoint, are the ones for which the reverse is the case, like bicycling, fishing, hiking, golf, downhill skiing, camping, hunting, and sailing. Usually, although not uniformly, these are outdoor recreational activities. Also, the fact that many people obviously do not participate in them as frequently as they might wish once more suggests the possible effects of barriers to participation.

To reiterate what was said earlier about measuring recreation, it is obvious from the Alberta and the Statistics Canada data that quite different conclusions emerge depending on the precise measure used. The national and Alberta statistics both illustrate different pictures of the relative importance of recreational activities in Canada when preference, participation rate, or frequency of participation is used as the yardstick. This means, as noted above, that planners must be extremely careful in selecting the most appropriate measure when assessing the public's recreation behaviour and preferences: if an inappropriate indicator is chosen, then there is the danger of overestimating the demand for some activities, while underestimating the demand for others.

Yet, there are benefits to be gained from measuring recreation from several perspectives. Only by comparing the results from different measures is it possible to draw conclusions about casual versus intense participants, about the potential influence of barriers to participation, and about the relative importance of outdoor recreation among the leisure pursuits enjoyed by Canadians. Inferences like this are impossible if we are content to use a single measure.

Patterns

A major difficulty with the preceding data, especially but not only those dealing with people's recreational preferences, is that many activities are not reported frequently enough to permit statistical analysis. This problem is widely encountered in recreation research, because the data usually come from surveys with relatively small samples, the cost of which escalates as the sample size increases. Therefore, it is desirable to classify recreational activities, if only to increase the numbers within categories, which can then be analyzed using statistical methods. But more important, if patterns of recreation can be detected and their underlying dimensions determined, then it is also likely that some fundamental explanatory factors will be uncovered. Indeed, it is often only as a result of classification that this deeper level of understanding becomes possible. However, the potential for classifying depends on the assumption that there are, in fact, underlying similarities, or patterns, between and among recreational activities, and on the belief that the loss of detail incurred by generalizing is more than compensated for by the ensuing new insights. Thus, the process of classifying recreational activities not only addresses a serious problem of data fragmentation, but also enhances the understanding of recreational choices.

Recreational activities, or more properly recreationists, can be classified in several ways. Broadly speaking, classification methods are of two types, conceptual and empirical. In conceptual methods, an *a priori* set of dimensions is constructed, and activities are allocated to predetermined classes. Perhaps the best-known example of a conceptual typology is the one developed by Hendee, Gale, and Catton (1971). These authors recognized five types of outdoor recreation, namely appreciative-symbolic, extractive-symbolic, passive/free-play, sociable/learning, and active-expressive. Conceptual methods have the distinct advantage of facilitating comparisons between studies conducted at different times and places. For example, the use of the Hendee *et al.* typology allowed Jackson and Schinkel (1981) to compare the activity preferences of residents and tourists in the Yellowknife region of the Northwest Territories with findings from McCool's earlier (1978) study in Utah. The typology was also used in a modified form by Buckley and Girling (1979) in their study of outdoor recreation in the Central Region of Ontario.

Conceptual methods, however, have been severely criticized because of their apparent subjectivity, particularly in how specific activities are allocated to general classes. This is probably why alternative, empirical techniques have been used much more frequently than conceptual methods in North

American and overseas recreation research. Empirical methods of classification include factor analysis (Allen and Buchanan 1982, Allen, Donnelly, and Warder 1984, Bishop 1970, Chase 1979, Chase and Cheek 1979, Chase, Kasulis, and Lusch 1980, Gudykunst *et al.* 1981, Yu 1980) and cluster analysis (Devall and Harry 1981; Ditton, Goodale, and Johnsen 1975, Knopp, Ballman, and Merriam 1979, Romsa 1973, Tatham and Dornoff 1971).

Empirical methods are frequently viewed as sharing several advantages, not the least of which is their apparent objectivity. Also, their use often validates the dimensions developed for conceptual typologies. For instance, a factor analysis of participation rates in eight outdoor activities (Jackson, in press) among the sample of Edmonton and Calgary recreationists referred to above verified a previously defined conceptual classification (Jackson 1986) of "appreciative" activities (canoeing, cross-country skiing, and hiking), "mechanized" activities (motor boating, snowmobiling, and trail biking), and "extractive" activities (hunting and fishing). Finally, the derived groupings may lead to new hypotheses about linkages between recreational activities. For example, Devall and Harry's (1981) identification of four clusters of activities at recreation sites in Oregon allowed the researchers to classify activities with reference to the technologies used in them, and subsequently to distinguish among the types of activities on the basis of their relative obtrusiveness.

Despite their advantages, empirical methods share one major limitation: the factors or clusters created in a specific analysis apply only to the data under investigation. Because the groupings are not necessarily replicated in different surveys, there are constraints on the possibility of comparing conclusions. Also, despite their apparent objectivity, empirical methods demand several analytical and measurement decisions on the part of the researcher, which in turn can influence the number and structure of the factors or clusters. Thus, as Johnston (1968) pointed out two decades ago, there is at least a degree of subjectivity even in supposedly "objective" methods.

Regardless of the classification method used, it is intuitively appealing that certain recreational activities share attributes which also serve to distinguish them from other activities. Mountain climbing, hiking, and back-country tent camping have much in common, while it would probably be inappropriate to classify curling or ice hockey with these activities. Groups of similar activities are thought to represent sets of "recreational interests" (Buckley and Girling 1979), "recreational activity packages" (Romsa 1973), or "market segments" (Romsa and Girling 1976, Tatham and Dornoff 1971). It is assumed that a recreationist who participates in one activity from a particular category would be more likely to select other activities from the same category than from other types of recreation.

In order to uncover such patterns, it is necessary to find out what other activities are enjoyed by people who enjoy a particular kind of recreation, and then try to identify some general, underlying, or fundamental characteristics of these activities. This was carried out by Wong (1979), who asked cross-country skiers and snowmobilers in Alberta about the other activities in which they participated. He found that cross-country skiers had higher participation rates than snowmobilers in hiking, bicycling, tent camping, canoeing, jogging, and downhill skiing, whereas snowmobilers had higher participation rates than cross-country skiers in fishing, trailer camping, motor boating, hunting, trail biking, and dune buggying. Reflection on these two sets of activities, however, allows us to go beyond the superficialities of the activities themselves and focus on some underlying characteristics. Thus, it might argued that the types of activities preferred more frequently by cross-country skiers are linked together by being passive, appreciative, self-propelled, non-mechanized, and low-impact, whereas those of snowmobilers are active, mechanized, consumptive, and, perhaps, environmentally more damaging (Jackson and Wong 1982).

Wong's results did not occur purely by chance, but were generally replicated in the 1984 Edmonton and Calgary survey referred to previously. Patterns of participation in other activities by cross-country skiers and snowmobilers resembled those identified in Wong's study, and similar patterns also emerged in a comparison of the other preferred activities of participants in canoeing and motor boating (Figure 2). The consistency of these patterns suggests that they are symptomatic of deep-seated recreational preferences. Thus, they may be related to other factors that vary simultaneously with recreational choices, such as motivations, environmental attitudes, and perceptions of conflict, which enhance the understanding of recreational choice and some of its implications, and are the focus of the next section of this chapter.

Figure 2: Participation Rates in Other Outdoor Recreation Activities: Cross-Country Skiers vs. Snowmobilers, and Canoeists vs. Motor-Boaters

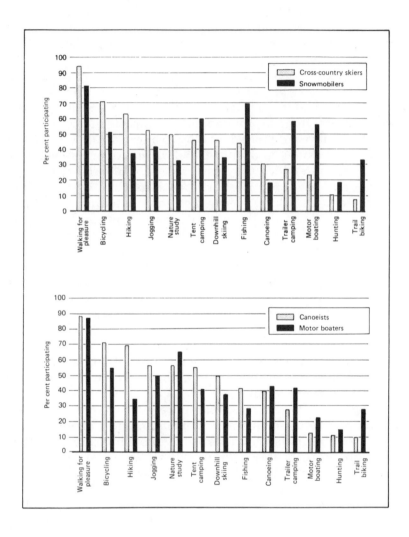

FACTORS RELATED TO THE CHOICE OF RECREATIONAL ACTIVITIES

Recreation researchers and practitioners alike are concerned with variables that help to explain patterns of recreation participation and preference. Researchers want to understand why patterns of human behaviour occur, while practitioners need to forecast future trends and to respond to recreationists' needs by providing the right mix and quality of recreation services. For both purposes, relationships between explanatory variables and recreation behaviour cannot be assumed, but must be measured explicitly. Ludicrous forecasts of participation rates can result if past and present trends are projected into the future without taking into account the underlying reasons that explain them (Driver and Tocher 1970, Knetsch 1970).

Three main sets of explanatory factors have usually been investigated in recreation research, namely, socio-economic variables, cognitive variables, and environmental attitudes and values. Socio-economic variables have most commonly consisted of age, sex, education, and income, but others, less frequently receiving attention in recreation research, might include occupation, household size and composition, and ethnic origin and race. Cognitive variables represent a complex set of factors such as people's individual needs, their awareness of recreational opportunities, and their preferences for man-made or natural environments as recreational settings. Here, they are exemplified by motivations (reasons for participating in recreation). Environmental attitudes and values, narrowly defined, summarize people's pro- or anti-environmental feelings, but more broadly defined, as they are below, also include measures of attitudes to technology and the quality of life.

While each of the three sets of factors can be examined individually and systematically, it is important to recognize that they are also interrelated (Figure 3). Thus, motivations and environmental attitudes are known both to vary with socio-economic variables and to be mutually interdependent. Furthermore, as depicted by the feedback loops, recreation behaviour can either reinforce or change motivations and environmental attitudes. In isolated and unusual cases, indicated in Figure 3 by the dotted line, an individual's socio-

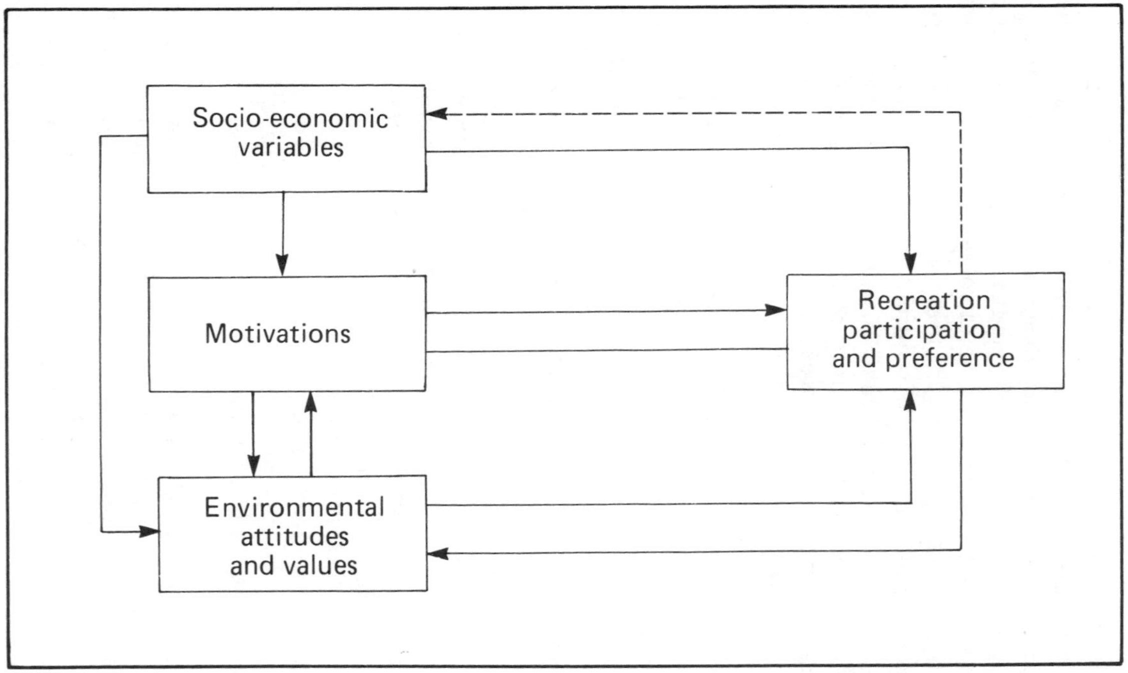

Figure 3: Relationships Among Factors Related to Participation and Preference

economic status might also change if he or she chooses an occupation with recreational opportunities in mind.

Socio-economic Variables

Of the variables related to recreation, the socio-economic characteristics of recreationists have probably been studied the most frequently. There are three main reasons why this is so: there are socio-economic variations in recreation behaviour, thus variables of this kind are of interest to researchers such as sociologists, who are interested in the social bases of recreation; an examination of socio-economic variations in participation can enhance the understanding of the process of recreational choice; and socio-economic variables can be used to forecast participation -- if not necessarily recreation demand -- in the future.

That there are indeed real social variations in recreation participation and other measures of recreation behaviour is well-known, because the issue has received much attention in the recreation research literature over the past couple of decades (Kelly 1980, White 1975, Zuzanek 1978). It is true that not all aspects of recreation behaviour can be explained with reference to socio-economic variables. For instance, while participation rates in many activities are known to vary quite consistently according to age, sex, education, and income, the latter variables do not correlate well with the frequency of recreation participation once non-participants are excluded from the analysis (Jackson 1980, Romsa and Girling 1976). Socio-economic variations in recreation participation *rates*, however, have been identified in many studies. They can be illustrated by an example from the 1984 Edmonton and Calgary survey, and specifically by age- and income-based variations in the participation rate in downhill skiing (Table 3).

About 30% of the sample had participated at least once in downhill skiing in the year prior to the survey, but the participation rate declined markedly with age. Just over half of the respondents aged twenty-five and under had skied, compared with only about 5% of those aged fifty-five or over. In contrast, the participation rate increased fairly steadily with income: the almost 40% participation rate of respondents with incomes in excess of $60,000 was roughly three times as high as the rate among respondents with incomes less than $15,000.

Table 3

**Age and Income-Based Variations in the Participation Rate
in Downhill Skiing**

	AGE *				
	<26	26-35	36-45	46-55	>55
	%	%	%	%	%
Participants	52.2	35.8	33.3	20.7	5.1
Non-participants	47.8	64.2	66.7	79.3	94.9
Totals (n)	(92)	(215)	(138)	(92)	(118)

	INCOME **				
	<$15,000	$15-30,000	$30-45,000	$45-60,000	>$60,000
	%	%	%	%	%
Participants	12.7	25.1	32.8	35.6	39.5
Non-participants	87.3	74.9	67.2	64.4	60.5
Totals (n)	(71)	(191)	(180)	(101)	(86)

*   Chi-square = 64.53; d.f. = 4; $p < .0001$
** Chi-square = 18.32; d.f. = 4; $p < .001$

Source: Original data collected by author (Jackson, 1985).

The identification and description of socio-economic variations in recreation behaviour are characteristic of the activity approach outlined earlier. In this approach, participation in downhill skiing would be said to be "explained" by variations in people's income and age. Little attempt is made to uncover *why* these variables influence recreation behaviour. Useful as it may be, therefore, this form of analysis does little more than generate socio-economic profiles of various types of recreationist.

In the behavioural approach to recreation, information of this kind is used in an effort to interpret the process of recreational choice: by asking the question "who?" we can tangentially address the question "why?" By simultaneously subdividing samples on the basis of a measure of recreation behaviour and one or more socio-economic variables, an understanding of the process or phenomenon for which the socio-economic variable is a concept indicator can be gained.

With reference to the data shown in Table 3, we might ask what it is about the circumstances created by income (or the lack of it) that enables people to participate in downhill skiing, or prevents them from doing so. One obvious factor is purchasing power. Beyond this, however, people with higher incomes might also be better educated, be exposed to different sources of information than the poor, evaluate this information in different ways, have better access to transportation, more free time available, a different set of motivations, mix with people of different lifestyles, and so on. In short, the focus is not so much on how increasing income *determines* the participation rate in downhill skiing, but rather on how having a certain level of income creates personal, social, and environmental circumstances, how these circumstances are variably perceived, and how the perceptions in turn influence recreational choices.

A similar set of questions is appropriate for interpreting the relationship between age and participation in downhill skiing. Again, there are some obvious reasons, such as declining physical ability with advancing age. In addition, though, people's perceptions of their physical ability, and even perhaps what they consider to be appropriate forms of recreation for their own particular age group, might constitute important influences. Thus, as in the income example, age does not determine recreation participation, but creates circumstances and perceptions which are ultimately responsible for recreational choices.

Turning now to forecasting, the use of socio-economic variables to predict recreation behaviour is based on four main advantages. First, as noted above, strong relationships exist between several socio-economic variables and many forms of recreation behaviour, especially outdoor recreation. Second, information about the socio-economic characteristics of recreationists is relatively easy and inexpensive to collect. Third, independent data about the socio-economic structure of society exist in the form of censuses, which can be used to create socio-economic forecasts for given points in the future. Last, the socio-economic model of recreation forecasting is simple to use and easy to apply (Wall 1981, 241-2).

Table 4 summarizes statistics which illustrate the socio-economic method of recreation forecasting, its advantages, and its limitations. The example shows downhill skiing and age, but for forecasting purposes, the method can be applied to any socio-economic variable that fulfils two conditions: it must be related to the activity for which forecasts are being made, and it must be expected to change in the future: gender would not be a useful predictor variable because the ratio of males to females is unlikely to change.

As outlined by Wall (1981), the socio-economic method of projections and forecasts involves three steps. First, the socio-economic correlates of participation in the recreational activity under consideration must be determined. The table shows such coefficients of participation for age groups of the Edmonton and Calgary population, derived from Table 3. Then, the number of people and their socio-economic characteristics must be calculated for the area in question for the time period of interest. Various assumptions must be made about the size and structure (in this case the age breakdown) of the population in the future (column D). In the example, a low-migration scenario is used, and comparable changes in the size and structure of the Edmonton and Calgary populations are assumed. Last, the predicted numbers of people in each socio-economic group are multiplied by the corresponding coefficients of participation, and the results of these calculations are summed. Column D is multiplied by column C, to derive column E, and the results are totalled.

The quality of forecasts of this kind obviously depends on the level of error in measuring coefficients of participation, as well as on the validity of assumptions about future population size, structure, and coefficients of participation. Despite these limitations, the method is preferable to the simple projection of

Table 4

Forecast of the Number of Participants in Downhill Skiing, Edmonton and Calgary Adult Population, 2000

A	B	C	D	E	F
20-24	15,7855	52.2%	90,775	47,385	-42.5%
25-34	23,8850	35.8%	191,271	68,475	-19.9%
35-44	129,740	33.3%	324,377	108,018	+150.0%
45-54	105,755	20.7%	222,982	46,157	+110.8%
55-64	77,125	6.2%	108,644	6,736	+40.9%
65+	75,260	3.8%	128,069	4,867	+70.2%
Total	784,585	29.9%	1,066,118	281,368	+17.0%

A   Age groups
B   1981 population, Edmonton and Calgary combined
C   Coefficient of participation in downhill skiing for each age group based on results of the "Recreation, Energy and Environment" survey, 1984
D   Projected population in the year 2000, Edmonton and Calgary combined, using forecasts prepared for the City of Edmonton, low immigration scenario, and assuming the same percentage and structural change in Calgary
E   Forecast number of downhill skiers in each age group in the year 2000 (Col. C x Col. D)
F   Percentage change in the number of skiers in each age group, 1984-2000

current average participation rates. Based on the assumptions underlying the projections shown in the table, the combined adult population of Edmonton and Calgary will increase to 1,066,118 between 1981 and the year 2000, or by 35.9%. Applying the current average participation rate of 29.9% to the forecast total adult population would yield 318,769 downhill skiers. However, if changes in age structure are taken into account, a more realistic forecast would be 281,638 skiers. Thus, an unstructured forecast could overestimate the number of downhill skiers in Edmonton and Calgary in the year 2000 by at least 37,000, or about 13%. Alternatively stated, the number of skiers will not increase by 35.9%, but only by 17.0%. If the data in Table 4 are even remotely realistic, and if downhill skiing is sufficiently similar to other outdoor recreation activities, then the anticipated ageing of the Canadian population (see chapter 9) could have profound effects on outdoor recreation participation in Canada in the future. The results of the analysis show that participation, at least in downhill skiing, is likely to grow much less rapidly than the rate at which the population as a whole is expected to expand.

Before a conclusion can be reached, an additional limitation of the use of socio-economic variables in recreation forecasting must be recognized. The results can rarely be generalized beyond the specific time and place for which the assumptions are created and the forecast is made. The Edmonton and Calgary forecast would not apply very well to the province of Alberta as a whole, and still less to the entire nation in the year 2000. In the opposite direction, because of the regional variations in recreation participation rates identified in an earlier section of this chapter, general forecasts which might apply to the nation as a whole would probably not be appropriate for regions, provinces, or smaller spatial units of analysis.

Some other difficulties associated with the use of socio-economic variables in recreation research apply not only to forecasting, but also to the other benefits of examining this class of variables. First, the measures tend to be fairly crude and are not always the best or most appropriate in all analytical and interpretive circumstances. For example, the number of years of formal education is the most common measure of the influence of the educational process on recreational choice, but many other dimensions of education could be used, such as the type of education received, particularly as it varies at the university level. Similarly, total household income may bear little relationship to a household's actual discretionary purchasing power, and therefore the amount of money which is available to spend on leisure, once an individual's or family's other financial commitments are accounted for.

The second general limitation is that the profiles used tend to be rather simple. The most common procedure has been to analyse the effect of each socio-economic variable individually, as opposed to classifying people with reference to a set of interconnected descriptors. The data summarized in the graphs shown in Figure 4 illustrate that neither age nor sex alone provides a complete explanation of recreational activity preferences. Rather, with some exceptions, changes in preference through the life cycle depend, at least partly, on sex. Conversely, recreational differences between males and females are partially dependent on age. Thus the two variables exert a conjoint influence on recreation preference. However, it should be recognized that the ability to construct more complex profiles of this type requires very large, and correspondingly expensive, samples.

Motivations

In the preceding section, it was noted that socio-economic variables can provide a partial, but only tangential, understanding of why people participate in various forms of recreation. Studies of motivations focus *directly* on why people participate in recreation and choose particular activities. They are useful because, as Beard and Ragheb (1983, 227) observe, "If different individuals responded in the same way to stimuli, there would be no need for bringing in the concept of motivation. However, individuals are driven to engage in leisure activities for different reasons, and the study of these different reasons [and] their origins . . . is central to the understanding of leisure behaviour." Motivations can be related to outdoor recreation participation at three levels of generality, namely: participation in outdoor recreation in general; preferences for particular categories of activity, for example, self-propelled, non-mechanized activities such as cross-country skiing, hiking, and canoeing; and participation in highly specific forms of outdoor recreation.

Research on recreational motivations has essentially addressed two questions: what motivations or combinations of motivations are most closely associated with particular activities or types of activity, and do certain motivations or

Figure 4: Age- and Sex-Based Variations in Preferences for Recreational Activities

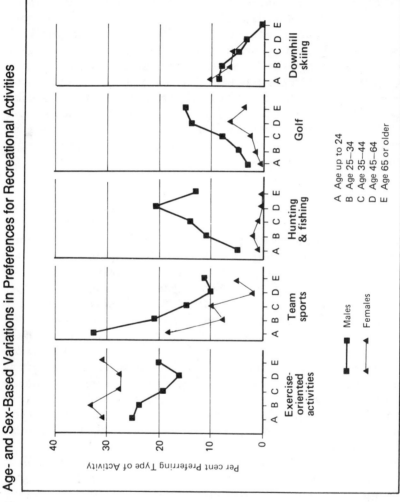

combinations of motivations distinguish between activities? These are, in fact, distinct, albeit interrelated, questions. Some motivations are both important and common to several activities. For example, both cross-country skiers and snowmobilers choose their activities partly because of the opportunity to fulfil desires for health and exercise, and rest and relaxation (Jackson and Wong 1982). While these reasons are important to most participants in both activities, they do not discriminate between them. Other motivations do discriminate, even though they may be less important. Snowmobilers frequently cite the adventure, challenge, and excitement of their activity, while these reasons tend to be much less important for cross-country skiers, whose interests may be more closely associated with solitude, peace and quiet, and a natural setting. Thus, the failure of a motivation to discriminate among activities does not negate its importance to many of the people who choose a certain activity. Conversely, even though a motivation may not rank highest among the list of reasons for participating in a given activity, it may still serve to differentiate this activity from others.

A major difficulty with motivations is that they cannot be directly studied independently of the recreationist. They can, of course, be inferred, but often only inaccurately. To measure motivations, it is necessary to question recreationists, and this in turn raises two further problems. First, are the questions used to measure motivations meaningful to the recreationist, as opposed to the researcher? Certainly, theoretical constructs such as self-actualization, which are commonly used in the research literature to label motivational dimensions, may not make much sense to most recreationists, but must be measured using more familiar, if mundane, terminology. Second, do recreationists even think in motivational terms? As Driver and Tocher (1970, 11) have observed, people are probably only rarely conscious of their own motivations, and do not explicitly canvass their needs when deciding to recreate, or when they are engaged in a particular activity.

In order to investigate the validity of the assumptions that some researchers have made with regard to these questions, Kroening conducted an in-depth study of the motivations of people who had visited the Canadian north for extended wilderness canoe trips (Kroening 1979, Kroening and Jackson 1981). She found that wilderness canoeists were, in fact, highly conscious of their motivations. More than 50% of her respondents felt that the following motivations were an important reason for choosing the activity: "to experience the out-of-doors intensely," "to see wildlife," "for the love of adventure," "to see beautiful scenery," "to see the ecology of different areas," "to use wilderness living skills," "to escape the routines of everyday life," "to see scenery that most others cannot see," and "to meet the challenge of physical endurance."

The sample of wilderness canoeists also felt that the questions Kroening asked were directly relevant to their own experience. However, because of the high levels of skills, experience, and planning associated with this most arduous and risky form of outdoor recreation, Kroening may have studied an unusually introspective group of recreationists. We do not know the extent to which her finding -- that motivational questions are indeed meaningful to recreationists -- also applies to more common, everyday recreational activities, especially those which have effectively become habitual. Yet, by and large, recreation researchers have tended to take for granted the relevance of their motivational questions to recreationists.

Another problem with motivational research concerns the number and content of the measures most appropriately used. Recreation researchers have usually developed their own motivational scales, and common instruments have rarely been employed in different studies. For example, Crandall (1980) reports on several studies which have used between twenty-one and thirty-nine statements to measure motivations, while Beard and Ragheb (1983) used as many as forty-eight. The 1981 Public Opinion Survey on Recreation conducted by Alberta Recreation and Parks (1982) used only sixteen statements, while a similar list of seventeen items was used in the Edmonton and Calgary survey (Jackson 1985).

On the other hand, despite variations in the range, content, and complexity of the motivational scales used in different studies, reasonably similar motivational dimensions have tended to emerge when the statements are classified using empirical methods, such as factor analysis. In the Edmonton and Calgary study, five motivational dimensions were recognized using this technique: a seven-item "challenge" dimension (including statements such as "to improve my skills or knowledge" and "for a sense of accomplishment"); a four-item "solitude" dimension" (for example "to be alone," "to enjoy peace and quiet"); a "change of pace" dimension, consisting of two items (for example, "to do something different from work," "for a change of pace"); a "socializing" dimension of three items (for example, "to socialize with others"); and a single-item dimension, consisting of the statement "for physical health or exercise."

Beard and Ragheb (1983) recognized four dimensions in a factor analysis of forty-eight motivational statements: their "intellectual" and "competence/mastery" scales resembled aspects of the aforementioned challenge and physical exercise dimensions, while their "social" and "stimulus avoidance" scales even more closely resembled the aforementioned socializing and change-of-pace dimensions respectively. Crandall (1980) delimited seventeen motivational categories, but again many correspond closely to those identified by other researchers, such as "enjoying nature," "escaping from routine," "social contact," "adventure, challenge, competition," and "physical exercise."

Most of the research on motivations for recreation has been conducted in the United States, but there is no reason to doubt that, broadly speaking, the findings apply equally well to Canadian recreationists. Research on motivations has demonstrated the multidimensionality of the recreational experience: rarely is a specific motivation exclusive to a particular activity, or vice versa; rather, it is combinations of motivations that distinguish among types of outdoor recreational activity. Motivations provide a useful explanation of recreational choices, and we now have a reasonably good understanding of the main reasons why people participate in outdoor recreation generally, as well as in specific outdoor activities or similar types of activity.

However, motivational research has been more successful from a theoretical perspective than in a practical context: the results are more difficult to apply in recreation planning than are those of research focusing on socio-economic variations in recreation. Certainly, it is difficult to see how this type of research could be used in recreation forecasting, because independent data do not exist on motivations comparable to the information provided by censuses and socio-economic projections. Despite this qualification, it cannot be denied that motivational research has contributed greatly to the understanding of recreational decisions, and practitioners would be well advised to appreciate the needs which their clients seek to fulfil in their leisure.

Values and Environmental Attitudes

Some recreation researchers and writers have recently begun to argue that a full understanding of people's recreation behaviour, and an ability to use this understanding to anticipate future changes, can only come about if research proceeds beyond the analysis of socio-economic and motivational variables. The fundamental values underlying recreation behaviour must be identified, measured, and investigated (Neulinger 1983). Yet little work based on an explicit attempt to assess the role of values in recreation has been published. Thus the influence of values on recreation is not well understood, partly because there is uncertainty as to what the relevant values are.

The problem has been addressed tangentially, according to Burton (1981), by using socio-economic variables as surrogate measures of values. Given the rapidity of social change and the growing complexity of society, however, traditional socio-economic configurations of values no longer exist. Socio-economically defined segments of society are now more frequently characterized by an internal value-based diversity than by consistency. Therefore, an alternative, or at least a complement, to socio-economic analysis is required, in which values are measured directly.

For this purpose, two distinct but interrelated questions must be asked: what values is it appropriate to investigate with respect to people's outdoor recreation choices, and how can they be measured? As far as the first problem is concerned, it has been argued that the most relevant values for outdoor recreation are those which distinguish between the so-called consumer and conserver societies (Jackson 1986). The notions of the consumer and conserver societies have begun to receive increasing attention in the literature, especially in Canada (Orfald and Gibson 1985, Science Council of Canada 1977, Thompson 1982), although mostly in a prescriptive vein. Some writers, however, believe that a long-term evolution of values can actually be detected. For example, Sewell and Mitchell (1981, 262) contend that "significant segments of the public at large are concerned about such matters as to what constitutes the good life. They wonder about the relative emphasis that should be placed upon the pursuit of high levels of economic growth, the attainment of a more egalitarian society, and the preservation of environmental quality. The traditional consumer society is now being challenged by a small but vociferous group which believes that a conserver society is superior."

It has also been argued that conserver society values will not remain those of a minority for long, but will eventually gain ascendance in Canadian society. Thus, Balmer (1979, 546) has suggested that, by the end of the twentieth century in Canada, "there will be a decline in values associated with materialism, private ownership, capitalism, and unqualified economic growth. Increasing emphasis will be placed on concepts such as quality of life ... [and] a new focus on the ecological ethic."

If value-based changes of this kind were to occur, what might be some of the implications for recreation? In a consumer society geared towards mass consumption, many forms of recreation impose severe impacts on the natural environment (Wall and Wright 1977) and place heavy demands on natural resources, especially energy (Foster and Kuhn 1983, Ritchie and Claxton 1983). Mechanized activities, such as driving for pleasure, snowmobiling, and motor boating, are obvious examples of the latter, but it is difficult to think of many other leisure pursuits that do not, in one way or another, require an appliance to be plugged in or a machine to be switched on.

In a conserver society, in contrast, according to Spry (1980, 145), leisure would be "simple . . . [and] without a great elaboration of apparatus." Jogging, cycling, and cross-country skiing are some examples cited by Spry, the popularity of which she interprets as signifying a shift towards conserver values. Other conserver society activities might include "gardening, crafts, carpentry, and all sorts of do-it-yourself activities . . . [which] may actually conserve material and environmental resources, since they combine recycling of materials with satisfaction of the instinct of workmanship" (Spry 1980, 145). In short, leisure in a conserver society would not demand "lavish expenditures" or "elaborate apparatus."

To summarize, the concepts of the consumer and conserver societies not only represent distinct constellations of competing values but, at the same time, imply diverging patterns of leisure and outdoor recreation. It may be concluded, therefore, that techniques designed to tap the essential beliefs that characterize these two opposing lifestyles will simultaneously help to shed light on some of the fundamental values that find their expression in recreational choices.

In this regard, the most useful work has been conducted by Dunlap and Van Liere, who have developed scales for the investigation of the public's fundamental value and belief systems, which they define as "paradigms" or "worldviews" (Dunlap and Van Liere 1978, 1984, Van Liere and Dunlap 1980, 1981, 1983). Broadly speaking, it is possible to distinguish between two such world views. At one extreme is a deeply rooted ecological world view summarizing environmentalist concepts, such as limits to growth, the idea that man is a part of nature rather than meant to dominate it, the importance of preserving the balance of nature, and the necessity for achieving a steady-state economy. Dunlap and Van Liere (1978) call this the "new environmental paradigm." At the other extreme is the "dominant social paradigm," characterized by a preference for material abundance and economic growth, and a profound faith in technology as the driving force for progress (Dunlap and Van Liere 1984). Since the former world view is expressed in pro-environmental attitudes, while the latter is associated with anti-environmental attitudes, scales designed to measure people's attitudes towards the environment offer an acceptable way of investigating the fundamental values relevant to outdoor recreational choices, if not to the entire spectrum of leisure pursuits.

The intuitively obvious relationship between outdoor recreation participation and environmental attitudes has received some attention in at least four previous United States studies, but with conflicting and generally disappointing results (Dunlap and Heffernan 1975, Geisler, Martinson, and Wilkening 1977, Pinhey and Grimes 1979, Van Liere and Noe 1981). However, using some improvements in the measurement of the key variables, as suggested by Van Liere and Noe (1981), the relationship was re-examined in the Recreation, Energy and Environment survey conducted in Edmonton and Calgary in 1984 (Jackson 1986).

Two hypotheses were tested, based on those originally developed by Dunlap and Heffernan (1975) and re-examined, with modifications, in the three other studies cited above: (1) participants in appreciative activities exhibit stronger pro-environmental attitudes than participants in extractive and mechanized activities; and (2) there is a stronger association between outdoor recreation participation and attitudes towards specific aspects of the environment necessary for pursuing such activities than between outdoor recreation participation and attitudes to more "distant" and general aspects of environmental issues.

The study provided support for both hypotheses. As shown in Table 5, the proportion of ecocentrists (respondents whose

Table 5

**Attitudinal Profiles of Cross-Country Skiers
and Snowmobilers**

	ENVIRONMENTAL SCALE		RECREATION SCALE	
	Skiers %	Snow-mobilers %	Skiers %	Snow-mobilers %
Ecocentrists	23.0	4.9	27.0	7.0
Moderate ecocentrists	37.4	39.0	38.3	20.9
Moderate technocentrists	28.1	36.6	27.7	44.2
Technocentrists	11.5	19.5	7.1	27.9
Totals (n)	(139)	(41)	(141)	(43)

*   Chi-square = 7.57; d.f. = 3; p<.05
**   Chi-square = 23.60; d.f. = 3; p<.0001

Source: Jackson, 1986.

attitudes were consistent with the pro-environmental position) was almost five times higher than the corresponding proportion of snowmobilers with reference to the general environmental attitudes scale, and twenty percentage points higher on the more specific recreational attitudes scale. Conversely, the proportion of moderate technocentrists and technocentrists combined was 56% among snowmobilers on the environmental scale (compared with 40% of skiers), and 72% on the recreational scale (compared with 35% of skiers).

The differences were not confined to these two activities. Generally speaking, participants in appreciative activities shared pro-environmental views which also served to differentiate them from participants in mechanized and extractive activities. Furthermore, when dimensions of environmental attitudes were analyzed, the best discriminators among types of recreationists were those attitudes which are simultaneously associated with differences between the consumer and conserver societies.

The findings are encouraging for two reasons: they represent a successful response to Burton's (1981) call for the explicit consideration of the influence of values on recreational choices; and they contribute to the small body of literature on the relationship between outdoor recreation participation and environmental attitudes.

Other than improving our knowledge of some of the factors that influence recreational choices, what practical value might be associated with the investigation of associations between environmental attitudes and outdoor recreation participation? What forecasts about recreation in the future can we make using these kinds of results? Important changes in outdoor recreation activity preferences will occur if those who foresee a shift from the consumer society to the conserver society are correct. Under conditions of a *voluntary* evolution of values, preferences for appreciative activities would become more widespread, while a decline would occur in preferences for mechanized and extractive activities. Similar changes would happen if a modification of values were *enforced* by resource or financial constraints, simply because participation in mechanized (and possibly extractive) activities would become more expensive than in appreciative activities. Consequently some participants in the former might begin to seek other, less expensive, pursuits.

Inferences of this kind are highly speculative, and it may well be that the current emphasis on consumer society values will continue, in turn supporting preferences for mechanized and extractive activities. As Butler argues in his concluding chapter, anticipating recreational futures is one of the most difficult tasks to confront researchers. Nevertheless, it seems reasonable to conclude that investigation of the attitudes and values associated with outdoor recreation behaviour offers a useful framework for stimulating discussion about how recreation in Canada and elsewhere might evolve, even if accurate predictions are still not possible.

OUTCOMES OF RECREATION PARTICIPATION

Of the many outcomes of recreation participation, we shall concentrate on three in this section: recreational satisfaction, social capacity, and conflict between incompatible recreational activities. Each is an important component of the "quality of the recreational experience." Before proceeding to a systematic discussion of each of these distinct aspects, a few words about their interrelationships and the treatment of the material are in order.

First, although satisfaction, capacity, and conflict will be examined in terms of differences among recreational activities, it is necessary to remember that these outcomes also depend on the antecedent variables which were discussed earlier, such as socio-economic variables, motivations, and attitudes and values. For example, while for organizational purposes, perceptions of conflict are most easily discussed as occurring between incompatible activities, we should also recognize that they stem from differences in the social class, motivations, and environmental attitudes and values of participants. Furthermore, feedbacks are involved which may ultimately affect recreational choices. Thus, the satisfaction of needs in a particular activity is likely to encourage continued participation, while a failure to achieve the desired level and type of satisfaction may influence people to seek an alternative type of recreation. Similarly, negative experiences with recreational conflict may influence subsequent recreational decisions, such as choosing a new recreational area, or perhaps even dropping out of the activity altogether.

Second, although the three aspects of the quality of experience to be discussed here are intimately interrelated and to some extent overlapping, they are not interchangeable concepts. Not all satisfaction studies involve questions about social capacity or conflict, despite the fact that the latter two concepts cannot be fully appreciated or measured without reference to satisfaction. Similarly, studies of the capacity of recreational resources often raise questions about inter-activity conflicts, but they also involve much more, while conflict studies focus on several issues beyond the scope of traditional social capacity research.

Satisfaction

The behavioural approach to recreation would be incomplete without the concept of satisfaction. This concept, which summarizes recreationists' own subjective interpretations of their enjoyment, is inherently a perception variable, and forges the necessary link between the numerical aspects of participation in the activity approach and the more qualitative aspects of the experience approach. Thus, the concept is valuable in a theoretical context. Satisfaction studies are also useful from a practical standpoint. A recognition of these important facets of recreation helps to avoid the pitfalls of relying only on the head-counting aspects of recreation participation, and thereby falling into the trap of narrowly defining the purpose of recreation management merely as the provision of recreation services without regard for their quality (Hawes 1978). Thus, managers are required to focus on what is, after all, the essential purpose of recreation -- enjoyment.

Satisfaction is a relative, not an absolute, phenomenon, because enjoyment depends on the nature and intensity of the expectations one has for an experience prior to participation (Bultena and Klessig 1969, Francken and van Raiij 1981). Expectations vary between individuals, and two people can differ quite markedly in their expectations about participating in what, to the outside observer, seem to be identical activities. A person with high expectations may fail to fulfil them, and thus becomes dissatisfied, whereas another person, perhaps starting out with lower expectations, is perfectly happy. Similarly, the same individual might have different expectations for a certain activity in different settings. A resident of Edmonton, for example, who decides to take a leisurely Sunday afternoon canoe trip down the North Saskatchewan River will probably have totally different expectations from those he would have for a month-long canoe trip on the Coppermine River in Canada's northern wilderness.

If satisfaction represents a congruence between expectations and enjoyment, it follows that complete and accurate measures of satisfaction should, in theory, include expectations as a base line against which to assess the degree of fulfilment. This causes enormous measurement problems, however, since it is often difficult, if not impossible, to ask people to reconstruct their expectations after a recreational engagement has occurred. Most recreation researchers, therefore, have sidestepped the expectations-fulfilment issue when attempting to measure satisfaction, and several different techniques have been reported in the literature. These include the sophisticated multi-item satisfaction scales of the sort used by Hawes (1978) and Beard and Ragheb (1980), and the somewhat less complex, but nonetheless quantitative, scale used by Alberta Recreation and Parks (1982), some results from which are described below. An alternative approach was taken by Vaske *et al.* (1982); in their study, respondents were asked to respond from "poor" to "perfect" on a six-point scale to the question: Overall, how would you rate your day/trip? More general measures were used by Foster in a study of campers in Alberta, and by Schinkel in a similar study in the Yellowknife region (Foster and Jackson 1979, Jackson and Schinkel 1981). In these studies, the researchers recorded campers' complete verbal descriptions of satisfaction with their stay at a particular campground, and responses were subsequently coded into categories labelled as high, neutral, or low satisfaction.

While the lack of common measures applied in a variety of settings to different behaviours limits the possibility of drawing generalizations about satisfaction in recreation, we can say that, broadly speaking, two main sets of factors influence satisfaction: those which are internal to the individual, and those which are external. Internal factors include some of the variables which have already been discussed, such as motivations, attitudes, and values, often strongly affected by past experience. Also grouped appropriately with internal factors are inter-activity differences in satisfaction, which have been investigated in several different ways, of which two instances are now described.

Differences in the needs satisfied by participating in different forms of outdoor recreation are illustrated by some of the data collected in the 1981 Public Opinion Survey on Recreation conducted by Alberta Recreation and Parks (1982). Responses to two of the eight "satisfaction of needs" statements included in the survey did not differ significantly among the five groups of activities shown in Table 6, but, for the remaining six statements, differences were both statistically significant and, in most cases, quite substantial. To choose just two examples from these data, a minimum of two-thirds of participants reported that the activity helped them to relax, but the proportion was twenty percentage points higher among campers, for whom it ranked a clear first, than among downhill skiers. Among this latter group, relaxation ranked as only the fourth most frequently satisfied need, after being in a pleasant environment, staying healthy, and experiencing physical challenge. A second strong difference occurred in the case of the need to socialize, which was reported as being satisfied twice as frequently among campers and downhill skiers as among people who prefer self-propelled activities like cross-country skiing and hiking. These data, like those from many other investigations (for example, Vaske, Fedler, and Graefe 1986), show that recreation participation can satisfy several different needs simultaneously. The findings are also consistent with the multidimensionality of motivations noted earlier.

Vaske *et al.* (1982) studied recreational satisfaction at a higher level of generalization than in the preceding study, by investigating how some fundamental characteristics of activities influence enjoyment. Rather than focus on specific activities, they classified them along a continuum. At one end of the spectrum they placed non-consumptive activities, such as viewing scenery and canoeing, which focus on an experience. At the other end were consumptive activities, like hunting and fishing, which focus on products. According to Vaske *et al.*, non-consumptive activities are characterized by diffuse goals and a high degree of control in selecting environments that provide the outcomes central to these goals. Consumptive activities, in contrast, are dominated by a clear and central goal, but with less assurance of fulfilling it. The two types of activities should differ, therefore, in the level of satisfaction achieved by their participants.

Pooling the data from a large number of investigations conducted at different locations in the United States, Vaske *et al.* found that consumptive recreationists expressed significantly less satisfaction than non-consumptive recreationists. Satisfaction ratings for successful hunters and fishermen were higher than those reported by unsuccessful consumptive recreationists, but were lower than those indicated by the non-consumptive user groups. Similar studies have not been conducted in Canada, but there is no reason to believe that

Table 6

**Needs Satisfied in Selected Outdoor Recreation Activities
Per Cent Responding "Often"**

Satisfaction Statements*	Downhill Skiing	Hunting and Fishing	Camping	Self-Propelled Activities	Mechanized Activities	Significant at < .05 Level
	%	%	%	%	%	
It helps me to relax	66.7	81.6	89.0	73.7	70.7	Yes
It helps me to stay healthy	76.9	59.0	62.4	83.2	63.9	Yes
The areas or places in which I engage in this recreational activity are pleasing to me	81.5	75.9	81.1	84.2	77.2	No
It gives me a sense of accomplishment	61.5	43.8	46.0	57.9	51.7	Yes
It is physically challenging	75.9	49.4	38.8	70.5	49.6	Yes
I socialize with others through this recreational activity	56.1	39.3	51.6	26.9	42.1	Yes
It increases my knowledge about things around me	26.6	62.6	54.7	49.5	47.1	Yes
It provides opportunities to try new things	48.1	39.6	51.1	44.2	43.7	No

* Listed in descending order of per cent responding "often" among the entire sample.

Source: Alberta Recreation and Parks, 1982.

Canadian recreationists would differ markedly from their American counterparts.

In summary, these studies lend support to the notion that satisfaction in recreation is dependent on several factors, including the specific activities which people select, some of the more fundamental characteristics of these activities, and the extent to which the goals associated with participation are fulfilled. From a theoretical standpoint, recreation satisfaction cannot be fully understood without taking variables of this kind into account, but they may be less important to recreation practitioners than are the external factors. Managers can do little to influence internal factors directly, except perhaps through information programs, but they ought at least to be aware of the desires that people have for, and the needs they fulfil by, participating in particular forms of recreation in particular settings.

External influences on satisfaction may be defined as the characteristics of the natural and social environments, summarized in the amount, location, design, quality, management, and use of recreation resources, facilities, and programs. Recreation managers can, and do, exert a considerable degree of influence over external factors, and indeed it is their mandate to do so.

Several studies have examined what people like and dislike about recreation resources and environments, and how these in turn influence satisfaction. For example, in a 1975 study in Point Pelee National Park (Grant and Wall 1979), the majority of visitors were very satisfied with the scenery, vegetation, behaviour of others, wardens, quietness, and so on. Only one major factor -- insects -- caused widespread dissatisfaction, but other aspects detracting from enjoyment for some visitors included litter, vegetation damage, and crowding. Similar findings emerged in the study of satisfaction in Alberta provincial park campgrounds mentioned above (Foster and Jackson 1979). Here, it was found that the cleanliness, maintenance, and design of non-random campgrounds (those with designated, distinct campsites) contributed to higher levels of satisfaction than were reported in random campgrounds, which were frequently described as dirty, poorly maintained, and noisy.

A fundamental principle in the behavioural approach to recreation, and one which practitioners must also recognize, is that environmental factors do not *determine* enjoyment; rather, the deciding influence on satisfaction is how recreationists *perceive* them. This principle is illustrated particularly well by the results of the Alberta camping study (Foster and Jackson 1979). The main focus in this study was on campground design (non-random versus random campgrounds), and on the adequacy of distance and the amount of vegetative screening between adjacent campsites. As illustrated in Figure 5, levels of satisfaction were higher in non-random than in random campgrounds, regardless of the perceived adequacy of spacing standards and the privacy afforded by vegetative screening. Beyond this, however, perceptions of the adequacy of distance and screening exerted a significant influence on satisfaction, even when the campground structure variable was controlled in the analysis. But the most important finding of the study was that no relationship emerged between objective measures of distance and screening and respondents' perceptions of these campground attributes, nor between the objective measures and reported levels of satisfaction.

This study, therefore, is of theoretical importance because it shows that satisfaction, which itself is a subjective concept, is influenced by factors which are perceived, or subjectively interpreted: satisfaction is not determined by them. Thus, it was not campground design, nor the interconnected aspects of vegetative screening or distance between sites, that affected satisfaction, but rather how these were perceived by campers.

The study is also of practical importance, because it demonstrates that managers cannot perform adequately unless they take into account the perceptions and preferences of the people for whom they are planning. At the same time, however, the findings illustrate one of the major difficulties of applying the results of recreation research, one which can be generalized beyond the specific study described here. If it is people's perceptions of environmental variables rather than the variables themselves that influence satisfaction, then it may be difficult to translate the findings into practice, in this case by developing uniform spacing, screening or design standards, but more generally by any kind of modification to the physical aspects of recreational resources and facilities.

Capacity

A second aspect of the outcomes of recreation behaviour, and indeed a theme which has received as much attention as any other in the recreation research literature (Schreyer 1984),

Figure 5: Satisfaction, Campground Design, Perceived Distance, and Perceived Vegetative Screening Between Campsites

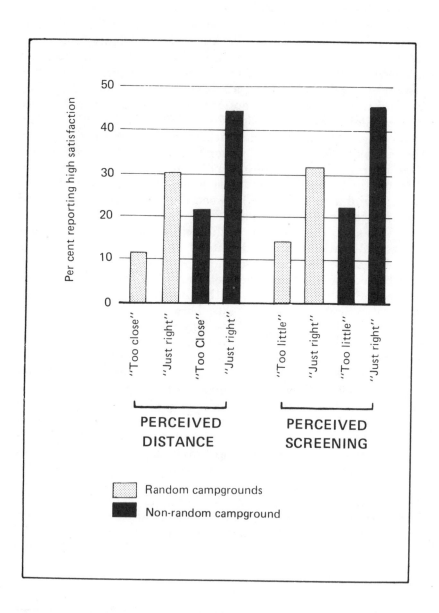

Source: Foster and Jackson (1979), Tables 6, 7, 9, and 10.

concerns the measurement of what has alternatively been referred to as "social carrying capacity," "social capacity," or sometimes simply "capacity." This intensive attention reflects a widespread concern that wilderness and back-country areas are threatened by overuse (Lucas and Stankey 1974).

To paraphrase and combine definitions produced by Lime and Stankey (1971) and Wall (1981), capacity studies aim to provide information to managers about the amount and character of use that recreational resources can sustain without unacceptable damage to the physical environment and without detrimentally affecting recreationists' enjoyment. Studies of this kind are of practical importance, because the ensuing information can potentially be used to decide how many people should be allowed access to scarce recreational resources, what activities should take place in particular recreational settings, and what timing restrictions, if any, should be imposed on recreational use (Stankey 1972).

Capacity studies also have a theoretical value. Like conflict studies (see below), capacity research illustrates the impossibility of achieving a full understanding of recreation behaviour without a holistic approach, in which many themes are synthesized. Pre-eminent among these is the quality of the recreational experience (satisfaction). However, the physical setting within which recreation takes place is also fundamentally important, in two complementary ways: the quality of the natural environment, or more properly how it is perceived, exerts a strong influence on satisfaction among many, if not all, recreationists; in the reverse direction, environmental quality is affected by recreational use. Also important to capacity are the level and type of recreational activity in a given area, not only because they affect environmental quality and impact (Wall and Wright 1977), but also because they influence the satisfaction of participants. Finally, capacity studies raise questions about appropriate objectives and practices in recreation management. How managers perceive users' needs and satisfactions, how they determine acceptable levels of environmental impact, and how they choose among management options, are also significant influences on the capacity of recreational resources.

When it was first introduced into recreation research, the concept of the social capacity of recreational resources represented a borrowing and extension of ideas about ecological capacity originally developed in range management (Mitchell 1979). The concept stemmed from the recognition that recreation can detrimentally affect the quality and processes of the natural environment, depending on the number of people using an area for recreation, the types of activities in which they are engaged, and the physical and biological components and characteristics of the recreational resource (Ohmann 1974). Initially, it was assumed that improved knowledge of all pertinent aspects of these man-environment relationships could result in numerical measures of the capacity of recreational resources, thus allowing managers to decide on a reasonable compromise between totally restricted and totally unrestricted access (Stankey 1982).

It quickly became apparent, however, that there was much more to social capacity than environmental impact alone. There were essentially four reasons why this was so. First, while the amount of environmental change can be measured objectively and scientifically, the definition of *acceptable* levels of environmental degradation reflects a value judgment by both managers and users (Frissell and Stankey 1977, Wagar 1977b). Furthermore, the threshold for irreversible change, as far as ecological processes are concerned, does not have to coincide, and in most real-world instances does not coincide, with what managers consider to be the threshold of undesirability, or the point at which users perceive their enjoyment to be detrimentally affected. For example, a forest area may have been logged to the extent that the aesthetic impact reduces its desirability as a setting for wilderness recreation, yet this negative impact does not necessarily imply a simultaneous irreversibility of the area's potential to support subsequent forest growth or to sustain forestry operations. Conversely, human activity may have significantly affected ecological processes, while the area can still provide quite satisfying experiences for the recreationists who use it. In summary, what is an acceptable level of ecological change, either for managers or users, is not objectively defined, but involves perceptions, preferences, and values.

Second, not only does the level of environmental change vary according to levels and types of use, but participants in different activities also frequently differ in their sensitivity to environmental quality, to the extent to which it has been changed by human activity, and how they define the acceptability of environmental change. For some users, a high quality of environment may be irrelevant to their enjoyment; for others, it may be the most crucial factor.

The validity of these propositions is illustrated by Lucas's (1964) classic study of the semi-wilderness Boundary Waters Canoe Area of the Superior National Forest in northeastern Minnesota, adjacent to Quetico Provincial Park in northern Ontario. Lucas investigated three elements of environmental perception: the importance of wilderness qualities relative to other potential uses; the area considered to be wilderness; and the essential characteristics of wilderness, particularly the types of acceptable use. All three elements differed among different types of recreationists.

Lucas found that wilderness was the main attraction for paddle canoeists, who viewed it as an area in which to travel and camp; wilderness per se was a less important attraction to other recreationists, who viewed it as a means to an end, such as the opportunity for fishing. Paddle canoeists had a much more demanding definition and spatial identification of wilderness than other recreationists. Also, other users tended to adopt a far more permissive attitude than paddle canoeists in their definitions of what uses of wilderness are appropriate, such as roads and logging, as well as about their encounters with other recreationists. Similar findings have been reported for Algonquin Park in Ontario by Priddle, Clark, and Douglas (no date).

The third reason why social capacity cannot be equated with ecological capacity is that environmental quality, in and of itself, is less important , at least from a recreation management standpoint, than how it affects the quality of the recreational experience. Thus, from this perspective, ecological thresholds provide only a necessary, but not sufficient, guide to recreation managers in establishing appropriate levels and types of use.

Finally, we must also recognize that other factors besides environmental quality influence the quality of the recreational experience. These include the presence, number, and behaviour of other recreationists, which therefore must also be taken into account when defining capacity. Stankey (1973), for example, demonstrated how wilderness users' satisfaction declined as more and more parties of recreationists were encountered. Equally important, he found that the relationship between the number of parties encountered and satisfaction varied depending on the activities in which the other parties were engaged. Thus, for paddle canoeists, satisfaction declined much more precipitously if the other recreationists were motor canoeists and particularly motor boaters, than if they were engaged in paddle canoeing. Similarly, for hikers, encounters

with horseback riders were more detrimental to satisfaction
than were trail meetings with other hikers.

To summarize the foregoing, we may modify slightly the
labels used by Lime and Stankey (1971) and define the social
capacity of a given area on the basis of interactions among three
components: visitors' activities, numbers, needs, and attitudes;
the characteristics, opportunities, and constraints of the physical
resource; and management objectives. Each exerts an effect on,
and is affected by, the two other components (Figure 6). Thus, for
example, spatial and temporal variations in physical resources
create simultaneous variations in appropriate recreational
activities; they also determine geographical differences in the
sensitivity of resources to recreational use. An area which
cannot sustain prolonged, high-impact, low-level use might be
perfectly suitable for many more users participating in low-
impact activities; types of recreational use that are inappropriate
on one resource could well be sustained indefinitely in another,
less ecologically sensitive, area. New management goals,
similarly, can lead either to more permissive or restrictive
attitudes towards appropriate levels and types of use, while
managers, when setting their goals, must take into account the
attitudes and preferences of the people who are likely to use
resources for recreation.

The concept of social capacity, then, is a dynamic one,
which means, in turn, that the capacity of an area for recreation
is not and cannot be fixed (Wagar 1974), but will similarly vary
as each of the aforementioned components changes (Graefe,
Vaske, and Kuss 1984, Lime and Stankey 1971). And it must be
re-emphasized that each component either summarizes, or
depends on, the perceptions of recreation managers and users.
Thus, the original search for a "magic number" of capacity was
the equivalent, in recreation management, of the quest for the
Holy Grail (Butler 1981).

Social capacity research has recently received several other
criticisms, some of which have been thoroughly discussed by
Stankey (1982). For example, many of the early findings were
derived from placing recreationists in hypothetical situations,
and were not based on observations of actual behaviour
(Peterson 1983). Recreationists were usually asked how their
enjoyment *might be* affected by the presence of varying
numbers and types of other recreationists, but more recent
studies, summarized by Graefe *et al.* (1984), have questioned
this assumed relationship between satisfaction and density or
use levels. Explanations include "displacement" (dissatisfied

Figure 6: A Dynamic Model of Social Capacity

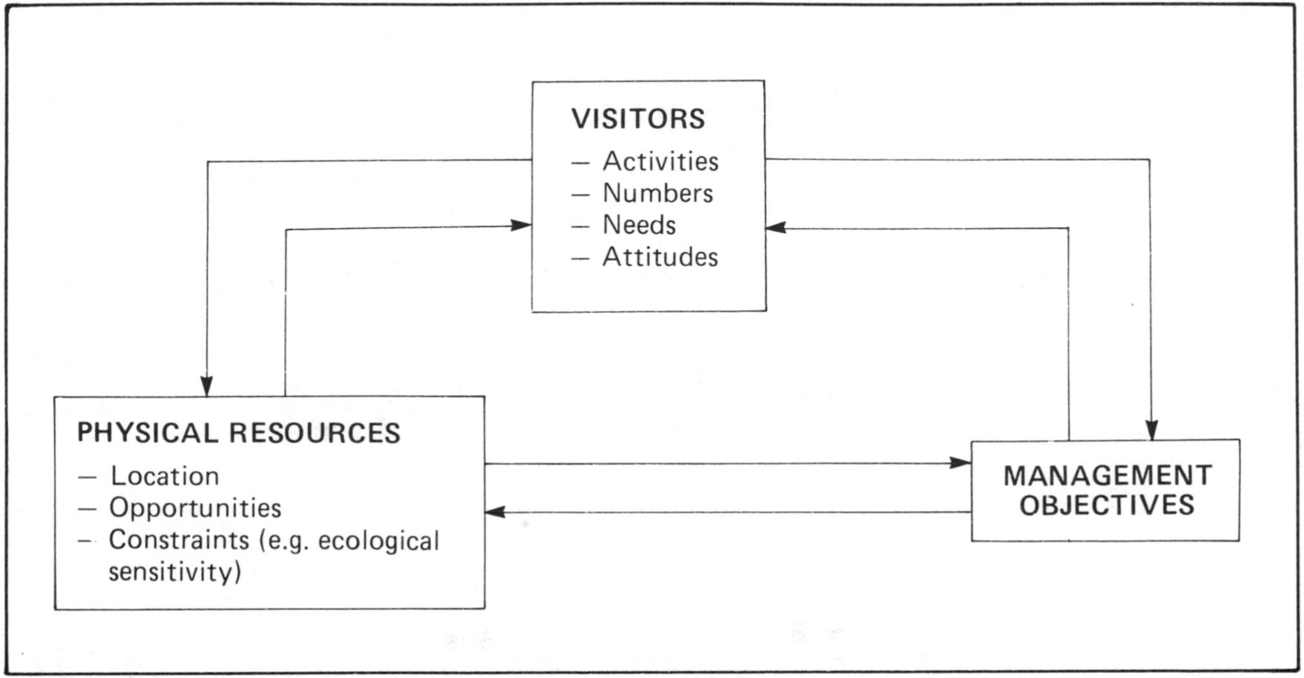

recreationists go elsewhere), and the fact that, for some forms of recreation, high use levels are perceived as an asset rather than as a detriment.

Also, many of the early studies were based on the responses of wilderness purists, so that the findings may not apply equally well to other recreationists, who do not place such high values on high environmental quality, solitude, and privacy, and to whom, indeed, such values may not only be irrelevant but perhaps even detrimental to their enjoyment. On the other hand, according to Wagar (1977b), the capacity concept was never meant to apply anywhere other than in wilderness or back-country areas like many of Canada's national parks and some large provincial parks.

Nonetheless, the capacity concept and the research associated with it have proven valuable in recreation research, if only because, as argued above, they illustrate the dynamism and complexity of recreation behaviour, and the necessity of viewing recreation and its outcomes as the product of perceptions. They have proven more problematic in recreation management, perhaps for exactly the same reasons that they have been beneficial in improving our understanding of recreation behaviour. Management decisions are much easier, though usually wrong, if they are based on untested assumptions about single or simple criteria. They are made much more difficult, however, when it is recognized that many dynamic and interacting factors must be taken into account.

This has necessarily been a brief discussion of one of the most important and thoroughly studied topics using the behavioural approach to outdoor recreation. More detail about the concept, research accomplishments to date, criticisms, and future research directions can be found in the papers by Becker, Jubenville, and Burnett (1984), Burch (1984), Shelby and Heberlein (1984), and Stankey and McCool (1984), in the special edition of *Leisure Sciences* (vol. 6, no. 4), which was devoted to a review of social capacity.

Conflict

Many types of conflict are associated with the recreational use of resources. Recreation often competes with other uses of land, like forestry, mining, and agriculture. The latter often preclude the use of land for recreation; in the reverse direction, as in the case of national parks and other reserves, setting land aside for recreation effectively represents the sacrifice of the benefits that otherwise would have accrued from the alternatives. Even where recreation and other land uses co-exist, the presence of mining activities or forestry will probably detract from recreationists' full enjoyment of the resource. The impact of recreation on ecological processes and environmental quality, noted in the preceding section, may be viewed as yet another form of conflict associated with recreation.

Notwithstanding the importance of these recreational conflicts in Canada and elsewhere, and the difficulties they cause for recreation planning specifically and resource management generally, the behavioural approach to recreation has typically been associated with research on one particular type of conflict -- that which occurs between incompatible groups of outdoor recreationists. Indeed, there are some writers, like Wagar (1977a), who believe that this form of recreation conflict poses even greater management problems than other kinds. Conflicts such as these are best exemplified by the case of cross-country skiers and snowmobilers, as in Knopp and Tyger's (1973) classic study. They are by no means confined to these two activities, however, but also occur between hikers and horseback riders, canoeists and motor boaters, and fishermen and water skiers, to name just a few examples (Devall and Harry 1981, Gramman and Burdge 1981, Lucas 1964, Peterson 1974, Stankey 1973).

Satisfaction, or more properly dissatisfaction, is the central construct in studies of inter-activity conflict, which emerges when recreationists are unwilling or unable to get along with one another. Conflict arises in any situation where the behaviour of some outdoor recreationists interferes with the achievement of the satisfactions desired by others (Buchanan and Buchanan 1981). An example might be a group of fishermen who wish to relax, enjoy the sights and sounds of nature, and get away from noise and people, but who are unable to do so because power boaters are running up and down the shoreline (Buchanan and Buchanan 1981). Thus, as defined by Jacob and Schreyer (1980, 369), "conflict can be viewed as a special case of user dissatisfaction, where the cause of one's dissatisfaction is identified as another group's or individual's behaviour."

Wong's study of perceived conflict between urban-based cross-country skiers and snowmobilers in Alberta is a good example of Canadian research on conflict between incompatible recreational activities (Jackson and Wong 1982). Perceptions of conflict were measured in several ways in this study. More than

90% of cross-country skiers stated that they prefer to meet other skiers rather than snowmobilers, whereas the type of recreationist encountered did not matter to the majority of snowmobilers (67% to 75%, depending on the nature of the encounter). Ninety-five per cent of cross-country skiers mentioned something that they disliked about snowmobilers using the same area, compared with only 29% of snowmobilers disliking the presence of cross-country skiers. Lastly, while 87% of snowmobilers agreed with the statement "skiers and snowmobilers can mix happily if both use common sense," 76% of cross-country skiers disagreed, most of them strongly.

Taken together, these and other measures included in the study demonstrate the asymmetrical nature of the conflict, that is, that the presence of snowmobilers detrimentally affects cross-country skiers' enjoyment, whereas most snowmobilers are indifferent towards, or even feel positively about, the presence of cross-country skiers in the same recreation area. However, there was also some evidence to suggest that a more symmetrical type of conflict has begun to emerge, not expressed in terms of on-site contacts, but more indirectly: some snowmobilers have developed a general dislike for cross-country skiers and their attitudes, based, perhaps, on the latter's apparent success in having snowmobiling banned from certain recreation areas in Alberta.

Other results of the study indicated that the roots of on-site conflict may be interpreted with reference to the incompatible goals and expectations that the two different groups of recreationists bring with them to their activities. The desires for physical exercise, tranquillity, solitude, and the absence of man-made features were significantly stronger among Wong's sample of cross-country skiers than among the snowmobilers, whereas socialization, adventure, and challenge were more important to snowmobilers than to cross-country skiers. It was concluded that conflict is felt among cross-country skiers because the presence, noise, danger, and other negatively perceived attributes of snowmobiles interfere with the satisfaction of cross-country skiers' needs, whereas the desires of snowmobilers are unlikely to be compromised, and might even be enhanced, by the presence of other recreationists, regardless of the activities in which they are participating.

Although Wong's is but one example of the many recreation-conflict studies that have been conducted in Canada and elsewhere over the past decade, it illustrates several common features of conflict between incompatible activities.

Indeed, one of the most striking aspects of recreation-conflict research is the high level of consistency that has emerged in different studies, despite variations in the specific activities which have been studied, the season in which the activities take place, and even the countries in which the research has been conducted. Although the majority of research to date comes from the United States and Canada (between which few, if any, significant differences can be detected), at least one overseas investigation, focussing on conflict between anglers and boat users in England, has produced similar findings (O'Riordan 1977).

Thus, most studies have confirmed the asymmetrical nature of on-site conflict: one type of recreationist is negatively affected by the presence and behaviour of another type, while the reverse is not always true. Recreationists who are perceived to cause a conflict are rarely disturbed by the presence or behaviour of others. However, as the conflict moves away from the specific site and enters the arena of competition over access to recreational resources, a growing symmetry is likely to develop. Second, the affected recreationists are most commonly those who participate in passive, appreciative, and self-propelled forms of recreation, whereas those who are perceived to cause the problem are the more active, faster, mechanized, and non-self-propelled types of recreationists. Third, the degree to which conflict is perceived depends on the number, location, and timing of encounters. Fourth, during the actual encounter, several elements may negatively affect the quality of the recreation experience, including the noise of machines, the fear of personal injury, discourtesy, perceived impacts on the environment, and perceived impacts on the quality of the recreational resource.

At a more fundamental level, we may conclude that conflict arising from the presence or behaviour of one group of recreationists causes dissatisfaction to another group because the motivations of the latter for recreating are frustrated. Gramman and Burdge's (1981) study of conflict between water skiers and fishermen supports this inference, as do various other studies cited by Buchanan and Buchanan (1981) and Jacob and Schreyer (1980). And finally, results from studies of differences in the environmental attitudes of recreationists whose activities conflict in the ways described above lend some support to the proposition that conflict occurs as a result of the distaste for the values that members of the conflicting group are perceived to hold, and the lifestyles they are presumed, rightly or wrongly, to prefer (Jackson 1986, Jacob and Schreyer 1980, Knopp and Tyger 1973).

It is not surprising that the body of inter-activity conflict research has grown markedly over the past decade, given its obvious theoretical and practical value. The necessity for interweaving many diverse threads in recreation research demonstrates the theoretical importance of conflict research: conflict cannot be fully understood without synthesizing knowledge about the choice of activities, the reasons that explain differences in activity choices, and other outcomes of recreation behaviour, such as satisfaction. In turn, the necessity for sharpening concepts and developing rigorous hypotheses derived from theory is amply illustrated in the excellent review essays by Jacob and Schreyer (1980) and Owens (1985), to which the reader should refer for a more detailed and comprehensive review of recreation conflict than is possible in this chapter. Conflict research is growing in practical importance, too, because recreation managers can decide if land use zoning, other forms of land use regulation, or other types of management are appropriate options for conflict resolution only if they know what activities conflict with each other, and how and why conflict occurs (Jacob and Schreyer 1980, Knopp and Tyger 1973, Owens 1985, Wagar 1977a).

CONCLUSIONS

In this chapter, it has been possible to discuss only a limited set of aspects of outdoor recreation that are consistent with the behavioural approach. In the interests of length, several other topics have had to be omitted, even though they constitute perfectly legitimate focuses of interest for research. They include non-participation and barriers to participation and enjoyment in recreation (Godbey 1985, Howard and Crompton 1984; Jackson 1988, Romsa and Hoffman 1980, Searle and Jackson 1985a, 1985b, Witt and Goodale 1981), the role of risk-taking (Cheron and Ritchie 1982, Foster 1986, Kroening 1979), and relationships between energy use and recreation (Foster and Kuhn 1983, Ritchie and Claxton 1983). Nevertheless, the topics which it has been possible to address should be sufficient to convey a sense of the behavioural approach to outdoor recreation, and to exemplify some of the important current themes in recreation research and management, both in Canada and elsewhere.

The pre-eminent theme, of course, which has been illustrated throughout the chapter, is the notion that recreational choices reflect an underlying set of preferences and perceptions, which enter into recreational decision-making in a variety of ways and at all stages of the process. Thus, any effort to understand recreation behaviour is incomplete unless these important influences are investigated. Without knowing about the factors that explain recreational choice, or about the outcomes of such choices, recreation research degenerates into the barren collection of information. If these elements are included, however, then the behavioural approach to recreation has the potential to make an important theoretical contribution, by which is meant an addition to knowledge and understanding.

In a practical vein, too, the behavioural approach provides useful applications. It has been demonstrated, at several points in this chapter, that recreation planners and managers are unlikely to make optimal decisions unless they are aware of recreationists' perceptions, needs, and preferences. However, an important limitation associated with applying the results of behavioural research must now be discussed.

There is a widespread tendency to believe that, if only more and better information is available (in this case about the needs and behaviours of recreationists), then resource planning and management problems will be resolved. The notion is fallacious for at least two reasons. First, there are many other important influences on recreational decisions, such as economic constraints, political questions, and the availability, quality, and ecological characteristics of physical resources. In any given case, politics, economics, or resource and environmental constraints might override public preferences.

Second, even if these considerations are set aside, knowledge about preferences will not necessarily eradicate planning problems. Indeed, in some cases it may well be that managers are faced with decisions that are more difficult than they otherwise would have been. In the absence of the kinds of information provided by behavioural research, recreation planners and managers must make assumptions about the public's demand for recreation, the needs and motivations which underlie it, and outcomes of the kind which have been described in this chapter. In this sense, recreation managers can follow their own biases and prejudices, which frequently may be in line with the public's requirements. More often than not, however, such biases are probably at odds with what the public really desires.

Furthermore, all of the aspects of recreation discussed in this chapter reveal that the public is a diverse, heterogeneous entity, characterized by simultaneous and consistent variations in participation rates, frequency of participation, preferences, social class, needs and motivations, and attitudes and values. What this means for planners and managers is that they must respond to many recreation publics rather than one single public alone. And, given limited resources, both physical and financial, it may not be possible to address the entire spectrum of public demand for recreation, especially in an era of restraint such as characterizes the late 1980s. Thus, planners and managers must make choices. While the data and information provided by research conducted from a behavioural perspective may assist in making those choices, it will not, by itself or automatically, solve recreation planning and management problems.

Chapter 5

Patterns

Jan Lundgren
Department of Geography
McGill University

Patterns

Earlier chapters of this book have examined two major
components of recreational phenomena: the attributes of supply
and the characteristics of demand. Supply and demand
combine through decision-making processes to result in
patterns of outdoor recreation. Patterns of recreation may be
defined as the spatial and temporal distributions of recreational
phenomena. These distributions are not random but exhibit
common characteristics and regularities which are the subject
of this contribution. Supply and demand are interdependent,
and it is through consumption that they are brought together to
produce distinctive configurations of people, facilities, activities
and, ultimately, impacts. Neither supply nor demand is static
so that decisions, behaviour, and the associated patterns have a
dynamic quality which varies considerably, but somewhat
systematically, over time and also spatially.

THE ROLE OF TIME

Patterns can be identified for both recreational supply and
demand. Clearly, these components have distinct spatial
variability reflecting the distribution of man-made,
locationally flexible facilities; natural-resource-based,
physical-landscape-dependent, locationally fixed recreational
opportunities; and the socio-economic characteristics of the
market. The market is concentrated in urban areas. However,
patterns of consumption change continually as recreational
preferences, when activated as participation, result in new
behaviours reflecting the changing life-cycle dynamics of the
population.

A fundamental factor underlying spatial patterns of recreation is the manner in which leisure is made available to potential consumers. Therefore, an analysis of the spatial implications of free time is a good starting point from which to outline the principal features of contemporary spatial patterns of recreation.

As countries became industrialized over the past 150 years, a process starting in Britain and gradually spreading to other European countries as well as to North America, Japan, and Australasia, leisure changed dramatically from being available in loosely defined blocks of time to being constrained within sharp temporal boundaries, often defined as non-work time. In the inter-war era leisure time expanded and, at the same time, became a set of increasingly structured time periods. This is of major significance for leisure behaviour and the associated patterns of recreation. It is now possible to distinguish three blocks of leisure time, each of which places distinct limitations on the range and types of recreational consumption. The consequences of this are presented in Figure 1, which illustrates the broad outlines of leisure space. The model consists of three spatial gradients associated with three different blocks of time. Together they encompass the leisure spaces of individuals within which all types of recreational pursuits occur, be it spontaneous visits to a local tavern or carefully planned and executed vacation travel to a distant, exotic destination. The daily, weekend, and vacation time slots of the model are relevant to both recreational supply and demand and exhibit characteristic patterns. Thus, daily leisure time occurs in small pieces but with high frequency and is usually associated with small, if any, expenditures and spatially restricted movements. Most such time is spent in the home or in its vicinity. To a large extent the leisure pursuits take place within the confines of home: watching television, reading, gardening, and entertaining are examples of common activities. In fact, of the twenty-five recreation activities listed in a paper by Wall (1979), two-thirds were home-based. In spite of the limited spatial range and small individual expenditures per occasion, the cumulated expenditures are large. Together they are sufficient to produce an economic base for the considerable array of commercial, urban recreational supply found in larger metropolitan centres, such as theatres, restaurants, stadiums, museums, and art galleries, which together constitute a substantial proportion of the service sector.

Figure 1: Recreational Land Use in the Quebec City Hinterland

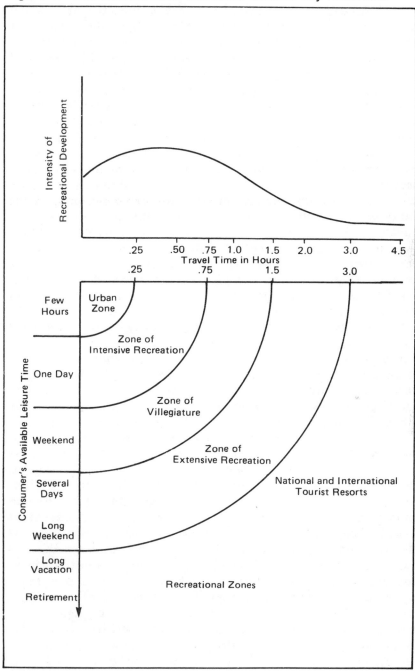

Source: After Freda Rajotte 1975.

The weekend leisure time gradient operates at a much lower annual frequency over a larger range of distances with usually a higher direct expenditure per occasion. Furthermore, in contrast to the fairly consistent year-round set of recreational pursuits for daily leisure, the weekend activities exhibit much seasonal variation. Admittedly there are some pursuits which take place throughout the year, but what is of most significance is the flux between summer and winter weekend activities that result in different patterns and economic impacts. In general, the weekend winter outdoor recreation pursuits have a higher cost per capita and per occasion than typical summer weekend activities: compare, for example, downhill skiing with family camping. The distance range may also be very different for summer and winter activities, reflecting the locations of landscape features able to support the various activities. Thus, for the Montrealer, access to high-class outdoor recreation opportunities for winter sports, notably alpine skiing, is available within a sixty- to ninety-minute travel range while the Torontonian has to travel considerably farther for an equivalent experience.

Not only do ranges and costs per occasion differ between summer and winter, but the directional stability of the trip patterns also varies. Summer sees a spatially diffuse pattern of recreational mobility as families make camping trips for which destinations may vary from one weekend to the next and where the trips may even consist of a series of circular tours. At the other extreme, a more stable, regular pattern of movement to cottages occurs as a function of property ownership: a regular, weekend rhythm of travel can be observed to cottages, which are usually within a travel time of less than two hours. In winter, the weekend pattern of recreational travel from metropolitan areas is characterized by flows which are more concentrated spatially. For example, the ski resorts in the Montreal Laurentians and around Collingwood in Ontario act as centres of attraction to which the market is pulled. Although there is bound to be some variability between destinations in the winter because some recreationists enjoy a diversity of experiences, and from week to week because of the vagaries of the weather, a strong effort is made by managers of the commercial enterprises to tie down consumers to their resort by such devices as season passes and ski programes. Obviously, this is a reflection of the need of all ski resorts to secure sufficient market base to cover the high capital, operation, and maintenance costs.

The daily and weekly blocks of leisure are a powerful force regulating the use of recreational space. According to national time budget studies, over 80% of leisure time falls within the daily and weekend time slots (Clawson1971). This makes them of extreme importance in both locational and economic terms. It also leads to the conclusion that the bulk of our leisure pursuits are confined within a fairly limited distance range within which activities in the urban environment are paramount and cumulative expenditures are large.

The above discussion could give the erroneous impression that the vacation time block is of only marginal importance to leisure and the use of recreational space. However, the fairly small annual proportion of approximately 10% of leisure devoted to vacations is one of the most influential forces in moulding recreational patterns beyond the consumers' home bases. This is partially due to the timing of vacations: there is great seasonality in demand, and the summer months, especially the latter part of July and the first two weeks of August, experience travel intensities which are between four and five times the annual monthly average. Such seasonal variations place strong pressures upon all aspects of recreational supply, including transportation, tourist accommodation in campgrounds, hotels and motels, and centres of attraction, be they beaches, historical sites, or amusement parks. It does not seem to matter greatly that the vacation time allotment is often divided into two to permit both a summer and winter break, for the demand peaks and temporary shortages of capacity are common characteristics of vacation time periods.

The economics of the vacation time period differ markedly from the other blocks of leisure. The expenditures per person per occasion are usually many times higher. Even a frugal family camping vacation cannot be obtained for less than ten dollars per day in direct expenditures, not counting equipment or transport costs. Low-priced resort vacations start at approximately one hundred dollars per week and, if the destination must be reached by air travel, an additional substantial sum of money must be expended. Thus, the vacation time slot not only has marked concentrations of seasonal demand, it also involves massive inter-regional, and even international, financial transactions. The vacation time slot also exhibits an extensive distance range: family vacations by car usually involve journeys approaching one thousand kilometres, and a large proportion of trips involve transcontinental or transatlantic travel to foreign destinations -- Florida, California, the Caribbean, and Europe. There is also considerable inter-city travel, but perhaps less of this in Canada than in Europe, where fairly short trips take the north German to Paris, the Dutch to Nice, or the Scandinavian, by inexpensive air charter, to Rome. In Canada inter-urban vacation travel may be less pronounced due to the long distances and high transport costs, and perhaps also to the comparative lack of unique places, with some notable exceptions, such as Quebec City, Victoria, and Halifax. As the discussion indicates, much of the vacation time slot is taken up with tourism. It is through the use of the vacation time slot that there is a drain on the Canadian travel balance, particularly to the United States and to a lesser extent to Europe, because of the large number of trips with southern destinations.

The large amount of vacation expenditures in popular tourist destinations constitutes much of the economic base for both domestic and international resorts, where Canadian dollars combine with those of other travellers to support resort establishments in such places as New England or, farther away, Barbados, where tourist development has depended to a considerable extent on Canadian vacationers. However, although the international part of vacation travel captures the imagination of readers of the travel sections of the *Montreal Gazette*, the *Globe and Mail* or the *Winnipeg Free Press*, much vacation travel is quite restricted spatially: only about 20% of Quebec vacations are taken outside of the province and, similarly, most Ontarians go to Ontario vacation destinations. Provincial loyalty is a common feature in the larger, more populous provinces, whereas small provinces in the east have a greater tendency to generate travellers for other provinces, thereby incurring considerable losses in their provincial travel balances.

AGGREGATE LEISURE SPACE

So far an analysis of patterns has been made from the perspective of individual leisure behaviour within the context of available blocks of time -- daily, weekend, and vacation -- and using place of residence as a base from which recreation is pursued. In order to arrive at a broader perspective on recreation patterns and their geographical implications it is useful to aggregate the individual patterns. This has been done by a number of geographers interested in differentiating the intensity of use of leisure space at different distances from major travel-generating urban areas, mostly located in the more densely populated ecumene in Canada or other western countries. In aggregating the individual patterns, the first step is taken in understanding leisure space within urban hinterlands and also on a national scale, encompassing the more recently developed and developing leisure space in the north. Thus, leisure patterns can be viewed in a holistic context as spatially hierarchical patterns of circulation. There is, however, a spatial continuum which is dominated at one end by high-frequency, strongly localized movements, and at the other end by extensive, long-distance pleasure travel, that is, tourism to both domestic and international destinations.

Christaller (1964) was among the first scholars to recognize the strong centre-periphery characteristics of tourist travel, applying the notion of centrifugal flows on a European continental scale. In Canada, Wolfe (1966) made somewhat similar observations in his research on the origins of visitors at Ontario parks, where the proportion of urban visitors from the highly industrial Great Lakes region was a prominent feature. Rajotte (1975) developed a metropolitan hinterland model of leisure-recreation-tourism space in her studies of the Quebec City hinterland (Figure 2). Her model was based upon detailed field observations of recreational land use in distance zones at varying travel times from central Quebec. Rajotte selected the northwestern sector of the hinterland for detailed analysis. This is a fairly homogeneous area of the Canadian Shield. In fact, it is in many ways a microcosm of the southern margins of the Canadian Shield, which stretches from Manitoba in the west to the Gulf of St. Lawrence in the east; an area which, because of resources and accessibility, possesses a leisure space zonation which is truly "Canadian." Thus, although the model has been developed in a specific geographical location, it is relevant to a much larger area. Rajotte emphasized the dominant distance decay characteristic of the hinterland leisure space in a manner similar to that of the land rent curve commonly employed in urban land use models. In the zone immediately beyond the built-up urban area, recreational intensity levels are slightly depressed. This area is surrounded by a zone of more intensive use, which corresponds approximately with travel time access considered acceptable for day trip recreation: 1.5 to 2 hours' journey one-way. As one moves away from the city and deeper into the periphery, the level of recreational utility declines until

Figure 2: Relationships between Leisure Time, Travel Range and Expenditure

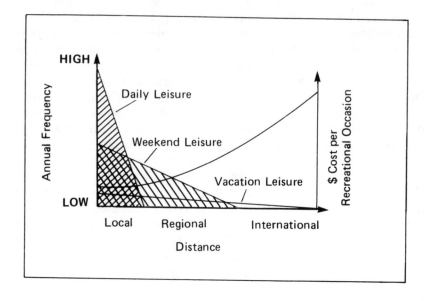

Source: J. Lundgren 1986.

there is little, if any, imprint of recreation upon the landscape. In the case of Quebec City, intensive forms of outdoor recreation are replaced with extensive forms, such as fishing and hunting, reflecting not only the poorer access but also the different space requirements for these recreational pursuits.

Rajotte's model was derived empirically but, nevertheless, it is amenable to a more strict, quantitative, spatial analysis. It established functional and spatial characteristics of leisure-recreation-tourism space for metropolitan hinterlands and has a good fit for many situations, including large areas of North America, parts of Scandinavia, and Australia, where population densities are low and long distances are traversed for recreation. Not surprisingly, deviations from the model can be found. The unique resort developments of the Montreal Laurentians and the Calgary-Banff-Jasper corridor do not fit well with the single-centred model design based upon Quebec City. In these cases, market demand is only partially derived from the nearby metropolis, and tourism from more distant locations, in addition to more localized recreation, produces a more complicated set of influencing factors.

A further omission from the model, although not ignored elsewhere in Rajotte's work, is the lack of explicit dynamic components. Over time, the recreational utility of destination zones is modified: metropolitan growth encroaches on the most accessible zone; new and improved transportation routes extend recreational pressures farther into the periphery and distort concentric patterns; excessive use and exploitation of natural resources in accessible locations displace participants to other locations; and new forms of transportation, such as light airplanes and off-road vehicles, allow recreation to take place in pristine areas. As a consequence, the outer fringe of the periphery is a highly dynamic part of the metropolitan recreational hinterland. Rajotte does refer to the gradual change that has been brought about by major historical changes in modes of transportation. Replacement of earlier forms of riverine transportation by steamship and rail changed accessibility into the hinterland and also transformed the role of Quebec City: from initially having generated the recreation and tourism demand largely by itself, the city eventually evolved into an important destination and transfer point for visitors en route to the hinterland or to the various resort areas along the Gulf of St. Lawrence. Murray Bay, Tadoussac, and Pointe-au-Pic on the north shore, and St.-Jean-Port-Joli, Kamouraska, Cacouna, and Métis-sur-Mer along the south shore, all reflect innovations in transportation prior to World War I. The concentric hinterland towards the north complemented the coastal, linear, and radially-extensive growth of recreational and tourist space in other directions, partially reflecting an environment with a potential for recreation which is far from homogeneous.

SPATIAL STABILITY AND INSTABILITY

A major question concerning the spatial patterns found in the Rajotte model is the degree to which they are stable. One can also ask how typical and permanent the patterns might be and the nature of the forces that might cause them to change. Few studies provide insight into the spatial dynamics of patterns of recreation, although some studies of the history of outdoor recreation touch upon the topic.

From both a historical and a contemporary perspective, the most critical forces impinging upon the recreational hinterland of urban areas, as presented earlier, are changes in transportation, the recreational potential of the physical environment or landscape, and innovations in the market, that is, changing recreational preferences. On the supply side, the patterns are affected by the relative location of sites and environments with recreational potential and by the forms and extent of capital investment in recreational property. Such investment may be by private entrepreneurs, as in the case of ski hill developments, and private individuals, as in the case of cottage ownership, or may be by the public sector, as in the establishment of parks, reserves, and other recreation sites. The above factors interact, each with different forces at different times, to produce rapid change or, conversely, a reinforcement of existing patterns depending upon the magnitudes of the forces involved.

The Montreal Laurentians is a metropolitan recreational hinterland that has experienced both stable and dynamic periods of development that span both historical and contemporary eras. Without going into the specifics of regional development and associated transformations, some of the more salient features will suffice to illustrate how spatial stability and change have alternated in the development process. The area was opened up in its full north-south dimension from Montreal to MontTremblant by the 1890s as the Canadian Pacific railway to Laurier became operational. Since that time the transportation corridor has been exposed to forces which emanated from outside of the region, such as changing demand, which was initially located largely in Montreal, and provincial strategies for transportation development and the management of land and water. How were spatial patterns of recreation affected by the factors which have been identified?

CHANGES IN TRANSPORTATION

The spatial configuration of recreational movements into the Laurentians was strongly influenced by the three major changes in mode of transportation and transportation infrastructure which the region has experienced since the 1890s. For a period of some thirty years the bulk of recreational pressures into the Laurentians was transmitted through the railroad. This tended to concentrate people, facilities, and impacts into nodes at the railheads and their more accessible environs. Of course, such areas also had to possess landscape attributes which would support non-urban types of outdoor recreation and tourism. The channelling of participation along the rail line was conducive to the establishment of major resorts that stabilized travel patterns. In fact, they became major nodes of attraction in the recreational hinterland. The same nodes also facilitated the creation of smaller, discrete local hinterlands in which privately owned summer cottages were a common feature. These were to be found along attractive shorelines and at scenic sites in the lake-studded landscape. Thus, the spatial stability fostered by the resort enterprises was reinforced by the increasing demand for development in the same areas, particularly around St.-Sauveur, at Ste.-Adèle and Ste.-Agathe-des-Monts.

As transportation modes changed in the 1930s with increased automobile travel over an upgraded road network, the earlier nodal pattern was modified. Pressures of use penetrated farther north and also extended laterally as secondary roads and dirt roads opened up more lake frontage and other areas which were favourable for cottages and commercial recreation developments, including camps, fishing and hunting lodges, and less expensive resorts. The outlines of the present recreational occupancy of the region could be discerned by the outbreak of World War II, for many of the more famous resorts, such as Tremblant, Chantecler, and Alpine Inn, were already in place.

Postwar affluence, increased car ownership, and the popularity of winter sports, especially alpine skiing, fostered further transportation changes: the Laurentian Autoroute was constructed between 1958 and 1975. Accessibility changed drastically with serious consequences for the commercial accommodation sector and the ski hills. From being predominantly a destination and a holiday region, necessitating an overnight or weekend stay in order to enjoy the various attractions, most of the region was transformed by the autoroute into a day-trip destination. Even the reasonably remote Mont Tremblant could be reached in ninety minutes from central Montreal. The La Verendrye wilderness park became much more accessible, although not as a day-trip destination from Montreal. The consequences of this improved accessibility were far-reaching for the supply of recreation opportunities, for a substantial proportion of the service provision, especially commercial accommodation, became redundant.

CHANGING PERCEPTIONS OF OUTDOOR RECREATION

Landscape diversity, specific elements of the landscape, convenience, and seasonality are among the factors which give the Laurentians an extremely rich recreational potential which exerts a strong pull upon the nearby metropolitan market. However, over the fairly long period of development as a recreational destination, the various attractions have not exerted an unchanged level of demand. Thus, the directional characteristics of recreational movements have evolved over time and altered in intensity, reflecting changes in consumer preferences for outdoor recreation.

Summer recreation and single season economics dominated both supply and demand for the Laurentians well into the 1930s. This was in keeping with the North American vacation tradition of seeking cooler upland environments and refreshing coastlines. The resorts and guest houses opened their doors in June and closed for the season in early September. The only exceptions were lodges catering to the sport hunter and fisherman. The single season economics meant that rates were quite high relative to other prices of the day, and therefore the market base from which visitors were drawn was narrow. For a long time the volume of recreational traffic was small and came from the wealthier districts of metropolitan Montreal.

Scenery in general, combined with select summer sports, was the major attraction.

The market was jolted into a different perception of the regional recreation potential with the introduction of winter sports, especially skiing. Alpine skiing drastically modified the recreational potential of the landscape attributes and thereby modified the attraction of existing resort locations. In consequence, new sites were explored and exploited during the 1930s, and these contrasted locationally with the patterns that had developed in association with summer-based recreation and tourism. Major resorts, such as Tremblant Lodge, Chantecler, and Nymarks Lodge, were developed at the foot of mountains, making earlier resort locations less competitive. The latter not only lost business; they also failed to attract the new market segments that were drawn by the novel activity. Thus, the former nodal pattern of recreation was weakened, and new capital-intensive facilities in new locations attracted an increasing number of visitors. The market changed towards greater appreciation of the winter season, slowly and then more rapidly changing the market base and exploiting more fully the potential of the metropolitan market.

RECREATIONAL INNOVATION

Activities and preferences for recreation are prone to change, as has been indicated above. Costs of participation play an important role in these changes, influencing both rates of change and their longevity. The two forms of skiing vying for prominence in the Laurentians provide a good example of how the cost factor works.

Although cross-country skiing was less expensive to pursue and had already been introduced in the 1920s before alpine skiing, it failed to take off as a major winter pastime until after World War II. Growth in participation was most rapid in the 1970s. Thus, the more glamorous and exciting downhill skiing was the development generator for the region for almost half a century, starting in the 1930s and, over time, activating an increasing proportion of the market potential. The rapidly growing equipment costs and daily expenses gradually changed the market around, making the alternative activity increasingly attractive from the perspective of price. At the same time, the growth in the popularity of cross-country skiing coincided with increased interest in physical fitness, which

came into vogue in the 1960s. The fact that the daily expenses for
a family engaging in downhill skiing, including equipment
and instruction for the novices, could amount to one hundred
dollars accelerated the turnaround. As a consequence, the
recreational utility of landscape features was modified again:
the resort focuses were weakened, and a much more dispersed
pattern was established as cross-country trail systems
crisscrossed the Laurentians.

Similar shifts have taken place in other segments of the
market. One of the best examples is water-based recreation,
especially boating. Until the advent of fibreglass, pleasure
boating, excluding canoeing, was a rich man's sport, with
considerable equipment, maintenance, and operating costs.
Prices started to decline in the mid-1960s with positive effects
upon participation. The introduction of simple, popular boat
designs, such as the Sunfish and Laser, and in the latter part of
the 1970s the sailboard, has revolutionized participation and
made sailing one of the most rapidly growing summer sports,
catering to a broadening age band at reasonable costs. Hence,
mass appeal has been established in the marketplace. Such
innovations have had their implications for the Laurentian
resorts. The lakeside resorts could attract a new clientele by
providing services for the new summer sports whereas, others
had no such options and were forced to look for alternative
attractions. At the same time, the new sports shifted recreational
participation to previously unused water bodies in the vicinity of
the metropolitan area, such as the La Prairie Basin on the St.
Lawrence Seaway, in central Montreal. Thus, again a
recreational innovation has produced a quick and dramatic
reassessment of dormant natural resources with implications
for established patterns of use.

TRANSFORMATION OF SERVICES

The consequences of the destabilizing processes that cause
changes in recreational patterns are most visible in the
restructuring that has occurred in the tourist businesses of the
Montreal Laurentians. Changing forces, particularly
modifications of transport and access, have produced a
shrinking market for the accommodation sector: the autoroute
reduced the need for overnight stays; new recreational pursuits
weakened the link to capital-intensive service facilities; price
developments for different types of recreation encouraged

customers to reassess past preferences and to consider alternative pursuits; and innovative, highly popular, almost faddish activities were introduced to the market. As a result, the region changed in recreation utility and became a day-trip destination for the metropolitan population at large and, secondarily, a longer-stay tourism destination. This transformation had considerable impact upon accommodation enterprises of all types.

The transformation has been documented in Lundgren's (1983) study of the Montreal Laurentians (Figure 3). From St.-Sauveur to Mont Tremblant the number of hotels declined from 190 to 103, and the number of rooms dropped from over 4,200 to less than 3,000. Massive reductions occurred in the central section of the corridor between Val David and Ste.-Agathe: many resort establishments closed and others were left with major reorientation problems and the need for complete refinancing. Some survived only by government intervention, while others, such as historic Gray Rocks, rode out the storm through skilful marketing and prudent management. The emergence of a buoyant, metropolitan-based convention trade in the 1970s has partially filled the gap left by the the reorientation of family vacations, and provided a supplementary income and a chance to regroup. Thus, the region survives as a recreation destination, but with a different economic base. This has resulted in the development of very different linkages to more distant, corporate markets in Toronto, Ottawa, and Quebec City, and these markets have become vital to the survival of the resorts.

DIMENSIONS OF THE CANADIAN LEISURE SPACE

The discussion of recreation in the Montreal Laurentians and Rajotte's model based on Quebec City consider metropolitan recreational hinterlands. It is possible to take an even broader perspective and position such hinterlands in a macro-geographic continental spatial framework or leisure space. By elevating the analysis of recreational patterns to a highly aggregated level, individual urban-based metropolitan hinterlands can be integrated into a comprehensive leisure space which is truly Canadian in character and which differs from the geographical circumstances within which recreational patterns function in most other industrial countries.

Figure 4: Commercial Fishing Lodges in Manitoba, Northern Ontario and Northern Quebec, 1985

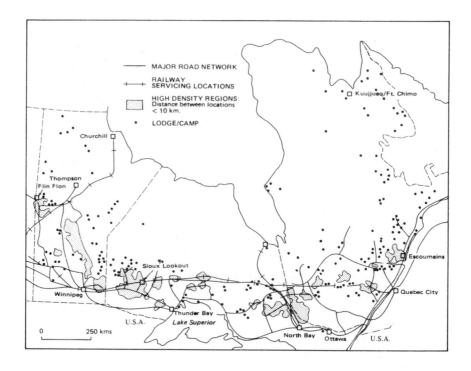

Source: Compiled by author.

The Canadian leisure space is presented in Figure 4. Among the many distinctive attributes of this leisure space, three outstanding features have been selected for more detailed discussion: distance decay characteristics, evolutionary spatial processes, and long-distance transport penetration.

1. Distance decay characteristics. The availability of leisure time and a more diverse supply of recreational opportunities in the Canadian ecumene tend to concentrate movements in and around the urban settlement system with its numerous, accessible urban and metropolitan nodes from coast to coast. The bulk of demand, supply, and consumption occur in this zone regardless of the type of time slot -- daily, weekend, or vacation. This leaves only a small fraction of total time spent in foreign destinations or in the vast, practically uninhabited areas north of the ecumene. If any recreational characteristic makes Canada unique it is the sharp contrast in the leisure space, with an extensive wilderness component in the leisure product seemingly so close and accessible to the domestic market. Nevertheless, much of the wilderness product is inaccessible in terms of travel costs for many potential Canadian consumers.

There is a rapidly declining recreational utility as one moves northwards towards the periphery of the domestic leisure space. Cost is undoubtedly one reason for this: as the traveller reaches the end of the road at Lac Albenal, Quebec; Windigo Lake, Ontario; and Sundance, Manitoba, any further northern advance requires a disproportionately large additional expense. As the model indicates, no low-cost transportation is available and only air services carry the traveller into more northern zones.

As a consequence of increasing transportation costs as one moves northwards, a second factor is activated: a shrinking market segment. A fishing week in road-accessible camp facilities rarely costs more than $200 for transport, since the camp can be reached by car. To this can be added a cabin rental of approximately $500 per week, which amounts to $175 per person when divided among a family of four. Expenditures for food should be added to this. Such expenses are affordable to a fairly large number of people. This is in sharp contrast to more northern experiences, for which both travel costs and living expenses are likely to be much higher. Fishing or hunting trips to Ungava Bay and the George River area of Labrador cost thousands of dollars; the return air fare alone from the south to Fort Chimo is over $500. In consequence, more northerly

Figure 5: A Conceptual Model of Tourist Destination Space: A Canadian Application

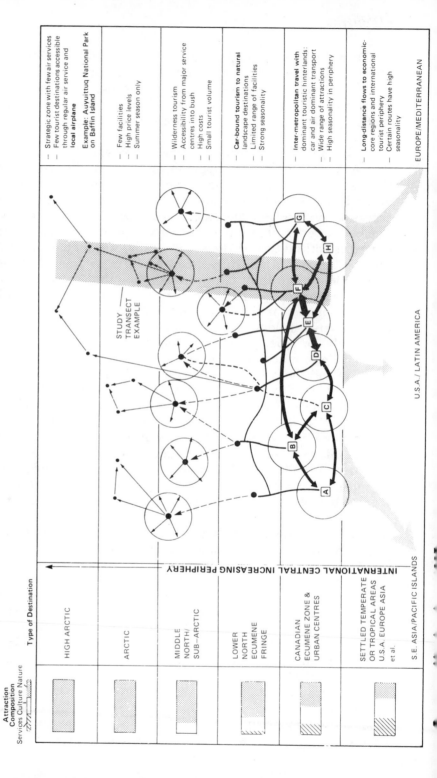

Type of Destination		Attraction Composition Services Culture Nature	Details
HIGH ARCTIC			– Strategic zone with few air services – Few tourist destinations accessible through regular air service and **local airplane** **Example:** Auyuittuq National Park on Baffin Island
ARCTIC			– Few facilities – High price levels – Summer season only
MIDDLE NORTH/ SUB-ARCTIC			– Wilderness tourism – Accessibility from major service centres into bush – High costs – Small tourist volume
LOWER NORTH ECUMENE FRINGE			– **Car-bound tourism to natural** landscape destinations – Limited range of facilities – Strong seasonality
CANADIAN ECUMENE ZONE & URBAN CENTRES			– Inter-metropolitan travel with dominant touristic hinterlands: car and air dominant transport – Wide range of attractions – High seasonality in periphery
SETTLED TEMPERATE OR TROPICAL AREAS U.S.A. EUROPE ASIA et al.			– **Long-distance flows to economic-core regions and international tourist periphery** – Certain routes have high seasonality

INTERNATIONAL CENTRAL INCREASING PERIPHERY

S.E. ASIA/PACIFIC ISLANDS

U.S.A./LATIN AMERICA

EUROPE/MEDITERRANEAN

recreation experiences tend to be exclusive and are affordable to only a small market segment. In order to compensate for the limited size of the domestic market resulting from high costs, northern camp operators rely to a considerable degree upon the United States' market, where a similar narrow segment exists but absolute numbers are much larger.

A further factor which works against a large volume of tourism in the north is the singularity of the attraction mix. In general, the number and variety of attractions decline with distance as one moves northwards from the ecumene. Although the north is not homogeneous in landscape or culture, the mix of cultural and natural features of the south is replaced by a relatively undifferentiated wilderness attraction which is accessible only in summer. The narrow resource base is a deterrent to much popular family recreation, and instead favours those visitors with highly specialized recreational preferences, such as the hunter, the fisherman, the keen amateur ecologist, and the researcher. Thus the market appeal, although it can be very strong, is restricted to a small number of potential visitors, too few to provide an adequate economic base for standard facilities. In fact, in many cases such visitors would not wish such facilities; they would rather rough it in the north and pay exclusive rates for the experience!

2. *Evolutionary spatial processes.* Although there are numerous stabilizing factors affecting the northern leisure space, including remoteness and the challenging environment, northern Canada has also experienced considerable changes in a manner comparable to those of the recreational hinterlands of metropolitan areas in the southern ecumene. Unfortunately, historical data do not exist for lodges. Such data would provide evidence of the northward extension of tourist facilities. In the circumstances, we can only make inferences about rates of change and the factors leading up to the present distribution of lodges (Figure 5). The current pattern of facilities highlights the heavy concentrations found along corridors of improved access at the northern perimeter of the ecumene and the sharp drop in numbers as one proceeds farther north. It also reveals the homogeneity and the singleness of purpose of the facilities, reflecting the recreational utility of the environment and the relative lack of diversity of recreational opportunities which it provides. In historical terms then, the evolution has meant more of the same in the north with little of the transformation of

Figure 3: Hotel Capacity 1965 - 1979

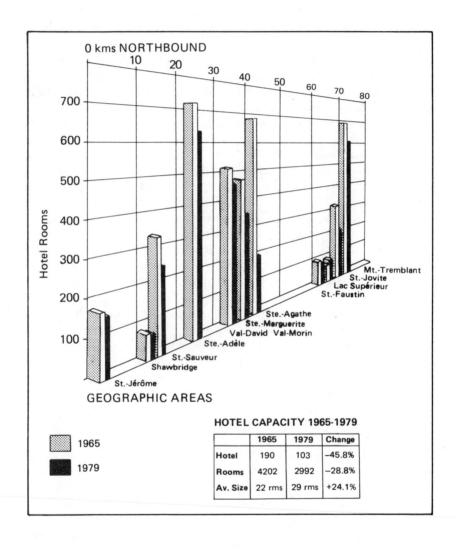

Source: Compiled by author.

land uses that can be observed in the more accessible zones of Rajotte's model.

3. *Long-distance transport penetration.* Transportation was a crucial agent of transformation in the metropolitan hinterland, as witnessed in the case of the Montreal Laurentians. It is obvious that it also affects the northern recreational periphery. However, it tends not to change use between alternative recreational activities in the north; rather it assists in opening up northern areas by making them more accessible to recreationists. The fringe dynamics are products of and reflect forces which are not directly related to recreation. Transportation networks have evolved to serve other forms of resource exploitation, such as the extraction of minerals, so that the forces of change differ from those which are found on the periphery of more southerly recreation hinterlands.

The exploitation of industrial resources did not affect the northern Quebec-Labrador region to any great extent until after 1945. Prior to this date, most of the lodge enterprises were located in close proximity to the east-west railway network, with the majority being concentrated on the Canadian Shield landscape of central to northern Ontario. Few northbound lines of penetration existed, the exception being the Ontario Northland railroad to James Bay. The drive for industrial minerals and, later, hydro-electric power got underway in the late 1940s and resulted in the installation of transportation facilities to serve the new developments. Later, in the mid-1950s, new defence installations in the north established more permanent service points at greater distances from the ecumene. More active governmental policies vis-à-vis indigenous people and the need to exert stronger geopolitical control throughout the north and Arctic accelerated high-speed transportation penetration in the form of air services, which indirectly affected tourist flows.

Nordair services out of Montreal constitute a good example of the magnitude, speed, and geographic extension of the penetration process (Figures 6A-D). Although a large proportion of the traffic has resulted from freight contracts for government projects and industrial shipments, a considerable tourist trade developed in the late summer and early fall, attracted by the excellent hunting and fishing opportunities. Lodge developments along the George River emerged during the late

Figure 6a: Nordair 1960

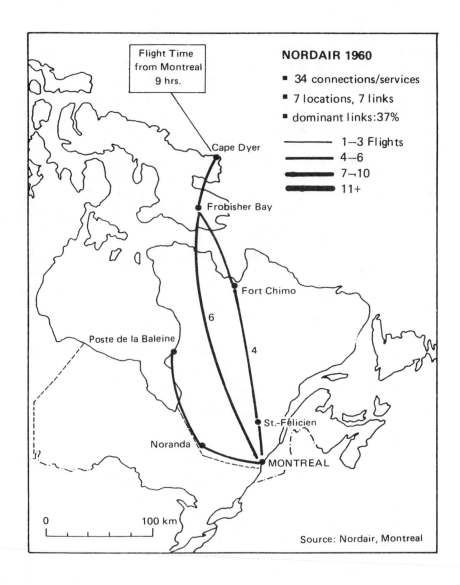

Figure 6b: Nordair 1965

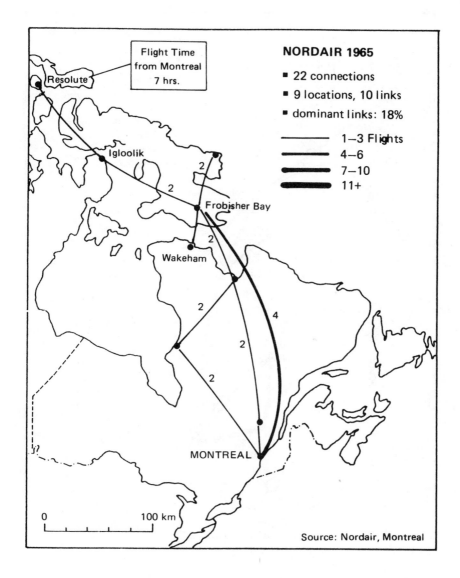

Figure 6c: Nordair 1975

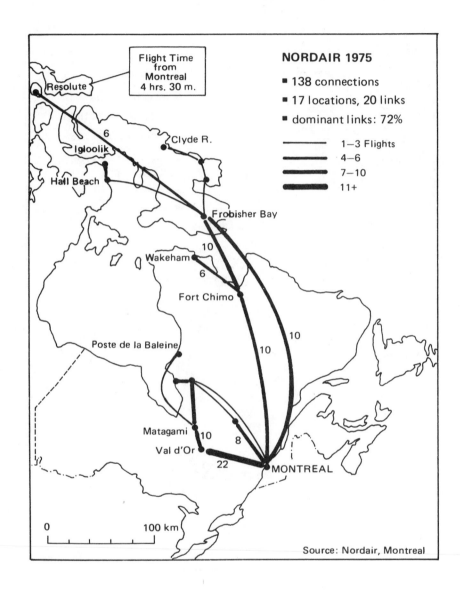

Flight Time
from
Montreal
4 hrs. 30 m.

NORDAIR 1975

- 138 connections
- 17 locations, 20 links
- dominant links: 72%

	1—3 Flights
	4—6
	7—10
	11+

Resolute

Clyde R.

Igloolik

Hall Beach

Frobisher Bay

6

10

Wakeham

6

Fort Chimo

Poste de la Baleine

10

10

Matagami

10

8

Val d'Or

22

MONTREAL

0   100 km

Source: Nordair, Montreal

Figure 6d: Nordair 1985

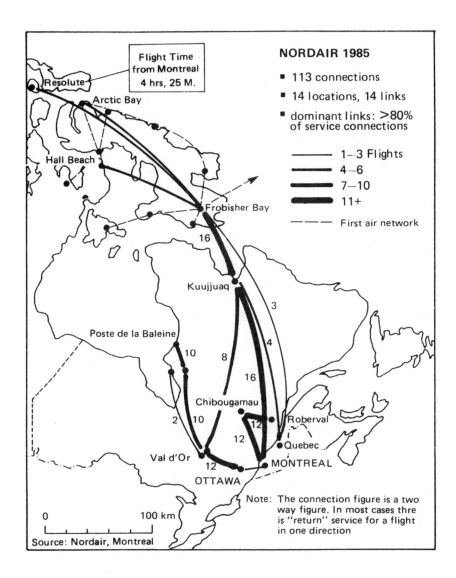

1950s and 1960s, with more recent establishments experiencing stricter controls because of pressures from the native peoples. However, the facilities were already in place, and by 1965 Nordair served the entire northern corridor from Montreal to Resolute Bay. In a sense the final phase of leisure space penetration has been reached for, from that time, no corner of the country could remain beyond the reach of the tourist. Since the mid-1960s, travel time reductions and improvements in comfort have attracted increasing numbers of visitors to northern lodges, northern parks, and northern experiences. Still, high transportation costs and, perhaps, the narrow range of attractions have deterred large numbers from venturing to these parts of the Canadian leisure space. The lure of the north attracts a particular type of visitor, and he is not the typical Canadian!

SUMMARY

The discussion of leisure which has been presented began with the fundamental premise that the distribution of discretionary time available to consumers in developed societies such as Canada has a major bearing upon the subsequent spatial patterns of recreation. With the addition of modifications in transportation technology and associated changes in mobility, plus changes in the market resulting from evolving socioeconomic characteristics, the most dominant explanatory factors are accounted for. None of these factors is unique to Canada; in fact they are typical of most of the world's developed countries as they have evolved since the Second World War. Thus, we can observe a trend among developed countries towards convergence of the patterns of leisure demand and supply, and spatial patterns of recreation.

Nevertheless, differences in leisure consumption should also be recognized. In the case of Canada, a highly important factor which is lacking in many other countries is comparatively abundant land for outdoor recreation and the relative proximity of such land to urban areas. This generalization applies even to those areas which have experienced substantial urban growth. Improved access to non-urban recreational supply has been of major importance for outdoor recreation development and has had considerable consequences for the shaping of Canadian leisure space.

A second observation concerns the stability of the spatial patterns which have emerged. The dynamic forces in postwar recreational developments have contributed to the intensification of use in existing areas and further penetration of non-urban leisure space in the periphery. More efficient transportation modes, and expanded and upgraded transportation infrastructures, coupled with higher per capita earnings and more available discretionary time, fostered these processes. However, it is doubtful if this expansive peripheral thrust will continue in the future. New trends in a rapidly changing market may give rise to exotic and untested destinations, while traditional family-based leisure may be modified as family structures change, and more diverse demands emanate from the yuppie generation and other consumer groups. Not only may new leisure patterns develop but, in turn, they may give rise to a new spatial stability: witness, for instance, the boom and massive personal investments in vacation condominiums within convenient travel distance from major urban centres.

A final observation concerns the future role of urban recreational supply. Increased popular awareness of the benefits of upgrading our urban environments has implications for the shaping of future leisure patterns. A more livable and pleasant urban recreational milieu is bound to influence individual leisure preferences, in the process redirecting leisure time, discretionary dollars, and leisure consumption to cities and towns. The allure of the woods and the wilds, a feature of contemporary Canadian leisure, may in consequence be in less demand. On the other hand, it is clear that the land will remain as a Canadian recreation resource, and it may attract tourists from those industrial countries where such land is in short supply. As a result, increased use of the peripheral zones of Canadian leisure space may occur as a function of both domestic demand and international travel.

Chapter 6

Economic Impacts

Peter Murphy
Department of Geography
University of Victoria

Economic Impacts

When most people think of recreation it is in terms of personal enjoyment and costs, not the economic impact such activity is having on the host community. Yet in this era of mass leisure more people have become dependent on the revenue and employment offered by recreation activities, and governments have started to question the cost of subsidizing recreation in light of the fiscal constraints facing them during the eighties. Whether we think about it or not, the economic significance of outdoor recreation has become an important component of the national economy and deserves some examination if we are to understand recent policy debates concerning privatization, multiple use, and facility investments.

Before undertaking such an examination it is necessary to recognize the complexity of the topic in terms of its definition and measurement. Economic impact is a term used to characterize the total income and taxes generated, and/or the number of jobs created, within a defined region, as a result of payments made for particular goods and services associated with a specific industry or activity (Travel Alberta n.d. IV-2). In this case the activity is recreation, where the traditional dictionary definition of "refreshment and relaxation of one's body or mind after work" (Webster 1984) provides a wide range of options to measure. For example, a facility offering recreation opportunities for local residents, such as an ice rink or golf course, can also serve as a site for spectator sport and become a tourist attraction when it draws visitors from out of town. The economic impact of the recreation, sport events, and tourism at such a facility can be substantial through equipment purchases, entry fees, travel and accommodation expenses. Given the interlinkage of these activities and their widespread contribution to the economy, this chapter deals with a broader perspective of recreation, including sport and tourism considerations. To paraphrase Berger (1983, 6) the recreation, sport, and tourism components will be treated as a "seamless web," using various economic impact studies to summarize the economic activity arising from these activities.

The chapter starts with an examination of economic measurement issues, followed by an examination of recreation impact studies, then moving on to consider some sport and tourism studies. The recreation studies focus on those activities engaged in by individuals or small groups, often using equipment and sometimes requiring professional assistance, such as guides. Sport is taken to be those recreation activities involving team organization, so the studies focus on amateur tournaments and sports events, with some consideration of professional sport. Tourism is viewed as the outdoor recreation and sport activities which lead participants beyond their home communities. This follows the conceptual perspective advocated by Mieczkowski (1981) and the practice of Statistics Canada, which classifies a person as a tourist when he is more than eighty kilometres or fifty miles from home (Murphy 1985, 7-8). Such a small range in fact places many recreation activities within a tourism perspective, such as hunting and skiing, or even an away in the local sports league.

Measurement Issues

The measurement of economic impact presents several difficulties because many recreation opportunities are supplied by the public sector, which makes the normal pricing system largely redundant. Even when entry or participation charges are levied they seldom reflect an accurate index of recreation's social value, because of the extensive government subsidization and difficulty in gauging the consumer's willingness to pay.

Economic impact can be examined in terms of the individual participant, who is the primary beneficiary, and the host community, where secondary benefits from the recreation activities accrue (Figure 1). The primary interest of individual recreationists is often the health benefits of physical exercise and relaxation, but they also receive economic benefits through being subsidized in the pursuit of their recreation activities.

Figure 1: Economic Impact Beneficiaries of Recreation

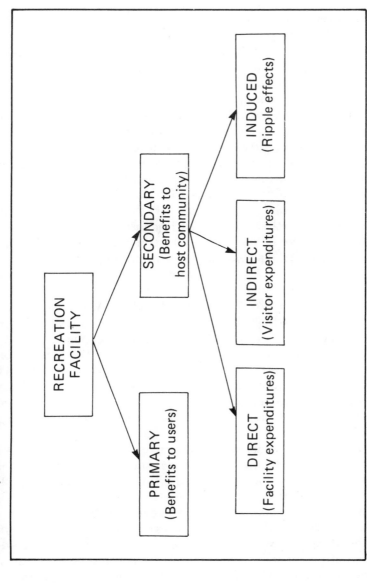

Source: P. Boggs and G. Wall 1984.

Such benefits can be calculated through consumer surplus estimates. These are generated from demand functions (see chapter 3, "Demand," Clawson 1959) or willingness to pay interviews (Fischer 1975), which Binkley (1977) has maintained are the most conceptually sound measures of recreation benefits, even if they do possess some limitations. The limitations basically become restrictive when specific activities or secondary considerations are examined, as in the case of alternative recreation options or the effects of congestion and aesthetic appeal on a demand function.

Community economic impact can be divided into three categories (Figure 1). The *direct impacts* represent a recreation facility's expenditure on goods and services within the community, plus its payroll contribution to the local economy. The *indirect impact* is visitor spending within the local economy containing the recreation facility and the revenue generated therein as a result of the recreation facility's purchases from other local industries and sectors. The *induced impact* represents the ripple effect of the direct and indirect economic activity, namely, the respending patterns which result from the wages and profits created. This impact is usually calculated using economic multiplier techniques, and its size is strongly influenced by the degree of leakage experienced by the local economy, which in turn is determined by the size and economic diversity of the community in question. In fact all community impact assessments are related to their scale of inquiry, which makes the categories and distinctions somewhat arbitrary. For example, at the provincial scale, federal taxes will be viewed as leakage, whereas some of those taxes may return as support programs elsewhere in the province (Murphy 1985, 90-5).

The actual terms and division of economic impact vary from study to study, but most respect the basic duality of impact on the recreation participant and the host community. The majority of studies referred to in this chapter focus on the community impacts and attempt to develop a general, or macro-scale, assessment of recreation's contribution to the local, often provincial, economy. One recent study which has attempted to assess both components of economic impact has been conducted by the Canadian Wildlife Service (Filion *et al.* 1985). In their study of the recreational economic significance of wildlife in Canada the authors broke the economic benefits into "1) direct benefits which are received by those who participate in wildlife-related activities; 2) indirect benefits resulting from the impacts

of the expenditures on the Canadian economy" (Filion *et al.*
1985, 1). In this case the direct benefits are the equivalent of the
individual's primary benefits. They were calculated by adding
the additional amount of money people were willing to pay to
participate in wildlife-related activities, over and above their
actual costs (Figure 2). The net value of the participants'
experience is expressed by subtracting the expenditures they
actually incurred from the amount of money they would be
willing to pay. "This net figure represents the economic value
of enjoyment received from wildlife activities that exceeds the
costs incurred. This is sometimes referred to as a 'consumer
surplus.'" (Filion *et al.* 1985, 1). The indirect benefits represent
an attempt to gauge the impact on the host community, in this
case Canada. They were calculated by combining the direct
expenditures of participants with the indirect and induced
economic effects, via an econometric model which determined
the proportional impacts on the national economy (Figure 2).
Thus, via a series of cost records, surveys to determine the
consumer surplus, and the application of computer models, the
study estimated that the 15.5 million people (84% of the Canadian
population) who participated in wildlife-related recreation
created an economic value of $7.8 billion in 1981. The figures
may seem surprisingly high until one considers that the
definition of wildlife-related recreation was very generous,
including incidental encounters, residential activities, and
indirect activities such as reading or watching films about
wildlife.

OUTDOOR RECREATION IMPACTS

The growing concern about tightening government budgets and
the realization that some decision-makers may look upon
recreation as an expendable frill in these tough economic times
are encouraging park systems around Canada to assess and
publicize their contribution to national or provincial economies.
Such a situation is not unique to Canada. Wilder (n.d., 1)
reports:

> Park and recreation departments around the nation
> [United States] are suffering a great deal of anguish
> over their financial plight, for this is a time of
> economic stress. Leisure services are hard to quantify
> and even harder to justify because the values are of an

Figure 2: Economic Impact Calculations by Canadian Wildlife Service

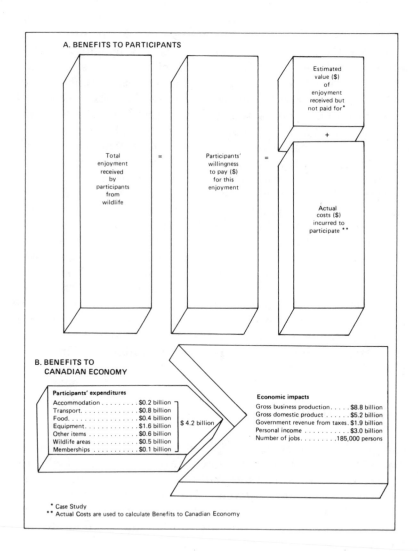

A. BENEFITS TO PARTICIPANTS

Total enjoyment received by participants from wildlife = Participants' willingness to pay ($) for this enjoyment = Estimated value ($) of enjoyment received but not paid for* + Actual costs ($) incurred to participate**

B. BENEFITS TO CANADIAN ECONOMY

Participants' expenditures
Accommodation . . . . $0.2 billion
Transport. . . . . $0.8 billion
Food. . . . . $0.4 billion
Equipment. . . . . $1.6 billion
Other items . . . . $0.6 billion
Wildlife areas . . . . $0.5 billion
Memberships . . . . $0.1 billion

$ 4.2 billion

Economic impacts
Gross business production. . . . . $8.8 billion
Gross domestic product . . . . . $5.2 billion
Government revenue from taxes. $1.9 billion
Personal income . . . . $3.0 billion
Number of jobs. . . . . .185,000 persons

* Case Study
** Actual Costs are used to calculate Benefits to Canadian Economy

Source: F.L. Filion, A. Jacquemot, and R. Reid 1985.

intrinsic nature, a social good, and subjective in nature. It is because of this subjectivity that the case for parks and recreation is often lost to a degree in the battle for budgets and for the shrinking dollar.

One response to this situation in Canada has been a series of impact studies to demonstrate the economic contribution of park systems.

At the national level, a Parks Canada study (1985) estimated that during the fiscal year 1982-83 visitor and Parks Canada expenditures amounted to $559.8 million which, after discounting imported goods, taxes, and revenues, produced a (net) final domestic demand of $516.7 million. Due to the infusion of this money into our national economy it was considered that the value added to the total goods and services produced in Canada (our Gross Domestic Product) increased by $821.3 million, and that an additional 28,700 person-years of employment were created, producing $535.3 million of extra labour income. On top of that, government revenues, in the form of taxes, duties, and royalties were estimated to have increased by $40.5 million.

Ontario's provincial park system of 137 parks plus their capital assets, excluding the land, was subjected to a similar economic analysis for its 1979 operating year (Ontario Parks and Recreational Areas Branch 1984). The study concentrated on the secondary benefits to local communities and restricted its measurement of benefits to areas within forty kilometres of each park. No attempt was made to gauge the expenditures on recreation equipment or to allocate a value to the park experience of visitors. Figure 3 illustrates the major contributions and linkages identified in this report. It can be seen, in the lower part of the diagram, that a modest budget of $24.4 million for direct park expenditures (the direct impact) generated a total spending impact of $230 million after it had proceeded through the indirect and induced phases. Furthermore, it was revealed that the Ontario government recovered 73% of its initial $24.4 million "investment" through taxes and revenues, so the net seed money needed to stimulate this large degree of economic activity was approximately $6 million.

A British Columbia Parks Division report on the economic impact of its 1983-84 operating, capital, and maintenance expenditures reveals an even more comprehensive picture of outdoor recreation's contribution to a provincial economy

Figure 3: Economic Impact of Ontario Provincial Parks, 1979 ($ millions)

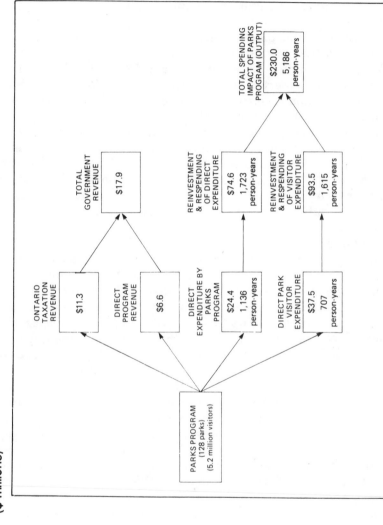

Source: Ontario Parks and Recreational Areas Branch 1984.

(Marvin Shaffer and Associates 1985). Table 1 indicates the principal findings of this report. It shows the $22.2 million operating expenditures of the Parks Division generated a direct income of $15.3 million and 620 person-years of employment. After the indirect and induced effects were calculated these figures rose to $25.7 million and 979 person-years.

When the capital and maintenance expenditures of $3.5 million were added to the calculation, an additional $0.3 million and 14 person-years were generated through direct impact. The lower figures in this case reflects the extensive use of outside contractors, which placed most of the impact into the indirect and induced categories.

Utilizing the figures in the upper part of Table 1, the authors calculated various multipliers to estimate the impact of parks-related activities on the British Columbia economy. The expenditure multiplier indicates the income or employment generated per dollar of expenditure in the British Columbia Parks operations of 1983-84. The income and employment multipliers show the levels of activity generated per dollar of direct income and employment. Shaffer and Associates (1985, 15) note:

> The income and employment multiplier is much higher for parks capital and maintenance than parks operations because contract labour and supervision is counted as an indirect not a direct impact. The expenditure multipliers appear to be lower for parks capital and maintenance because of a proportionately higher import content than parks operations.

This illustrates very clearly the effect of category classification and study area size on the calculation of economic impact, as noted in the introduction to this chapter.

Three provinces have examined the question of economic impact as part of a more comprehensive review of their recreation and sport activities. In Ontario there have been two such studies. Ellis (1982) assessed the impact of sport, recreation, and fitness activities, while Berger (1983) attempted to identify the economic impacts of programs and services provided by the Recreation Division in the Ministry of Tourism and Recreation. Ellis calculates that the economic volume arising from sports, recreation, and fitness in Ontario is $4.92 billion which, with a provincial multiplier of 1.88, translates into a total economic impact of $9.25 billion in 1981 (Table 2).

Table 1

Economic Impacts of B.C. Parks Division Expenditures in 1983-84

($'000, 1984)

	Operating Expenditure	Capital and Maintenance	Total Expenditure
Parks Expenditures	22,164	3,490	25,654
Income			
Direct	15,334	291	15,625
Indirect	2,980	1,925	4,905
Induced	7,353	766	8,119
Total	25,667	2,982	28,649
Employment			
Direct	620	14	634
Indirect	158	59	217
Induced	201	21	222
Total	979	94	1,073
Multipliers			
Expenditure (Income)	1.16	0.85	1.12
(Employment)	44.17	26.93	41.83
Income	1.67	10.25	1.83
Employment	1.58	6.71	1.69

Source: M. Shaffer and Associates, 1985.

Table 2

Economic Volume Arising From Sports, Recreation, and Fitness in Ontario

Source	Estimate ($ million)
42 Recreation activities (including alley bowling, cricket, football, horseback riding, recreational bicycling, swimming, water skiing, etc.)	1,058
9 Fitness activities (including walking, yoga, skipping rope, general exercise, etc.)	85
Fishing	675
Hunting	67
Camping	450
Motor boating	550
Recreational snowmobiling	220
Recreational trail biking, motorcycling, flying, etc.	60
Cottaging	440
Movies, amusement parks, racetracks, etc.	735
Total recreation spending by Ontarians	4,300
Spending on recreation by Ontario Ministry of Natural Resources and Ministry of Culture and Recreation	103
Net municipal parks and recreation operating expenditures	315
Capital construction in recreation in public and private sectors	205
Provincial sub-total	4,923
Economic multiplier effect (1.88)	4,432
Provincial total	$ 9,255

Source: J.B. Ellis, 1982.

Compared to Ontario's gross domestic product of about $110.6 billion, this equates to 9% of the provincial economy, and in the process supports approximately 200,000 person-years of employment per year. In addition, Ellis (1982, ii) notes that all this activity "yields a provincial tax component of about $950 million. This is over 9 times the amount spent directly by the province on recreation through the Ministries of Natural Resources, and Culture and Recreation." Berger's study concluded that "the economic impact of expenditures by the Recreation Division is 1:9.07; that is, every dollar spent by the Recreation Division, including staff salaries, generates $9.07 in additional expenditures throughout the provincial economy." (Berger, 1983, 4). This figure was calculated as follows:

- Direct private expenditures on recreation $4.60
- Composite provincial multiplier   4.00
- Value of volunteer time   0.47

                TOTAL: **$9.07**

Although Berger's calculation appears to be more comprehensive with the introduction of a valuation for volunteers, he maintains the estimate is still incomplete; for the ratio still "does not take into account economic benefits in the fields of physical and mental health and work productivity and performance, which are closely related to recreation activities and therefore affected to a greater or lesser extent by the programs of the Recreation Division," (Berger 1983, 19).

It is interesting to note that these apparently independent studies, using data from different years (1979 Ellis, 1981 Berger), relating to different ministries, and using different methods to derive their economic impact assessments have detected a similar ratio between government expenditures and economic activity in Ontario -- namely 1:9. Such a ratio indicates a substantial return on recreation "investment" in Ontario, which compares favourably with the ratios for provincial parks (1:3) and culture (1:2.6) according to Berger (1983, 3).

In Western Canada a study by Burton (1984) estimated the recreation expenditures during 1983 in Alberta amounted to $3.89 billion which, with the addition of a multiplier effect of 1.67, produced a "total economic significance" of $6.49 billion. Of the direct recreation expenditures, $174 million came from municipal governments and $185 million from provincial

government agencies.   This represented 9.3% of all direct
expenditures and 5.5% of the estimated total economic
significance.   Once again we have a good indication of
substantial economic returns on the government's initial
expenditure. In British Columbia a survey of various Statistics
Canada figures was used to calculate the economic significance
of recreation and sport in that province (British Columbia,
Recreation and Sport Branch 1985).   This statistical
compendium estimated British Columbia's direct recreation
expenditures for 1982 amounted to approximately $5 billion, and
when a multiplier of 1.67 was applied, the total economic impact
became an estimated $8.45 billion.   This study noted that
municipal government expenditures on recreation, culture,
tourism, and related activities in 1980 were $236.3 million,
while the provincial contribution was $89.6 million. If these
figures are summed and compared to the 1982 expenditure
estimate, the resulting percentage of 6.5 reveals a substantial
degree of economic activity beyond the government's direct
contribution.

In addition to system-wide recreation economic impact
studies there have been several examinations of individual
recreation activities. Examination of specific activities permits
more in-depth analysis, focusing on factors such as the
contribution of equipment purchase and maintenance, plus the
differences between resident and non-resident consumption
and impacts.

A study of recreational boating in British Columbia
(Shaffer et al. 1977) revealed what a strong allure the coastal
waters have for West Coast residents and how, in the process,
they have supported a substantial business activity. Using 1976
Statistics Canada data on recreational boating ownership, the
study reports 152,000 households, almost 20% of British
Columbia's households at the time, owned one or more
recreational boats. This compared with a national average of
14%. Of the estimated 176,000 boats owned in British Columbia,
almost 70% were owned by Georgia Strait residents, with
sailboats and outboard motorboats (runabouts) predominating.

This interest in boating proves to be costly for participants
and rewarding for the Canadian and British Columbia
economies. Boat ownership has long been equated with "owning
a hole in the water down which you pour money," and the study
confirms this. The capital expenditure for recreational boating
in British Columbia was between $78 and $85 million in 1976,
and operating costs were estimated to be an additional $70

million, bringing the total expenditure to $148-$155 million. In addition it was estimated that non-owner residents spent $2.5 million on renting boats, while visitors spent approximately $1.2 million for the same purpose. When the study calculated the total indirect and induced expenditure impacts on British Columbia, it developed an estimate of over $300 million income contribution from this one recreational activity (Table 3).

Moving to a winter sport that is also equipment= and capital=intensive, Travel Alberta (n.d.) conducted an economic survey of its 1976 ski industry. The study found that Alberta residents spent $20.5 million a year or $11.06 a day on downhill skiing, while non-residents contributed $4.1 million, and $28.00 per day. On top of these operating expenses a random survey of retail ski outlets provided an estimate of $15.3 million spent on ski equipment, clothing, and accessories during the 1975-76 season. This spending, however, was not included in the overall impact assessments "because Albertans may purchase equipment locally and spend ski vacations abroad . . . [and] . . . import leakage is high in view of the absence of local manufacture" (Travel Alberta n.d., 17). Even without consideration of equipment expenses the expenditure impact of skiing was considerable, with an overall estimate of $66.79 million.

One recreation area where the difference between resident and non-resident activity has become an important economic consideration is hunting. Successful hunters take their trophies or game home, which in the case of out-of-province hunters means the loss of provincial resources. This is partially compensated by the creation of a dual pricing system, requiring non-residents to pay a premium for their hunting permits. In Alberta: "residents are the owners of the province's wildlife, but non-resident hunting supports several small industries and provides income for numerous businesses. As a result, non-resident-hunters are allowed to hunt in Alberta but pay higher fees and hunt with less freedom than residents" (Boxall 1985, 6). The higher fees range from two to twelve times the cost to a resident, depending on the species being hunted, and the loss of freedom refers to a mandatory guide for non-resident hunters.

A comprehensive survey of hunting practices in British Columbia during 1981 revealed that resident hunters spent almost 1.5 million days in the field, hunting a wide variety of species but with the greatest effort being spent on hunting deer, moose, and elk (Reid 1985a, iii). Based on survey results, resident hunters were estimated to have spent almost $90

Table 3

Summary of 1976 Recreational Boating Expenditures in British Columbia

Source	Estimate ($ million)	
	(Low)	(High)
Direct Expenditures		
Owner capital expenditure	78	85
Owner operating expenditure	70	70
Renter expenditure	3.7	3.7
	151.7	158.7
Indirect Expenditures		
British Columbia	52.7	55.8
Canada	54.5	57.6
B.C. Taxes	6.5	7.0
Canada Taxes	18.0	19.0
	131.7	139.4
Induced Expenditures		
British Columbia	19.0	20.1
OVERALL EXPENDITURE	302.4	318.2

Source: M. Shaffer, R. Hale, J. Lyle, 1977.

million on hunting-related expenditures. This translated into an average annual expenditure of about $557 per hunter, or $58 for each day of hunting. A companion study of non-resident hunters in the same year found 4,000 non-residents spent over 46,000 days hunting in British Columbia during 1981. They, too, hunted all major game species, but with particular attention being paid to moose and black bear. Based on survey data, the non-resident hunters were estimated to have made gross expenditures of $13 million on their hunting trips, with much of this money being spent in peripheral regions of the province where guide fees, transportation, and accommodation charges provided a useful contribution to the local economies. The incomes of provincial residents were estimated to have increased by almost $8 million as a result of this non-resident hunting after deductions for costs and expenses, which the author translates as being the net economic value of non-resident hunting to the province.

Of particular interest in this study was the attempt to discover the scope of consumer surplus in hunting, with questions relating to willingness to pay. The resident and non-resident hunters were asked to indicate at what additional daily expenditure they would stop hunting. For non-resident hunters the average amount by species ranged from an additional daily expenditure of $25.00 for deer to $82.10 for mountain sheep. While the ranking of species was "quite similar for resident and non-resident hunters . . . for each species, non-resident hunters were willing to pay a greater daily increase than were resident hunters." (Reid 1985b, 10). The difference ranged from a low of 5% for deer hunting to a high of 77% for black bear and mountain sheep hunting. This indicates the consumer surplus is considerable for the non-resident hunter to British Columbia, who is apparently willing to pay a premium to hunt in one of the few remaining wilderness areas of North America.

SPORT IMPACTS

Although sport has been an element in some of the outdoor recreation activities discussed in the previous section, it generally did not involve the organized team activities and commercialization associated with major sports events today. In this section, therefore, attention will focus on the growing feature of our affluent urban lifestyle, namely, organized sport and spectator sports. Given the seamless-web situation in recreation, it is difficult to separate sports events into separate categories, for even the old divisions between amateur and professional have become blurred. It is no surprise to find some sports events designed for amateur participation have snowballed into major commercial attractions, complete with political overtones -- as evidenced by Summer Olympic Games and Commonwealth Games boycotts.

Sports events can take on many forms. They range from amateur invitational tournaments or leagues designed to bring together recreation enthusiasts for fun on and off the field of competition, to national or international championships where competition and skill take precedence over socializing, with competitors performing in front of large numbers of spectators either directly or via the media. Examples of the first category are more numerous, but because of the fun and recreation emphasis more attention has been paid to the social rather than the economic impact (Manson-Blair 1984). More research along economic lines has been undertaken with regard to larger-scale events because of their more apparent economic significance and commercial sponsorship. For example, the cost of television coverage rights for the Olympic Games has grown dramatically over the past decade. The contract for the Montreal (1976) Summer Games was for $5 million, for the Lake Placid (1980) Winter Games $15 million, for the Los Angeles (1984) Summer Games $224 million, and for the Calgary (1988) Winter Games $305 million (Yates and Lee 1984, 14).

One of the few Canadian impact studies of a small-scale sporting event was carried out by Marsh (1984) in Peterborough, Ontario. His study of the Peterborough Church League Atom Hockey Tournament of 1982 revealed that even a minor amateur event of this nature can have a significant local economic impact. Over three thousand players, coaches, spectators, and parents were drawn to Peterborough for the four-day event, coming from other parts of Ontario, from Quebec, and from some points in the northeastern United States. The spending pattern that resulted was considerable, with an estimated $165,000 entering the local economy those four days in January (Table 4). The community involvement in this tournament was exemplified by the use of thirteen local hotels, local billet and entertainment, and the use of local recreation facilities (rinks), which ensured a widespread diffusion of the generated expenditures. Given such a favourable impact at very minor cost to the community, Marsh (1984, 54) was encouraged to suggest that "greater recognition should be given to the

Table 4

**Total Expenditures for Peterborough Church League
Atom Hockey Tournament, January 1982**

Source	Expenditure
Distant teams *	$130,637
Local teams	11,374
Spectators	2,704
Players, and spectators, children	8,481
Households supplying Billets	2,666
Tournament team entry fees	9,303
TOURNAMENT TOTAL	$165,165

* Distant teams were those whose adult participants used hotels.

Source: J.S. Marsh, 1984.

economic impact of this event and similar events in the city by city business, politicians and tourism planners, and that such events and their organizers should receive all possible community support."

The economic potential of such sporting events has not been missed by some jurisdictions, which actively encourage and facilitate the development of regional and national meetings. One example is the Recreation and Sport Branch of British Columbia, which published a report entitled "Capitalizing on Sports Events" (Lee and Yates 1984). The report noted that the 1979 Canada Winter Games in Brandon, Manitoba, recorded a capital expenditure of $3.99 million and operating expenses of $1.77 million, which resulted in the further impact of $1.06 million on the Brandon economy and $1.89 million on the Manitoba economy. In 1984 the Canadian Men's Curling Championship, popularly known as the Labatt Brier, attracted 3,950 spectators, 80 participants, and 100 media personnel to Victoria, British Columbia. The direct visitor expenditures were estimated to be $1.34 million, but when other impacts such as committee and sponsor expenses were added, the total impact on the Victoria economy was estimated to be $3.46 million for this eight-day event (Lee and Yates 1984). With this type of evidence, the authors developed a computer model to estimate the economic impact of sports events. Their model includes input from competitor and volunteer expenditures, operating and capital expenditures, the value of sponsor contributions, as well as various government contributions. Table 5 indicates the level of economic return that could be expected from a large multi-sport event, in this case a projected economic impact of $11 million from a two-week event involving seven thousand participants.

Turning to larger-scale international events the potential economic impact increases dramatically. For example, there has been considerable interest in the host community, Calgary, in the economic significance and repercussions of the 1988 Winter Olympic Games. One study (DPA Group 1985, 3) estimated that "total incremental expenditures of approximately $647 million," would occur. This figure was derived primarily from the direct expenditures on construction costs, operating costs, media commitments, and visitor spending. Examples of the construction bonanza are the Olympic Park ($68.4 million), the Olympic Saddledome ($97.3 million), the University of Calgary speed skating facility and accommodation ($107 million), the Nordic Ski Centre near Canmore ($15.4 million),

Table 5

**Projected Impact of a Large Multi-Sport Event
Using Computer Model Data**

Input			Outputs & Multipliers	
1	Number of Participants	7,000	Participant Days	98,000
2	Number of Spectators	15,000	Spectator Days	210,000
3	Number of Event Days	14	Total Attendance Days	308,000
4	Number of Volunteers	2,000	Competitor Expenditures	$7,350,000
5	Volunteer/Person Expenditure	$200	Spectator Expenditures	$21,000,000
6	Estimated Days Expenditure			
	per Competitor	$75	Visitor Expenditures	$28,350,000
7	Estimated Days Expenditure			
	per Spectator	$100	Volunteer Expenditures	$400,000
8	Event Capital Expenditure	$20,000,000		
9	Induced Cap. Expenditure	$5,000,000	% due to event	0.25
10	Direct Operating Exp.	$25,000,000		
11	Total Operating Revenue	$25,000,000	Operating Profit	0
12	Value of Sponsor Cont.	$10,000,000	Sponsor Multiplier	0.3
13	Municipal Contribution	$10,000,000	Employment Multiplier	0.000102
14	Provincial Contribution	$15,000,000	Municipal Revenue Coefficient	0.018
15	Federal Contribution	$15,000,000	Province Revenue Coefficient	0.033
16	International Contribution	$5,000	Federal Revenue Coefficient	0.083
			Municipal Revenues	$2,329,488
			Province Revenues	$4,270,728
			Federal Revenues	$10,741,528
			Total Visitor Impact	$43,942,500
			Total Volunteer Impact	$616,000
			Total Construction Impact	$31,160,000
			Total Induced Construction Impact	$697,500
			Total Operating Exp. Impact	$40,000,000
			Total Sponsor Impacts	$13,000,000
			TOTAL IMPACT	$129,416,000
			NET MUNICIPAL YIELD	$-7,670,512
			NET PROVINCIAL YIELD	$-10,729,272
			NET FEDERAL YIELD	$-4,258,472
			TOTAL PROVINCIAL RETURN	$111,016,216
			EMPLOYMENT GENERATED	5,482.5

Source: J. Lee and B. Yates, 1984.

the Mount Allan alpine ski facilities ($25.3 million), and the city of Calgary infrastructure and transport facilities ($20 million). In addition the study noted that there would be further, but less tangible, positive impacts:

> The games will leave a legacy of unique facilities which will continue to be used by world-class athletes and will be open for public use after the event ... Such facilities as Canada Olympic Park will become tourist attractions in their own right . . . the Olympic Arts Festival in conjunction with the new Calgary Centre for the Performing Arts will improve the attractiveness of Calgary as a centre for cultural activities.
>
> (DPA Group 1985, 6)

Furthermore, it was expected that the media coverage of the Olympics would create a positive viewer image of the Calgary region that would encourage tourists to visit after the games concluded; and that the development of sports facilities and a Sports Medicine Facility in the University of Calgary will draw athletes from across North America for training and rehabilitation.

The prior statistics are estimates of likely impacts and they were made before the event took place. Detailed information is now available on what actually transpired (Kolsun, 1988). The Calgary Tourist and Convention Bureau has conducted a study that indicates that approximately two-hundred thousand local spectators and one-hundred and thirty-four thousand spectators from elsewhere attended the Winter Olympics, and another two and a half billion people were exposed to the Olympics, and Calgary, by viewing the events on television. The economic impact of the Olympics in Calgary was dramatic: the research suggests that $158 million was spent on accommodation, food and beverage, retail sales, entertainment and transport in Calgary by visitors attending the Olympics.

Professional sport for most of us is a spectator activity, and this vicarious form of physical recreation generates not only "couch potatoes" but a lot of revenue and status for the cities involved. An indication of the money and status is the struggle in Oakland, California, to keep the Raiders at home, and in Vancouver's to secure a baseball to team in the magnificent but underutilized stadium. Gratton and Taylor (1985, 250) maintain professional team sports in North America is "a commercial activity" interested in maximizing profits and achieving commercial success. They quote El-Hodrini and Quirk who state that:

> the essential economic fact concerning professional team sports is that gate receipts depend crucially on the uncertainty of the outcome of the games played within the league. As the probability of either team winning approaches one, gate receipts fall substantially, consequently, every team has an economic motive for not becoming too superior in playing talent compared to other teams in the league.

(Gratton and Taylor 1985, 238)

This approach explains North America's search for parity between teams by structuring the college drafts in reverse order of league standing and setting stringent compensation rules for the transfer of talented players to ensure the wealthier clubs do not dominate. The commercial aspect of these sports also means the game rules can be altered in the pursuit of excitement.

Despite the economic significance of professional sports in Canada there have been few published reports about this "industry." One recent attempt to examine some economic aspects of a professional sport occurred in the Geddert and Semple (1985) examination of hockey franchises. They noted that acceptance of the profit maximization concept for major hockey franchises had directed the N.H.L. to focus on major metropolitan areas as franchise locations. They point out, however, that fan interest and loyalty at times can compensate for the lack of a large population base, and accordingly promote the cause of Saskatoon as a potential franchise site.

TOURISM IMPACTS

The economic impact of recreation becomes most apparent in the area of tourism. As far back as 1885, Van Horne appreciated the economic value for his railroad of recreation trips to the Rocky Mountains. "If you can't export the scenery, you have to import the tourists" was his credo and the Canadian Pacific Railway worked with the Canadian government to create the Banff park reserve (Leighton 1985). Since then, governments and individual entrepreneurs have attempted to capitalize on the scenic and recreation opportunities of the Canadian landscape to an ever-increasing degree (Nelson 1973, Gunn 1976, Marsh 1983). Their success can be seen in the Canadian government estimates of 1982 tourism receipts, totalling $16.8 billion; direct employment that year was estimated to amount to 458,000 jobs (Tourism Canada 1985, x). The regional breakdown for these figures is presented in Table 6.

Individual provinces have developed their own assessments of tourism's economic impact, as in the case of British Columbia, where the industry currently stands third to forestry and mining in terms of revenue generated. But it is expected to move to second place in the not too distant future, as commodity prices remain low and the tourism industry maintains its recovery from the recession of the early 1980s. In 1984 British Columbia's tourism generated $2.3 billion and approximately 100,000 person-years of employment, counting both full- and part-time positions (British Columbia 1985). These figures show the remarkable resilience of tourism in a province hit hard by the recession, so it comes as no surprise that British Columbia used a tourism megaproject in the form of Expo '86 to help lift it out of the economic doldrums.

Much of the vacation demand in Canada has been related traditionally to the outdoors and recreation opportunities there. In terms of international travel, "the detailed image, created by Canada as a holiday destination, is that of a beautiful country with outstanding scenery and vast open spaces that would be particularly good for a touring holiday, a holiday based on outdoor activities, or a sporting holiday" (Taylor 1983, 37). Parks Canada undoubtedly is part of this allure, and it estimates that "2% of all tourism spending by Canadian and foreign visitors is due to the existence of national parks, national historic parks and sites, and historic canals" (Parks Canada 1985, i). In 1982 this translated into $270 million in tourism spending attributable to Parks Canada (Parks Canada 1985, 23). This same study estimates that 1.8 million foreign visitors were attracted to the Parks Canada system, spending $40.8 million in the process, or approximately 1% of our foreign revenue.

One recreation activity which has generated a great deal of tourism interest in Canada is skiing. For example, the 1978 Travel Industry Development Subsidiary Agreement (TIDSA) between British Columbia and the federal government, which was designed to improve the tourism appeal of the province, allocated $16 million, or 32% of the funds, to ski-resort

Table 6

Provincial Tourism Economic Impacts, 1982

Province (receipts ranked order)	Tourism Receipts ($ million)	Direct Employment (1,000 jobs)
Ontario	5,791	172
Quebec	3,063	76
British Columbia, plus Yukon and N.W.T.	2,771	75
Alberta	2,308	56
Saskatchewan	764	19
Manitoba	669	20
Nova Scotia	585	17
New Brunswick	358	11
Newfoundland	302	8
Prince Edward Island	140	4
TOTAL	16,751	458

Source: Tourism Canada, 1985.

development (Montgomery and Murphy 1983, 188). The philosophy behind much of this ski investment was to create major ski resorts that would keep more British Columbia residents at home and lure more visitors from out of the province, especially from the United States and overseas. In this way it was hoped to make better use of the province's resource potential and reduce the travel budget deficit in the process.

According to McKay (1985,115-17) government investments in skiing through TIDSA and other programs have amounted to $24 million which, in turn, has generated a total investment of $403 million, plus construction employment of 6,089 person-years and operating employment of 5,560 person-years. One of the keys to British Columbia's success, according to McKay (1985, 121) was its emphasis on ski-resort development: The key competitive factor in British Columbia over areas in Washington and Alberta has been the provision of the on-mountain accommodation. After 4 to 6 hour drives for a 3-5 day stay, people have been demanding to stay on the mountain without the requirement of driving a car again until the day of departure." The fostering of Whistler near Vancouver, Mount Washington on Vancouver Island, and Big White in the Okanagan provided regional attractions that lured distant travellers as well as British Columbia residents,   thus illustrating the symbiosis between Canada's outdoor recreation potential and the tourist industry.

Canada has even more to offer tourists than its scenic beauty and recreation possibilities, a fact that has been recognized in the recent change of emphasis in Tourism Canada's advertising to the United States market (MacLeans 1986). The Canadian government apparently feels there is latent tourism demand for the leisure and recreation opportunities existing in our cities, a belief that has received some support from the few studies of urban tourism impacts.

Two tourism impact studies of Toronto have revealed the visitor appeal of urban recreation and cultural facilities. Wall and Sinnott discovered a wide range of urban facilities had tourist appeal (Table 7), and that their visitors contributed a great deal to the Toronto economy. For example, the "average group of out-of-town visitors at the Art Gallery of Ontario spent $18 per person per day during their stay in Toronto, much of this on food, accommodation, entertainment, shopping and transportation. Comparable figures for the Royal Ontario Museum, Ontario Place, the Zoo, and the Science Centre were

Table 7

**Visitor Origins to Five Leisure and Cultural Centres
in Toronto, 1978**

	Visitation Rates to Attractions (Percentage)				
Origins	Art Gallery of Ontario	Royal Ontario Museum	Ontario Place	Metro Toronto Zoo	Ontario Science Centre
Metro Toronto	53	48	56	36	21
Ontario, within 100 km	6	9	13	21	7
Ontario, 101-200 km	3	4	3	4	5
Ontario beyond 200 km	5	5	3	5	9
Other Canada	7	8	4	10	10
U.S. Border states (N.Y., Mich., Pa., Ohio)	14	14	11	14	31
U.S. Other States	7	8	3	7	11
Other Countries	6	5	8	4	7

Source: G. Wall and J. Sinnott, 1980.

$13, $8, $10 and $12 respectively" (Wall and Sinnott 1980, 58). When these figures are multiplied by the millions of visitors who come to the city the total economic impact is considerable, and the authors cite one estimate of $1.25 billion for 1979.

A more detailed examination of one cultural exhibit illustrates the appeal and economic significance of this aspect of recreation. During the months of November and December 1979, Toronto was fortunate to play host to the travelling Tutankhamun exhibition. Wall's (1981) examination of this exhibit revealed that 43.9% of the visitors were Toronto residents, who spent an estimated $3 million. Out-of-town day visitors, primarily from other parts of Ontario, comprised 37.5% of the visitors and spent an estimated $6 million, while those out-of-town visitors who stayed overnight comprised 18.6 percent of the visitors and spent around $11 million. Hence this two-month event generated $20 million in visitor expenditures, most of it from out-of-town visitors.

The link between tourism and culture has not been lost on the arts community, and as government grants have been reduced over the past few years more arts groups are actively pursuing a working partnership with tourism. A good example of the new attitude can be seen in Backerman's survey (1983) of Vancouver's non-profit cultural industry, in an aptly named report "Arts Mean Business." The study was undertaken because "arts compete with other activities in the city for financial support . . . and . . . the cultural industry must continue to demonstrate its economic benefit to the community" (Backerman 1983, 2). As a result of his survey Backerman estimates that over two thousand people were employed in the cultural industry on a full- or part-time basis, and that direct spending by non-profit arts organizations amounted to $17.4 million. A more recent assessment of the arts in Victoria, British Columbia, claims that area has a "50 million dollar industry" (Segger 1986), which would not surprise anyone who has visited its numerous galleries and antique and craft shops, or attended one of the many concerts and plays that are offered in this relatively small community.

In addition to its natural and cultural attractions Canada has also demonstrated there is a potential market for quality artificial attractions. In the east Canada's Wonderland, which opened in 1981 and is located about thirty-three kilometres northwest of downtown Toronto (Cameron and Bordessa, 1981), has had "a substantial impact on the economy of the Toronto region," according to a study by Boggs and Wall (1984, 45).

According to their calculations its total economic infusion is anywhere from $67 million to $87 million, depending on the measurement assumptions used. In the west a combined retail-recreation complex has created a great deal of interest. The West Edmonton Mall with its amusement park component has definitely become a tourist attraction, drawing package tours from as far away as the West Coast, and a commercial success, spawning projected clones in the Minneapolis-St. Paul area and possibly in Ontario.

The tourism potential of culture and sports is not limited to the big newsworthy shows of major cities. A study in Saskatchewan illustrates that small-scale events designed primarily for local residents' consumption have considerable tourist appeal, if one uses the standard Statistics Canada definition of a tourist as being anyone travelling eighty kilometres away from home. Murray and Associates (1985, x) found that on average "only 38.1% of attendance (at Saskatchewan's 1983 events and festivals) were drawn from the host community." There was considerable variation around this average, with cultural festivals and arts and crafts events being primarily local in appeal, while theme shows like the Agribition and sports events like the National Figure Skating Finals (Skate Canada) drew more out-of-town visitors than locals. Most of the tourists came from elsewhere in Saskatchewan, but Alberta accounted for 10% of the tourist travel to these events. The estimated tourism expenditure for the events surveyed was $140 million, or 14% of the total tourism expenditure in Saskatchewan that year.

DISCUSSION

The purpose of this chapter has been to survey the literature on the economic impact of recreation in Canada and search for patterns and generalizations within that literature. It soon became apparent that in this task the usual narrow focus on specific types of recreation would be inappropriate. What was local recreation for one was a tourist trip for another, what was a leisure pursuit for some was a business venture for others, and what was the peak of amateur sports competition for some was an economic opportunity and image boost for the host community. Thus one can accept Berger's seamless web analogy, but one must divide the recreation phenomenon into outdoor recreation, sports, and tourism in an attempt to reveal the economic impacts of what, for most of us, is primarily a time for fun and unwinding.

One of the first trends to emerge from the literature review has been a recent surge of interest in the economic significance of recreation and recreation-related activities. Many of the cited studies are consultant reports commissioned by various governments, mainly at the provincial level, during the late 1970s and early 1980s. The parallel between this interest and rising unemployment during the same time period cannot be ignored. It would appear that more governments are investigating the business side of recreation as a major component of our post-industrial economic revival. This leisure business potential has been predicted by futurists like Kahn (1979) and has been foreshadowed by our growing dependence on the service sector and small business for employment and economic growth. For example, "in the past 20 years, 80% of all new jobs in B.C. have been created in the tourism and service industries" (B.C. Central Credit Union 1983, 1)

One may consider that the future is already here when one examines the economic claims of many studies. Throughout this chapter the reported economic impact is consistently in the millions of dollars with hundreds of person-years of employment generated. It is difficult to gauge the comparative contribution of these recreation activities because the studies seldom provide the relevant information. Those that do, such as the Parks Canada and Ontario studies, suggest that as substantial as the current economic impact is, there is plenty of room for growth and a long way to go to catch up with some of our current major industries.

Despite the present contribution of recreation to Canada's economy and its potential for growth, some caution should be exercised in the interpretation of the cited statistics. First, there are some major difficulties in assessing the total impact of recreation on national or regional economies. Second, the focus on economic impact should not be taken as a balanced accounting, for it does not consider the costs.

Unfortunately recreation is not identified as a single activity in the standard industrial classification system employed by Statistics Canada, so researchers must construct their own expenditure and employment estimates through proportionality calculations across a wide range of industrial sectors. The accuracy of these calculated proportions depends in turn on the results of individual surveys, which in themselves are time= and place=specific and consequently not the best basis for generalizations. The result is that many recreation impact studies to depend on secondary sources or parallel studies to guide their estimates for the multipliers intended to reflect the indirect and induced impacts.

It is interesting to note how the multiplier was calculated in some of the cited studies. Ellis's Ontario study (Ellis 1982) makes use of previous Ontario Ministry of Industry and Tourism input-output studies, focusing on those multipliers in sectors "for which recreation dollars are destined" (Ellis 1982, 31). The value, presumably an average, selected from this sample is 1.88 -- which "turns out to be one of the higher ones in Ontario's economy" (Ellis 1982, 31). In the Alberta study Burton derives his income and employment multipliers from "seven recreation-related Albertan industries" (Table 8). In order to be conservative in his calculations Burton excludes the two highest multipliers and averages the remaining five to derive a value for recreation. This produces a recreation income multiplier of 1.67 and a recreation employment multiplier of 1.55. The British Columbia study simply adopts Burton's income multiplier without comment. Presumably it was selected because it was a recent calculation and considered relevant to a neighboring provincial economy.

The emphasis on economic impact within the cited studies was intended to demonstrate the actual and potential contribution of recreation-related activities to our economy, and should not be construed as an attempt to reach a balanced assessment, because costs have seldom been considered. In a nation of finite space and resources wishing to maintain or improve the standard of living for its growing population, hard trade-off decisions invariably will be needed. The opportunity costs of forsaken alternative land uses and investment decisions are becoming a major concern. For example, the lobbying for parks and wilderness runs counter to the interests of the forestry and mining industries in several areas. In some cases the selection of a recreation use over other uses necessitates compensation for foregone opportunities, as recently occurred when Ottawa agreed to pay British Columbia "$32 million in compensation for forest lands set aside in Pacific Rim National Park 17 years ago." (*Vancouver Sun* 1986, B4). Similarly, investment in projects like Expo '86 have been criticized for diverting funds from other sectors such as education and forestry (Blackorby *et al.* 1984).

Table 8

Multipliers for Recreation-Related Industries in Alberta Considered by T.L. Burton

INDUSTRY	MULTIPLIER	
	Income	Employment
Beverage industries	2.300	2.517
Clothing industries	1.638	1.491
Printing and publishing	1.686	1.721
Wholesale and retail trade	1.674	1.512
Business Services industry	1.893	1.557
Accommodation and food services industry	1.730	1.426
Other personal and miscellaneous services industry	1.730	1.426

Source: T.L. Burton, 1984.

As geographers, we are also interested in the environmental and social costs of recreation. When an area becomes an attractive magnet for recreational pursuits, some modification of the environment is inevitable because large-scale recreation, like any other industry, requires management to maintain its long-term viability. This situation has been recognized both with regard to the physical environment (Wall and Wright 1977) and the social environment within host communities (Murphy 1985). In most cases the cost is an eroded landscape or lifestyle, which requires some form of management policy to balance local recreation opportunities with their respective environmental and social carrying capacities.

One final caveat that should be kept in mind when reading this chapter is that while the economic impact of recreation is important, it is not in itself a complete measure of recreation's value. Some feel that it is not possible, or even desirable, to attach a price to the personal fulfilment of aesthetic experiences or the physical benefits of exercise. It is certainly very difficult to do so. But beyond that, recreation can and does mean more than the economic value of an activity that has been stressed here.

While the economic impact may help to justify the provision of recreation and sports facilities in Canada, for many it is the physical and mental benefits which are of prime importance. The physical and mental well-being provided through recreation become especially important at times of stress. In his examination of the Sault Ste. Marie, Ontario recreation system, Berger (1983, 37) noted:

> recreation plays a key role in community life, and personal life, particularly during times of economic recession. The high priority given by the public to recreation activities and programs, and the increasing demand for such programs, indicates the high priority which individuals give to recreation activities--a priority which is supported by municipal politicians and staff.

This author noticed the same phenomenon in Edinburgh, Scotland, where a working class suburb with unemployment exceeding 25% was given an important morale boost through the recreation and workshop programs of its recreation centre in the early eighties.

SUMMARY

There can be no doubt that recreation is big business in Canada, and that, as we move more into the post-industrial society, it will have an even bigger impact on our economy. While there is no single data source to provide an overall view of recreation's economic impact, the limited studies and surveys cited in this chapter suggest Canadians and visitors are willing to spend a great deal in pursuit of their exercise and relaxation within our boundaries. We have much to offer in terms of scenic beauty, abundant outdoor recreation opportunities, cultural and arts attractions, plus a growing list of recreation and tourist facilities to supplement our traditional outdoors attractions. Individuals and companies are investing in leisure industries and recreation-related activites as never before. It is not surprising, therefore, that various governments have become aware of the size and potential of the recreation "business," and that they are beginning to approach it as both a social and economic investment as it matures into a growth industry of the service sector.

Chapter 7

Environmental Impacts

Geoffrey Wall
Department of Geography
University of Waterloo

Environmental Impacts

INTRODUCTION

It is a paradox that participants in recreation are drawn to attractive environments, whether natural or built, but that their mere presence is likely to result in the modification of those environments. There is a real possibility that the environment can be loved to death! Increased concern can be seen in the titles of recent conferences, which include the words "conflict or harmony?" (Canadian Society of Environmental Biologists 1986) or, in more titillating fashion, "progress or prostitution?" (Downie and Peart 1982). On the other hand, the provision of recreation opportunities provides a persuasive rationale for the preservation and creation of attractive environments. The tension between use and preservation of such places has long been acknowledged in Canada but is given more poignancy with the realization that burgeoning recreation is a mixed blessing.

The environment may be both the object of and setting for recreational experiences. Particular elements of the landscape, such as viewpoints, mountain peaks, fish or historic sites, may be the specific objects of recreational attention and their attainment and appreciation the major goal of the recreational activity. In other cases, the environment may constitute the backdrop or context in which the activity takes place. Thus, the presence of a lake or an ocean vista may make an area particularly attractive to picnickers or campers even though they may have no wish to engage in water-contact activities. In either case, whether the environment is object or setting, the presence of people participating in outdoor recreation will bring about modifications to the environment. Impacts of recreation on the environment are both purposive and accidental. Areas are set aside and managed for recreational use, structures are erected to entertain and accommodate recreationists, and new environments are created, such as theme parks, which cater to the whims of the recreating public. Many of these areas, such as national parks, are relatively natural, whereas others, such as many resorts, may be far removed from a natural state.

There is a large and growing literature on the impacts of recreation and, in order to present a structured perspective on a vast quantity of interrelated materials, it is necessary to organize the information through the use of a simple logical framework. This is done in Figure 1. The type and extent of impacts will be greatly influenced by the characteristics of the environments in which recreation takes place. This topic is discussed in the next section, which defines terms and examines the nature of the environment. For convenience, impacts upon the environment are viewed as being created by three interrelated factors which can be considered as generators of change: the development of attractions, the provision of associated infrastructure, and the visitors as they journey to the site and participate in activities. Each of these three subjects will be examined in turn. These sections are followed by a discussion of the difficulties of measuring environmental impacts. Next, the impacts themselves will be presented and changes in geology and soils, vegetation, water, air, and wildlife will be discussed and illustrated through reference to case studies undertaken in Canada. Finally, an assessment will be made of the significance of environmental impacts.

THE NATURE OF ENVIRONMENT

The word environment encompasses all aspects of the world around us. According to Nelson and Butler (1974), it is a comprehensive term which overlaps in meaning with ecosystem. The latter is a biological concept which can be defined as the elements and processes interacting with an organism or organisms. Ecosystem dynamics, which is concerned with the processes of energy flow and cycling of phosphorus, nitrogen, carbon dioxide, and other nutrients necessary to maintain organic life, implies that an organism is an integral part of its own ecosystem, and that the distinction between organism and ecosystem is a false dichotomy. However, from an anthropocentric perspective and for present purposes, it is convenient to define the environment as the sum

Figure 1: A Framework for the Examination of Environmental Impacts

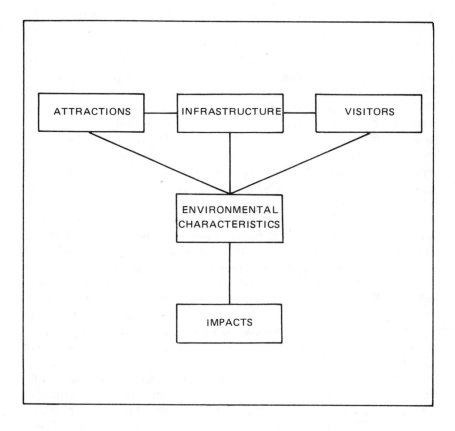

total of conditions which surround us. Evidently environment is an all-embracing term which defies analysis in its full complexity.

We respond to and manipulate environments both as individuals and as groups or societies. We may, as individuals, decide to visit a national park, but we decide as a society to allocate resources to the provision and maintenance of such parks. Furthermore, the interaction between human beings and environment is a two-way process: the environment provides opportunities and constraints as human beings attempt to satisfy their needs and desires and, at the same time, human beings have the ability to modify the environment, a situation which has become more prevalent with growing population and modern technology.

The word environment is often employed with associated adjectives. The natural environment usually refers to nature, more specifically aspects of nature which are natural in that they have not been modified by human beings. In fact, the impact of human activity is so pervasive that there are no truly natural environments. Natural environments are contrasted with man-modified environments, such as urban environments, which are often called built environments. Natural and built environments may both be termed physical environments, although some use the terms *natural* and physical interchangeably. Others use the term *physical* environment to contrast with the socio-cultural environment, which refers to the attributes of individuals and societies which impinge upon us. This chapter will be concerned primarily with physical environments, whether natural, modified, or predominantly man-made. The chapter which follows is devoted to social impacts.

Recreational activities take place in many different environments, spanning the whole spectrum from remote, pristine locations to congested city centres. Some recreations, such as downhill skiing, are very specific in their environmental requirements, whereas others, such as walking and picnicking, can be undertaken in a diversity of settings. It is self-evident that the impacts of recreation on forests, tundra, wetlands, dunes, mountain slopes, and marine and lacustrine shores vary markedly both because of the elements which comprise these environments and the activities which they support. Some environments are more resilient than others and can support more users over longer periods of time. However, although the ability to support recreational use on a long-term basis is a desirable characteristic, it is not necessarily the same as the ability to provide a high-quality experience.

GENERATORS OF IMPACT

As suggested above, the forces generating changes in the environment have been divided into three components: attractions, infrastructure, and visitors (Figure 1). Of course, this threefold division is somewhat arbitrary, for it is virtually impossible to consider the impacts of attractions in the absence of the necessary supporting infrastructure or role of the visitors. Nevertheless, the division is convenient and useful for descriptive purposes.

1. *Attractions*

The word impact often has a negative connotation and is frequently associated with undesired changes, but not all changes are bad and the environment is often modified in order that the requirements of human beings may be met more satisfactorily. It is common practice to change existing environments and to create new environments to make them more suitable for particular types of visitors. An extremely wide variety of attractions exists, spanning the entire spectrum, from those which are predominantly natural in origin to those which are almost entirely man-made. Examples of attractions include parks, resorts, ski areas, cottages, waterfronts, historic sites, museums, concert halls, theme parks, and stadiums. The first four items in this list will be discussed by way of illustration.

Parks

Most people regard parks as relatively natural environments. However, in most parks, particularly in urban parks with their play equipment, facilities for sports, paths, manicured grass, and carefully tended flower beds, considerable changes to the environment are made. In fact, some landscape architects specialize in designing modifications to parklands in an attempt to enhance their attractiveness to users (Rutledge 1971). Even most wilderness parks are managed: trails are introduced, campsites are designated and constructed, and information and interpretive centres may be built. Although policies are slowly changing, it was once fashionable in most parks to suppress all fires. Prescribed burns may now be used to replace natural fires, but their timing and location is carefully controlled. The mere designation of a park may draw attention to the attractiveness of an area and pull in visitors who would not otherwise have come, thereby changing the level of use and associated impacts.

Resorts

There is a substantial literature on purpose-built recreational environments, commencing with the pioneering work of Gilbert (1939, 1954). Much of this research is focused upon the morphology of spas (Patmore 1968, Lawrence 1983, Roark 1974) and seaside resorts (Lavery 1971, Stansfield 1972, Meyer-Arendt 1985). There is general agreement that seaside resorts have evolved with particular characteristics which are summarized in Figure 2. Intensity of land use diminishes with increasing distance from the pier, which marks the most accessible point from the railway station. A strip fronting the coast consists of amenities and hotels, and these are backed by a street of souvenir shops and entertainments running parallel to the coast. Resort morphology has evolved with changes in transportation technology, varies with distance from markets, and continues to change with the development of instant resorts, spawned by charter flights and the wide-bodied jet.

In Canada, urban resorts have been less important than in Europe or the United States. Although both the Atlantic and Pacific coasts have played, and continue to play, an important recreational role, they have not been host to seaside resorts on the scale of those of Europe. However, numerous communities on the St. Lawrence River and the Great Lakes have appended a recreational function to their other activities. The large international literature on spas and seaside resorts is not matched by similar works on Canada. Perhaps this is because spas (with the major exception of Banff) and coastal resorts have not had the same significance in Canada as in Europe. There is a substantial literature on Banff (Scace 1969), and Wall (1983b) has written on Preston Springs and Radium Hot Springs (Wightman and Wall 1985), and has reviewed the status of Canadian research on water-based recreation (Wall 1982c). Wolfe (1952) examined the evolution of Wasaga Beach and its "divorce from the geographical environment" and Stansfield

Figure 2: Theoretical Accommodation Zones in a Coastal Resort

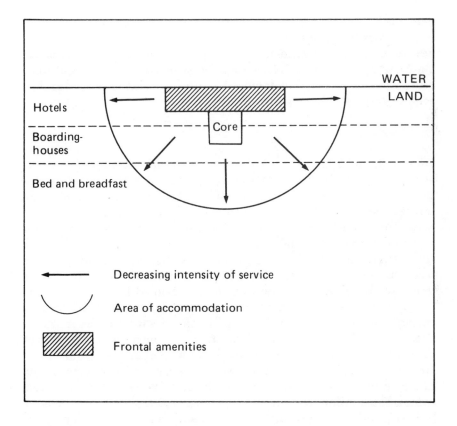

Source: After Barrett 1958.

and Rickert (1970) have described the peculiar character of recreation business districts, using Niagara Falls as an example. However, the recent publication of popular articles on St. Andrews, New Brunswick (Rees 1988), and on resorts along the St. Lawrence (Lanken 1987) suggests that interest may be growing, at least from a historical perspective.

Ski Areas

Similarly, the increasing number of studies of the environmental consequences of skiing (Bayfield 1974) and the development of ski resorts in Europe (Barker 1982, Mosimann 1985) is not matched by comparable Canadian investigations, although ski resort developments have generated considerable controversy in this country.

Cottages

One form of recreational development which is very much associated with Canada, particularly Ontario and Quebec, is the cottage. However, it is not confined to Canada, and similar landscapes may be found in the United States and in Scandinavia, where there is a forest-lakes complex comparable to that of the Canadian Shield. Initially, cottages tend to be isolated or clustered around points of access and almost all possess shore frontage. As growth continues, infilling takes place so that lakes become completely fringed by cottages, and subsequently second, third, and even fourth and fifth tiers of cottages may be built back from the shore without direct water access. Wolfe (1977) has described the early stages of this process for Lower Shebandowan Lake, near Thunder Bay, Helleiner (1983) has documented the process for nearby Loon Lake, and Désy (1967) and Michaud (1967) have provided somewhat similar evidence for Quebec. Lack of public access to built-up lakes, shoreline modification, water pollution, and other environmental problems of existing developments which have been exacerbated by the trend to winterization, have encouraged the search for new styles of cottage colony. Suggestions include condominiums and mosaic developments in which building is concentrated and some lakes are left undeveloped and zoned for different recreational uses (Jaakson 1970, 1974). Such developments would add new components to the morphology of cottage lands, but as yet it is not clear how these ideas will be received by the public and, consequently, how widely they will be adopted.

Summary

The potential for commercial exploitation and for environmental modification, both purposive and accidental, is influenced by the nature of the resource. In the case of spas, the resource can be considered to be a point, the spring, and visitors and recreational developments are clustered around that point. The high density of visitors creates the potential for commercial exploitation of the resource, the development of an urban resort, and a high degree of environmental modification. Banff and Niagara Falls provide examples of this phenomenon.

Much the same was true of seaside resorts. In the early years of their growth, the key location was that point of the beach most accessible from the railway station and, as described above, it acted as a focus around which visitor services clustered. As personal mobility improved, resorts expanded along the coast, so that a pattern formerly made of points became a linear one, particularly as resorts coalesced. Many of these points also apply to cottages when considered at the scale of an individual lake.

In contrast to these point and line characteristics, many Canadian recreational resources are areal in character. The forest-lakes complex of the Shield and other "wilderness" areas are less amenable to commercial exploitation than point resources and impacts on the environment are more diffuse. Even where limited access points cause visitors to congregate, they spread out across a larger area and may actually try to avoid others. As a result, visitors and their purchasing power are widely distributed with a diminished likelihood of concentrated commercial development or environmental modification.

2. Infrastructure

A considerable quantity of infrastructure must be provided in order to get participants to their recreation sites efficiently and to support them while they are there. Examples of such infrastructure include accommodations (Wall, Dudycha, and Hutchinson 1985, Nelson and Wall 1986), restaurants (Smith 1985), transportation, waste disposal and water supply facilities, and signage. Each of these elements has its own implications for the environment.

Peaking of demand causes considerable problems for the provision of infrastructure. If facilities are provided to cater to peak demand they will be oversized and underutilized for much of the time. On the other hand, if peak demand cannot be met, then facilities may be overtaxed at such periods, as occurs on occasion with waste disposal systems at Banff, with detrimental consequences for the Bow River.

The provision of increased infrastructure, particularly more extensive and upgraded road systems, has permitted more people to penetrate farther into the wilderness and has thus extended the zone of impact. The extension of both roads and rails in the western national parks has been among the most contentious environmental issues in Canada in recent decades (Canada, Federal Environmental Assessment Review Office, 1979, 1982a, 1982b, 1983).

One example of possible implications is provided by Carbyn (1974). He has suggested that although predator control programs have ceased in the Canadian national parks, other human activities have increased in the parks with detrimental implications for wolves. Of four specific effects which he identifies, three are directly related to infrastructure. These are the impacts of highway and trail construction on denning sites, the disruption of normal predator-prey relationships as a result of the attraction of ungulates to seeded right of ways or other human structures such as townsites and campgrounds, and the killing of wolves along highways. The fourth effect, disturbance of young at nursery dens by human visitors is, in many ways, similar to the first. Recognition of the destruction of animals on highways has caused fences and underpasses to be constructed in an attempt to reduce the carnage of wildlife on the roads (Leighton 1988).

3. *Visitors*

The factors which influence the impacts of visitors on the environment are very similar to those which Keogh, in chapter 8, has suggested have implications for social impacts. They include the number of visitors, their length of stay, the activities in which they engage, and the season of the year. The first three factors determine the magnitude of the impacting forces and the latter factor influences the vulnerability of the environment.

The population of Canada continues to increase and participation rates in outdoor recreation have expanded in recent decades, so that the potential for environmental impact has grown. The majority of Canadians now live in cities and are not very familiar with rural and wilderness environments and, in consequence, they may not be aware of the types of behaviour that are appropriate in such places. In consequence, some participants, such as those who pick flowers, chop down trees, and use fire carelessly, may simply not be aware that their behaviour is potentially damaging. In other cases, the impacts may be due to vandalism. Priddle and Wall (1978) examined depreciative behaviour in Ontario provincial parks and concluded that the problem is highly concentrated spatially in parks relatively close to urban areas and, temporally, on long weekends in the summer, particularly the Victoria Day weekend.

Not surprisingly, not all activities have the same potential to degrade the environment and to detract from the experience of other users. For simplicity, activities are often divided into mechanized and non-mechanized categories with the former having the greater likelihood of causing environmental consequences. Although it may be only a fleeting impact directly, few would deny that some forms of mechanized outdoor recreation create sounds which may disturb wildlife and which may be disruptive to other people. A series of studies by Kariel (1973, 1980a, 1980b), undertaken in a number of western national parks, confirms that noises associated with modern technology may be annoying. However, there is some evidence to suggest that participants in different activities may have different degrees of tolerance. While there is a considerable literature on noise, and few would deny that a proportion of airport or highway noise is attributable to recreation, as in the case of air quality which is discussed later, very little of the research is specifically concerned with outdoor recreation.

Space does not permit the detailed evaluation of all outdoor activities. However, some comments will be made concerning an activity which, while not restricted to Canada, could be regarded as being Canadian. The snowmobile is a Canadian invention and snowmobiling is a Canadian contribution to the outdoor recreation experience (Butler 1982). However, not only are the machines dangerous when used by unskilled drivers, death and injury being a not uncommon occurrence, they also have considerable environmental implications, if only because they permit their users to penetrate into previously inaccessible areas. Growing concern over the impacts of snowmobiling prompted the staging of conferences on the topic in both Canada (Butler *et al.* 1971) and the United States (Chubb 1971), and a number of academic papers have been published upon the topic.

Neumann and Merriam (1972) examined the environmental effects of snowmobiles in the Gatineau Park, Quebec, and the western suburbs of Ottawa. They concluded that specific gravities of snow were doubled and sometimes tripled, greatly increasing thermal conductivity and reducing insulating effects. The direct mechanical effects of snowmobiles on vegetation at or above the snow surface were found to be severe. On trails which received high intensities of use, all vegetation above the compacted snow surface was mechanically eradicated. Browsing animals used some of the vegetation broken down by snowmobiles, although activity data suggested that snowshoe hares avoid snowmobile trails. Conversely, red foxes were much more active close to the same trails.

More recently, Keddy, Spavold and Keddy (1979) have examined the impact of snowmobiles on field and marsh vegetation in Nova Scotia. They concluded that snowmobiling can have a significant effect upon natural vegetation but that field and marsh vegetation are affected differently, the ice cover on the marsh reducing the magnitude of impact. They suggested that because the first pass of the snowmobile causes most compaction, encouraging the use of trails is more appropriate than attempting to diffuse use.

Other useful studies of impacts of snowmobiling have been undertaken in various parts of the northern United States, and their findings are likely to be equally applicable to Canada (Walejko *et al.* 1973, Dorrance, Savage and Huff 1975, Richens and Lavigne 1978, Eckstein *et al.* 1979).

THE MEASUREMENT OF IMPACTS

Assessors of changes induced in the environment by recreation are faced with similar challenges to those common to all types of impact research (Wall and Wright 1977). These include the problems of defining a base level against which change can be measured, of distinguishing between human-induced and natural change, of spatial and temporal discontinuities of cause and effect, and of incorporating the full complexities of direct and indirect effects.

It is extremely difficult to determine what a place would be like in the absence of recreation, particularly if it has been used for recreation for a considerable period of time, but in the absence of such information it is impossible to be certain of the role which recreation has played in modifying it. Furthermore, environments are not static but evolve naturally: vegetation succession takes place, lakes silt up and animal populations respond to changes in their habitats. Activities of human beings may modify energy balances and speed up processes which occur naturally at a slower rate. Thus, weathering (the breaking up of rock into small particles) and erosion (the transportation of those particles downslope under the influence of gravity), which are natural processes, may increase in recreation areas and may become management problems.

In many cases, the limits of a recreation site do not contain the full causes or effects of change. Thus, many recreational areas may feel the consequences of acid rain or global climate change derived from activities beyond their borders and, conversely, impacts of recreation may extend beyond the recreation site. For example, inadequate waste disposal and leaking septic tanks may pollute river water and cause fish-kills downstream, and destruction of the habitat of migratory species will influence the population elsewhere in the range. Furthermore, impacts are both direct and indirect, and it is seldom possible to trace the full impacts of recreation as they reverberate through the complex linkages of an ecological system.

A number of other problems which are more specific to recreation can be added to the common difficulties of impact research. The diversity of recreational activities presents a challenge for students of environmental impact, making generalization about the environmental impacts of recreation difficult. Clearly, the consequences of skiing are likely to differ greatly from the changes caused by boating or the environmental disturbances caused by the recreational use of all-terrain vehicles. To compound the problem, as has already been suggested, recreation takes place in many different environments, each with its own characteristics and susceptibility to change: obviously, a grassy sward is different from a beach, ski hill, or alpine meadow, and possesses different potentials for change.

Faced with the above problems, investigators have adopted a diversity of research methodologies, each with its own strengths and weaknesses. Three major types of study can be identified:

after-the-fact analysis, monitoring, and simulation. Most studies are of the first type (see, for example, Willard and Marr 1970). Impacts are measured after they have occurred and impacted sites may be compared with sites experiencing no recreational use or impact, the differences between the two being attributed to recreation. Such studies are relatively cheap and easy to undertake and results are achieved quickly. The methodology is excellent for identifying locations where remedial measures are required, but the investigations are undertaken after the changes have occurred so that they are akin to shutting the barn door after the horse has bolted. A further deficiency of such studies is that, while they often provide very detailed information on environmental changes, it is only the occasional study which provides comparable information on levels and types of recreational use. The manager of a recreation site needs both types of information if wise decisions are to be made for both the environment and visitors are open to manipulation.

Monitoring studies have the potential to overcome the latter limitation. It may be possible to measure and relate levels of use and associated environmental changes over considerable periods of time, and this may be particularly instructive if sites can be monitored from the moment that that they become used by visitors (see, for example, LaPage 1967). While such studies are intellectually appealing and are often among the most informative, they are also very time-consuming and expensive to undertake, so that they constitute only a small proportion of all investigations of recreational impacts.

Simulation studies exhibit an experimental approach (see, for example, Weaver and Dale 1978, Keddy 1979). Experimental and control plots are exposed to known volumes and frequencies of recreational use and the consequences are measured and compared. This approach has the great advantage of examining use and impact at the same time. The studies are relatively cheap to undertake, and they are becoming relatively more common. They also lend themselves to the examination of recovery rates since environmental changes can be monitored after the impacting forces have ceased (Willard and Marr 1971, Bayfield 1979), something which may be difficult to arrange in areas actively used for recreation.

THE NATURE OF IMPACTS

Whether recreating in natural or built environments, in small or in large numbers, and regardless of activity, recreationists have side effects upon the environment, and it is these side effects which have received the most attention from researchers and which will be discussed next. The literature on this topic is large and growing rapidly, but fortunately a number of fairly comprehensive reviews are available (Speight 1973, Satchell and Marren 1976, Wall and Wright 1977, Hammitt and Cole 1987), as well as conference proceedings (Ittner *et al.* 1979), and review papers on specific topics. For example, Liddle (1975, 1988) and Kuss and Graefe (1985) have assessed the impacts of trampling upon vegetation; Seabrooke (1981) has drawn together the literature on water-based recreation; Howard and Stanley-Saunders (1979) have compiled an annotated bibliography on impacts on streams; Manning (1979) has examined riparian soils and vegetation; and Liddle and Scorgie (1980) have reviewed the effects of recreation on fresh-water plants and animals. Although participants in recreation also erode the built environment, as has occurred at Stonehenge (Bainbridge 1979) and some cathedrals in England (English Tourist Board 1979), the results of the numerous studies on the impact of outdoor recreation on relatively natural settings will receive the majority of attention in the remainder of this chapter. There are a number of possible ways of organizing these materials: by activity, considering the impacts of different types of recreation; by ecosystem, reporting upon studies undertaken in different environmental contexts; and by environmental element, discussing the implications for particular components of the environment, such as rocks, soil, vegetation, air, water, and wildlife. The latter structure will be adopted here, and a brief synopsis will be provided of a more detailed discussion which is available elsewhere (Wall and Wright 1977).

Geology

In most environments recreation has few implications for geology. However, in certain special environments the implications can be severe. For example, rock hounding and collecting fossils can lead to the destruction of interesting geological sites, and the removal of stalagmites and stalactites can diminish the appeal of caves. Mountaineers cut holds and leave pitons on rock faces, and others carve names and paint messages on rock surfaces. These are not major ecological problems, but they do diminish the quality of the recreation experience for those who follow. However, rock inscriptions, such as petroglyphs or Indian paintings, may be valued if they are sufficiently old and it is not clear at what point undesirable graffiti become a valuable archaeological resource.

Soils

Most work on recreational impacts has concentrated upon soils and vegetation, particularly in campsites and along trails. The studies indicate that users compact soils, increase the proportion of water running off the surface rather than percolating down through the soil, modify soil moisture and temperature regimes, reduce organic matter and nutrients in the soil (although these may also increase locally due to the deposition of waste materials), increase erosion, and reduce the number and diversity of soil organisms. Changes in soil chemistry resulting from recreation have been confirmed by Rutherford and Scott (1979) in an investigation in Brown's Bay Provincial Park near Kingston Ontario.

As in the literature as a whole, a substantial proportion of the recreation impact research in Canada has been conducted upon trails and campgrounds. For example, Root and Knapik (1972) examined conditions along part of the Great Divide Trail of the Rocky Mountains of southwestern Alberta and adjacent British Columbia. They measured the thickness and types of surficial deposits, bedrock lithology, local topography and aspect, ground-water and surface water drainage; the proximity, extent and meltwater effects of snowbanks; and vegetation. They concluded that trampling by horse and foot traffic is the initial cause of damage, and this is particularly noticeable in wet areas adjacent to lakes, streams, snowbanks, and groundwater features. Subsequent erosion by running water is the major cause of trail damage. Where damage is sufficient to inconvenience horse and foot traffic, new trails are worn parallel to the old trail, creating a continually broadening series of unsightly ruts. Trail orientation and slope are important in influencing damage by running water, and soils with a high silt content are highly susceptible to erosion. The authors' many recommendations include the use of switchbacks, culverts, bridges, water bars, and stepping stones to prevent water from running down the trail; the avoidance of wet areas; and the separation of horse and foot traffic.

Kariel and Jacks (1980) describe the success of some of these measures on meadows and trails in Yoho National Park.

Vegetation

Vegetation is modified directly through mechanical damage caused by recreationists and their vehicles coming into contact with plants, and indirectly through changes in the soil. The results are that vegetation is destroyed and bare patches may be created; growth rates and reproduction rates may be reduced; the age structure of the vegetation may be modified; species composition is changed as certain more resilient and often weedy species obtain a competitive advantage; and species diversity is reduced. Although these changes are usually considered to be negative, in some cases habitat diversity may increase as areas are opened up for recreation, and light is allowed to penetrate along trail and campsite edges in areas that were formerly entirely forested. Unfortunately, different researchers measure different variables (for example, biomass, species diversity, percentage cover) so that comparisons between studies are not easy to make, and it is not clear which measures are of most significance to managers. The situation is extremely complex, for the amount of impact is not influenced only by the numbers and types of users, but also by such factors as the season of the year, the amount of soil moisture present, soil type, species morphology, and the successional stage of the vegetation.

Trottier *et al.* (1976) examined impacts on the Mount Kerkeslin campground in the Athabasca Valley of Jasper National Park. Their study included a consideration of vegetation, wildlife, and soils. The objective of their study was to assess the likely environmental impact of possible campground expansion and to identify means by which adverse impact could be minimized. They recommended that any expansion should be in the aspen cover type, excepting sites underlain by stony substrates, rather than into the riverine, pine, or mixed-wood types. They suggested that wide buffer zones should be left between sites to provide cover for small mammals and birds, and deadfall and standing dead trees should not be removed unless they were a direct threat to public safety, because they are an asset to some forms of wildlife.

Somewhat similarly, impacts of recreation on vegetation and soils have been examined in Rushing River Provincial Park (Mackintosh 1979, James *et al.* 1979, Monti and Mackintosh 1979). The park is in the boreal forest of northwestern Ontario. The authors concluded that intensive recreation leads to soil compaction, increased bulk density, reduced infiltration rates, loss of leaf litter, and increased exposure of roots. Diameter growth of jack pine is significantly reduced in campsites when compared with adjacent undisturbed areas, probably as a result of water stress associated with soil changes. Reductions in needle area and dry weight indicated deterioration of the crowns of trees in high-impact areas. Changes in the species composition and diversity of understory vegetation was greatest in areas of greatest use. There was also extensive mechanical damage from the collection of firewood, vandalism, and motor vehicle collisions. Mackintosh suggested remedial actions through site rehabilitation, improved campground design, and modified management policies, which included zoning for different uses and the education of users.

In a very different environment, Trowell (1987) has described the consequences for dunes on the shore of Lake Huron of visitors to the Pinery and Ipperwash provincial parks in Ontario. She suggested that a path is created on the dune after fifty pedestrian passes and that much of the vegetation is killed after an additional three hundred passes. Park managers are rehabilitating the dunes through the planting of native species, the closure of some parts of the parks to the public, and the construction of boardwalks on heavily used routes.

Air

There are few studies of the influence of recreation upon air quality. In deep valleys, such as Yosemite in the United States where large numbers of automobile exhausts combine with the smoke from campfires, the air quality can become uncomfortable. A study has been undertaken of the ability of air masses to disperse pollutants in ski areas in Colorado (Kirkpatrick and Reeser 1976). However, the impact of recreation upon the atmosphere is not considered to be a problem in most situations. Nevertheless, few would deny that automobile exhausts are a substantial contributor of pollutants, and if it is acknowledged that a large proportion of automobile use is for pleasure, then it follows that recreation is a substantial cause of air pollution. However, there is little literature to substantiate this assertion and the author is unaware of Canadian studies on the topic.

Water

Lakes "age" naturally, and the impacts of recreation are likely to differ on oligotrophic and eutrophic lakes. Most of the evidence of the adverse effects of recreation on aquatic ecosystems is circumstantial. Water is mobile and it disperses and dilutes pollutants, often making it difficult to link cause and effect with absolute certainty. Few would deny that recreation can contribute to lower water quality and increased concentrations of pathogens through inappropriate waste disposal and leaking septic tanks. Many cottagers are concerned about water quality in lakes as increased use of lakeshores contributes to nutrient enrichment, especially of nitrogen and phosphorus compounds, leading to greater plant growth and diminished oxygen supply. Although there are simulation studies which indicate that as much as four out of every ten gallons of gasoline may be discharged directly into the water from outboard motors (Barton 1969), there are surprisingly few quantitative studies of cause-and-effect relationships between recreation and water quality.

Wildlife

Wildlife constitutes the quarry for some types of outdoor recreation, and hunters and anglers aim to have an impact upon wildlife as the objective of their activity (Reed and Boyd 1984). Nevertheless, many among their number claim that because they are concerned about the maintenance of populations of desirable species, their overall impact is benign. Many species adjust quite well to the presence of humans, and most readers will have experienced how tame (and dependent upon human food) many animals and birds can become. There is a substantial literature on bears and bear management which has been developed in response to concerns about human-bear encounters in recreation areas (see, for example, Marsh 1970,

Mundy and Flook 1973, Payne 1978). It does seem unfair that it is usually the bears who are considered the rogues and who are relocated while the invading visitor remains unchastised.

Impacts of recreation on wildlife take three forms: direct influences on numbers by killing or stocking, alteration of habitat, and disturbance. In all three cases this may lead to changes in population numbers and species composition. However, animals are mobile so that it is often difficult to distinguish between death and out-migration. Although there are a very limited number of exceptions (see, for example, Busack and Bury's (1974) study of the impacts of off-road vehicles on lizards in the Mojave Desert, California), most studies lack population counts taken prior to the incidence of recreation, and there are very few longitudinal studies. This would seem to be essential where much impact is likely to be indirect through habitat modification.

Recent Developments

The preceding review is a synopsis of an assessment undertaken by Wall and Wright in 1977. Their work is summarized in Figure 3. Research has continued to flourish since that time, and numerous additional studies can be added to their bibliography. There have not been major methodological innovations. Rather, the trend has been to apply existing methods to new environments and new activities. Following the example of Bates (1935, 1938, 1950), many of the early studies were undertaken in temperate grassland and sand dune settings in Britain, but the range of environments which have been investigated now encompasses temperate and tropical forests, deserts, wetlands, coastal and riverine areas, and coral reefs, as well as high=latitude and =altitude locations. Of course, not all of these environments are found in Canada.

As has already been suggested, most of the early studies concentrated upon the implications of trampling on trails and campsites. These studies are still very valuable, for the impacts of most activities are derived from the cumulative pressures applied by a succession of feet and vehicles. Impacts of canoeing, for example, are few while the craft is on the water but are concentrated at the shoreline where camping takes place and where the canoe is introduced to and withdrawn from the water. The trampling studies were soon joined by

Figure 3: Recreational Impact Interrelationships

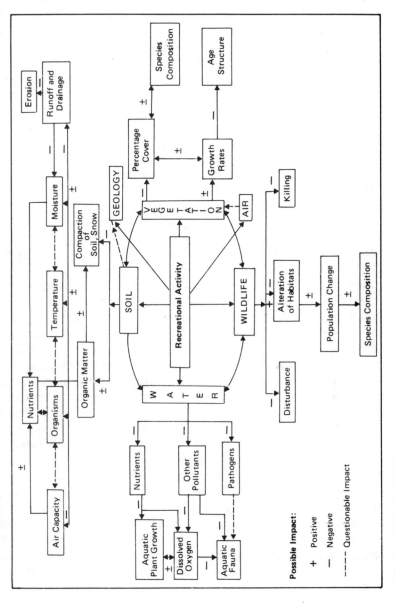

Source: Wall and Wright 1977.

investigations of skiing and snowmobiling, and they, in turn, have been complemented by examinations of off-road vehicles, river rafting, boating and reef walking. Most studies still concentrate upon soils and vegetation and none attempts to trace the full range of direct and indirect impacts as they reverberate through the ecosystem. Nevertheless, the growth in the number of studies and their extension to new environments and locations represents a substantial degree of progress in the acquisition of information on the impacts of recreation on the environment.

Research results obtained in different environments and using varied methodologies are all pointing to important generalizations. At a conceptual level, interactions between human beings are now being viewed in a more sophisticated manner. Thus, for example, Liddle and Tothill (1984) have suggested that such interactions can be seen as a three-stage process, termed alpha (communication), beta (contact), and gamma (response). The alpha process includes all of the signals that are received before physical contact takes place. The beta process begins with first contact and ends when contact ceases. The gamma process commences when a response to the beta process takes place. Also, terminology is beginning to be used in a more precise manner. Thus, a distinction can be made between resistance or the ability to resist mechanical damage (in the case of plants), tolerance or the ability of a species to survive over a given period, and resilience or the regrowth and proliferation of individuals and/or parts of plants after damage has occurred. Perhaps the most significant practical implication of the studies is the recognition that impacts on the environment occur at relatively low-use intensities and successive increments of environmental change diminish in magnitude with additional increments of use. In other words, much impact occurs with relatively small numbers of visitors. Furthermore, rates of recovery may be slow, particularly in high latitudes and altitudes, and take considerably longer than the time required for the impacts to occur. These findings have considerable implications for managers. They suggest, for example, that unless managers have a very large area at their disposal, it will be difficult to rotate areas of use, designating some as off limits to visitors while they recover.

THE SIGNIFICANCE OF ENVIRONMENTAL IMPACTS

The purpose of this section is to examine the significance and implications of the impacts which have already been discussed. Many of the impacts of recreation which have been described are individually small, although cumulatively they may result in substantial changes in the environment. While it has been common for concern to be expressed about the adverse effects of other developments on recreational environments, (witness, as was mentioned above, the public hearings about the extension of road and rail networks in the western national parks), the impacts of recreation have often been viewed, sometimes erroneously, as relatively benign, particularly when recreation takes place at low densities. In consequence, they have not usually been of major concern in most legal assessments of environmental impact.

Major tourist developments, without question, can have adverse impacts upon the environment, and specific recreation projects, such as the development of ski areas in the national parks of western Canada (Bella 1987, 121-7), have been the object of much controversy. Although requirements vary considerably from place to place, many countries now require environmental impact statements to be prepared in situations where projects or policies appear as if they might put the quality of the environment at risk (Mitchell and Turkheim 1977, Mitchell 1979, 228-55). In Canada, both the federal and provincial governments have legislation requiring environmental impact statements to be prepared in certain circumstances and, even if projects are legally exempt, the climate of opinion is such that most major projects will have their environmental consequences scrutinized in one way or another.

Most recreationers are gregarious. While there is a minority who stray far from the beaten track, even in wilderness settings the majority are concentrated in a relatively small area. This means that most impacts are also highly concentrated spatially. However, there is a tendency for visitors to congregate in highly valued areas such as shorelines and viewpoints, so that while most impacts of recreation are relatively localized they often occur in highly valued places. Nonetheless, most visitors appear not to be adversely affected by many of the changes which have been described above, for they continue to return to the same locations. Conversely, the quality of the experience of a minority of users may be destroyed by quite small modifications to the environment which they deem to be unacceptable.

Both accidental and purposeful environmental modifications which are acceptable to most users of an urban park may be deemed by the same individuals to be inappropriate if found in a wilderness setting. Also, there may be little relationship between the magnitude of impacts as measured quantitatively by scientists, and their salience to users with very different goals and objectives. In fact, the recreating public may even employ different measures from the scientist. For example, in the case of water quality, the scientist may be measuring turbidity, pH value, coliform counts, and biochemical oxygen demand, whereas the recreating public may take their cues from colour, smell, temperature, and the quantity of debris in the water. The interpretation of the significance of results may also vary dramatically, as is shown when people continue to bathe at placarded beaches (Barker 1971); users may be prepared to accept the risk, and the probability of being harmed by the degraded environment may be less than the probability of being involved in an automobile accident on the way to the beach. Thus, relationships between human behaviour and environmental modifications are not straightforward, and management of the interactions between the environment and people at leisure continue to pose challenging questions for researchers and for the managers of recreation sites.

The degree to which environmental modification is acceptable to potential users is a function of the experiences which they hope to gain from use of the resource. It is common for goals to vary to such a degree that real conflicts occur between potential users whose objectives are so antagonistic that compromise may not be possible. Recreation may be viewed as competing with other potential uses of the scarce resources of land and water. Conflicts between preservation and use; between forestry, mining, and recreation; between commercial and sport fishing; between agriculture and the development of second homes; and between hunting for sport and subsistence are just some among numerous possible examples of competition between recreation and other types of resource use. Careful management may permit the co-existence of different activities and a sharing of resources.

Multiple use of resources usually involves the segregation of users spatially, as in the case of buffer zones to separate active logging from recreation, or temporally, when snowmobiling takes place on agricultural land during the winter season. Where true multiple use takes place, such as the simultaneous use of lakes for recreation and flood control, there is usually some loss in utility for each function, although total net benefits to society may be greater than from allocation of the resource to a single use. However, tensions between users are seldom completely eliminated and conflicts over the allocation of resources between recreation and other uses are usually resolved through the political process.

Recreation researchers have devoted greater attention to conflicts within recreation than to investigating conflicts between recreation and other resource uses (Owens 1985). Lucas' (1964) study of users and managers of the Boundary Waters Canoe Area in Minnesota was one of the earliest studies in this genre and, as Jackson has pointed out earlier in this volume, it still merits attention. Since the publication of Lucas' study, a growing literature has evolved concerning the environmental perceptions of recreationists. Much of this literature has considered individuals participating in different types of recreation, often making a distinction between mechanized and non-mechanized activities. Attention has been drawn to differences in the experiences sought and resulting conflicts between such groups as snowmobilers and cross-country skiers (Jackson and Wong 1982); sailors, power boaters, water skiers, and fishermen (Owens 1977, Gramman and Burdge 1981); hikers and riders of trail bikes; and campers using different types of equipment (Clark, Hendee, and Campbell 1971). The research has generally confirmed the broad findings of Lucas. However, there is a danger that injudicious reporting of survey results may lead to the development and perpetuation of myths. For example, it is usually concluded that mechanized forms of recreation are more demanding than non-mechanized activities. This is a half-truth. While mechanized recreations usually require larger areas and may make greater environmental impacts than non-mechanized forms, their devotees are less likely to require a pristine environment and are more likely to be tolerant of the presence of large numbers of other users. But to conclude that they do not appreciate the environment is to perpetuate a falsehood. Rather, they prefer a different relationship with the environment and their preferred experience may be derived from a different mix of personal, environmental, and social components.

Similarly, wilderness camping with fly-in access, space blankets, and freeze-dried food may be just as dependent on modern technology as other forms of camping. Nor is it clear to this author why those who appreciate a comfortable bed should, automatically, fail to appreciate a natural environment. A well-designed lodge may be much less taxing on the environment than many of the eyesores which currently masquerade as campgrounds. The moral is that wilderness devotees, who have been responsible for much of this research, should be more careful to separate their own values from those of their respondents than has sometimes been the case in the past.

Some researchers, such as Dunlap and Heffernan (1975) and Jackson (1986, 1987), have examined more broadly based values held by participants in different recreations and their attitudes towards the environment and environmental issues, and McKechnie (1977) has developed and tested an instrument for measuring environmental dispositions. Jackson discusses environmental attitudes in some detail in this volume so that, other than to draw attention to the imprecise use of terminology, which continues to plague the whole area of so-called "perception" research (Schiff 1971), the reader is referred to his contribution for a thorough discussion of this topic.

Careful analyses reveal that participants in the same activity may have very different expectations and experiences. Bryan (1979) developed the concept of specialization to provide some order to this topic. He proposed that levels of specialization can be distinguished within any activity. He defined recreation specialization as "a continuum of behavior from the general to the particular, reflected by equipment and skills used in the sport and activity setting preferences." (Bryan 1979, 29). Roggenbuck, Smith, and Wellman (1980) used recreational specialization as the conceptual basis for their study of Virginia canoeists, Graefe (1980) employed it in an investigation of fishermen, Kauffman and Graefe (1984) applied it to canoeists, O'Neill-Mayer (1985) to scuba divers, Donnelly, Vaske, and Graefe (1986) to boaters, and Williams and Huffman (1985), with mixed success, to hikers. Grimm (1987) has provided a useful review of this literature, linked it to depreciative behaviour (Roggenbuck, Smith, and Wellman 1980; Christensen and Clark, 1983), displacement and succession (Schreyer 1979; Becker 1981; Anderson and Brown 1984), and examined these concepts in the context of Nahanni National Park Reserve.

Managers have a number of options open to them in manipulating the recreation-environment interface in an attempt to provide recreational experiences compatible with their mandates. They can modify the environment, for example, by planting vegetation, seeding and watering campsites, stocking fish, or improving habitat for desired species. Also they can attempt to modify the behaviour of visitors. Such an approach can be divided into two main strategies: manipulative and regulatory. Regulatory controls define where, when, and how people may recreate. Manipulative strategies are more subtle and, in many ways, more attractive. They are "less obtrusive practices that control the intensity of use without directly interfering with the user's perceived freedom of choice" (Gilbert, Peterson, and Lime 1972, 136). A bewildering variety of management strategies has been suggested as appropriate to wilderness areas, and many of these have been reviewed by Hendee, Stankey, and Lucas (1978). However, this author is not aware of any systematic attempt to assess the extent to which various strategies have been adopted, their relative success, and the circumstances which influence their usefulness.

Much of the literature on the environmental impacts of recreation has developed with the notion of carrying capacity in mind. Carrying capacity, as mentioned by other authors in this volume, has been variously defined but can be considered to be the maximum number of people which an area can support without an unacceptable decline in the quality of the environment or the quality of the recreational experience. The carrying capacity concept is particularly interesting in that it is an attempt to combine human and environmental components within one measure. Shelby and Heberlein (1986) have provided one of the more comprehensive discussions of the topic from a behavioural perspective, including consideration of the tenuous relationship between crowding and satisfaction. Unfortunately, while interest in carrying capacity generated a large literature on environmental impacts and drew attention to the need for managers to specify the goals for their sites with clarity, the failure to develop satisfactory methods for measuring capacity and, more basically, the growing belief that areas do not have an inherent capacity, have led to the notion of carrying capacity falling into increasing disfavour (Wall 1982b). Limits of acceptable change (Stankey and McCool 1984) and, particularly, the recreation opportunity spectrum (Driver *et al.* 1987) are concepts which incorporate a continuum of recreation-environment interactions and which are attracting an increasing number of devotees, particularly in the United States. However, they are not the only contenders in the quest to develop an integrated and widely applicable conceptual base for the planning and management of recreation-environment interactions. Others include the Visitor Impact Management framework (Graefe, Kuss, and Loomis 1985) and the Visitor Activity Management process (Graham, Nilsen, and Payne 1987), which is in process of application by the Canadian Park Service. Thus, research on environmental aspects of outdoor recreation is currently in a transitional stage. However, both from the perspective of the development of conceptual bases to further the understanding of interrelationships between recreation and the environment, and from the viewpoint of providing planners and managers with tools which will assist them in their decision-making, there is strong evidence that considerable progress has been made.

CONCLUSIONS

The large land and water area and the relatively small population of Canada may lead one to think that the environmental impacts of recreation are less pressing in Canada than elsewhere. It is true that that Canada still possesses large areas with attractive outdoor recreational environments, but this should not be a cause of complacency, for many of these areas are not very accessible to the majority of the people. The population of Canada is concentrated in a small number of places on the southern margins of the country and many of its needs, including most demands for outdoor recreation opportunities, must be satisfied in close proximity to a few urban centres. Population continues to grow, both naturally and through immigration, standards of living are very high relative to most countries, and pressures for resource exploitation are increasing from many directions, not only recreation. Great vigilance, careful management, and public education will be needed to ensure that recreational areas within reach of most people are not degraded.

Furthermore, Canada is a northern country. Many areas have thin soils, short growing seasons, and slow rates of regeneration. Once such areas are damaged, they take an extremely long time to recover. Nowhere is this more true than in areas of permafrost, where complete recovery may take centuries, rather than years or decades. In such situations, we would be wise to consider very carefully the best way to play the game.

Chapter 8

Social Impacts

Brian Keogh
département de géographie
Université de Moncton

Social Impacts

INTRODUCTION

Since both outdoor recreation and tourism involve travel, participants are often brought into contact with other individuals and groups, either during the travel phases of their experience or at the destination area. The values, perceptions, and attitudes of participants may differ significantly from those of the people they meet so that the social transactions arising from such encounters can have important effects on the lives of both parties involved, contributing over time to modifications in lifestyles, family and community relationships, value systems, behaviour, and even cultural characteristics. For the indigenous populations of destination areas, these effects may be compounded by more immediate changes in their lifestyle brought about by the creation of an infrastructure to cater to the needs of the visitors. Such social consequences of tourism and recreation are collectively referred to as socio-cultural impacts or, more commonly, social impacts.

Though the impacting process is not one-way and impacts may accrue to both visitors and those they encounter (for example, World Tourism Organization 1984), from a general planning perspective the most significant impact is that felt by residents of the destination area. If visitors experience negative impacts from encounters with others on a trip, they can avoid such impacts in the future by not repeating the experience. However, for the residents of destination areas who experience negative social impacts the solution is obviously not so simple. Frequently, such impacts are imposed upon them and can have an important effect on their attitudes towards tourists and the tourist industry. Social impacts must therefore be carefully monitored if tourism involving host communities is to be a truly renewable resource (Murphy 1983).

It is not surprising, then, that most social impact research to date has concentrated on the effects of tourism and outdoor recreation on the indigenous population of destination areas, and it is this form of impact which is the concern of the present chapter. More specifically, the chapter attempts to identify the major types of social impact arising from tourism and outdoor recreation within Canada and to assess their implications for planning and management. To achieve these aims, however, it is first necessary to better define how such impacts arise. With this in view the subject will now be placed within a wider context and provided with an appropriate conceptual framework.

Although the tourism and recreation industry has been one of the world's leading growth industries since World War II, studies dealing with the social impacts are relatively recent, most appearing over the past fifteen years. In the 1960s, in Canada as elsewhere, most analyses of tourism were of an economic nature, and by means of economic growth charts tourism was more often than not presented in a very favourable light. As a result, planning tended to be very much demand-oriented and focused largely on how to attract visitors to an area rather than on the consequences of their demands on the destination areas.

It was not until the work of Young (1973) that attention was drawn to the fact that tourism could have consequences other than economic blessings. The pendulum then tended to swing the other way, with many studies of the 1970s taking a more critical and sometimes negative look at tourism's impacts. Sociologists and anthropologists began seriously researching the human aspects of tourism development, bringing with them an entirely different perspective from that of the economists of the previous decade. As Thurot (1975) observed, for the social anthropologist the golden age of many host societies was past and commercial tourism was threatening the last vestiges, while for the economist the golden age was yet to come for those societies opting for tourism development.

The excesses of optimism and pessimism of the 1960s and 1970s prompted Mings (1978) to call for more meaningful impact studies and a more balanced view of tourism's consequences. His call appears to have been heeded, for today a fairly substantial literature exists from which a more balanced perspective is beginning to emerge. In the field of social impact, particularly noteworthy contributions have been the reviews by de Kadt (1979) and Noronha (1975, 1979). Such contributions have also had an effect on planning, as different levels of government have begun to recognize the need to incorporate resident attitudes into socially responsible tourism development programs.

The growing number of case studies and syntheses of empirical research has also enabled conceptual and methodological difficulties to be identified and has encouraged clearer thinking and a more unified approach to research. In this area, both Butler (1979) and Mathieson and Wall (1982) and Murphy (1985) have made most useful contributions. The work of these authors provides a basis for the development of the conceptual framework presented below.

CONCEPTUAL FRAMEWORK

As suggested above, the social impacts of tourism and recreation on destination areas arise in two main ways (Figure 1): from the encounter between residents (host population) and visitors and infrastructure development.

The impacts arising from the encounter between residents and visitors are influenced on the one hand by the characteristics of the visitor and on the other by those of the destination area and its residents.

Visitor Characteristics

The visitor characteristics of most significance to social impact studies are those which influence the degree, frequency, and type of interaction with the host population. These may be identified as follows: i) socio-economic characteristics;   ii) type of activity;   iii) length of stay;   iv) number of visitors.

i)   Socio-economic   characteristics: Include   levels   of affluence, attitudes, behaviour, expectations, and desires. Encounters between visitors and residents sometimes reveal substantial differences between the two groups, which may be potential sources of impact. Material differences, for example, may encourage exploitation of the visitors or foster a servile attitude on the part of the hosts. Furthermore, as de Kadt (1979, 66) observes, tourists often adopt a standard of living while on vacation which is above their normal level during the rest of the

Figure 1: Social Impacts -- A Conceptual Framework

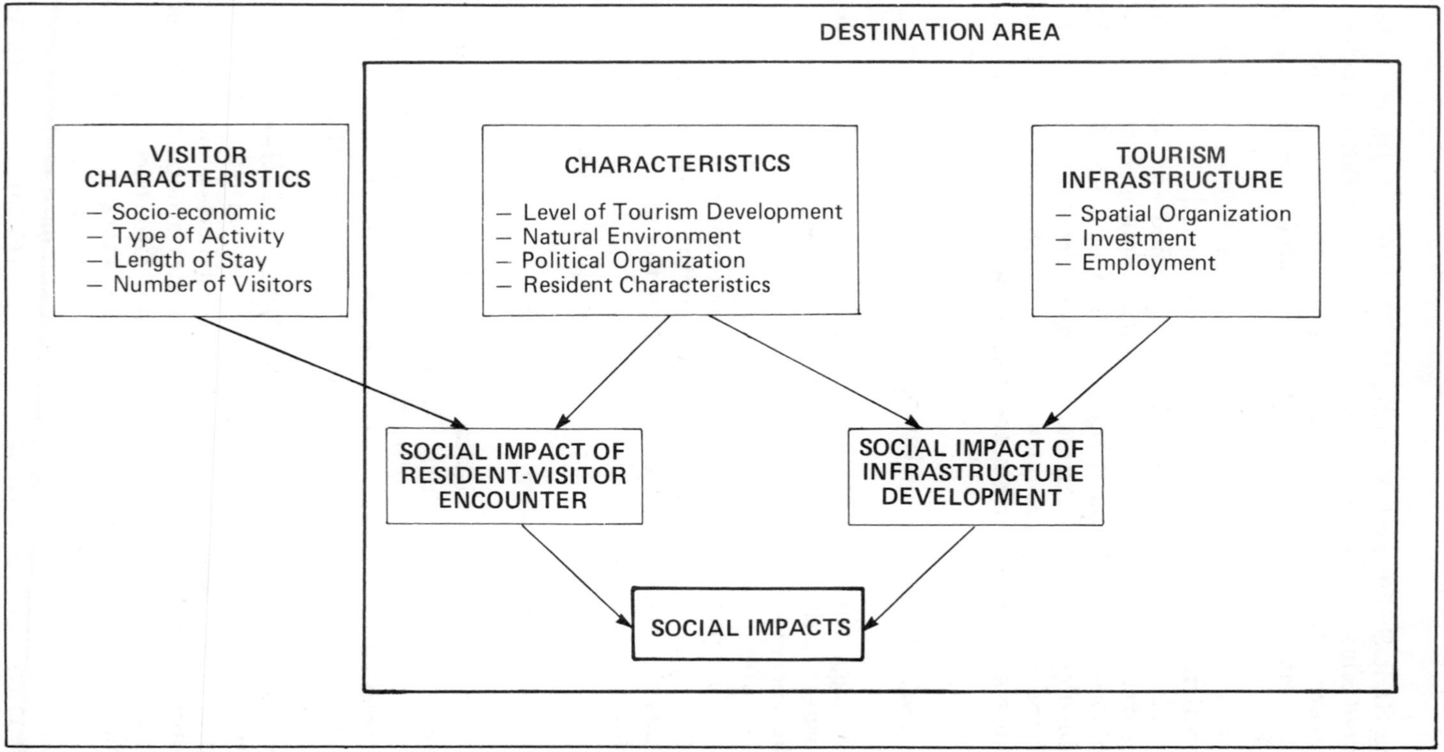

year, thereby exaggerating the differences in living standards between themselves and the indigenous population. Although in Canada the differences in the standard of living between hosts and visitors is not generally as great as in developing countries, the freer spending habits of tourists can engender unhealthy levels of commercialization among host populations, as Cheng (1980, 78) has observed in Banff.

Differences in attitudes and behaviour between visitor and resident populations reflect, in part, the general cultural or subcultural differences between the visitor-generating region and the destination area. Thus, in a study of tourism on Manitoulin Island, Ontario, Owens (1981, 139) suggested that many aspects of tourism acknowledged by residents as having a negative impact, such as the demanding attitudes of tourists, were associated with visitors' urban lifestyles. Attitudinal and behavioural differences are also partly due to the different perspectives of host and visitor at the time of the encounter, in that one is in the home environment and not necessarily at leisure, while the other is away from home and at leisure. As Butler (1979: 372) notes:

> Visitors to an area are transient and temporary, and are there for the pursuit of pleasure, relatively free of responsibilities, and under little or no sense of obligation to or dependence on the local area. The indigenous population, especially those not involved with recreation, often the majority of the population in many areas, perceive the area as their home, the source of their livelihood and a place in which they often invested time and money to shape in a particular way.

It has also been suggested that visitors' attitude and behaviour patterns are influenced by expectations and desires. Visitors' expectations are related to the images they hold of the areas they visit (de Kadt 1979, 53, de Burlo 1980, 25-31). In the case of mass tourism, the image of an area's attractions tends to be standardized and often unauthentic or staged (Cohen 1979a, 26), having been created specifically to fit a "tour package" (Duncan 1978). Here the role of intermediaries in the tourist industry (tour operators, travel agents, guides) is particularly important, though it is equally certain that the images marketed by most government organizations responsible for promoting tourism do not always correspond entirely to reality. Thus Papson (1981), in an analysis of tourism development policies in Nova Scotia and Prince Edward Island, has suggested that socio-cultural reality is redefined by the governments' marketing techniques and becomes "spurious." The impact of such images on tourist behaviour and attitudes is not clear, but, as Listfield (1979) noted in a study of American visitors to Quebec City, they may contribute to negative behaviour as the tourists finds that their preconceptions of the culture they are visiting are not confirmed.

Visitors' behaviour and attitudes may also be strongly governed by their motives or desires in visiting an area. Experiences sought are many and varied an observation which has inspired a number of tourist typologies (Plog 1972, Cohen 1972, Smith 1977, Cohen 1979b). In general, the experience sought is reflected in the way the visitors organizes their trip, their style of travel, and, more important from the point of view of social impact, their ability to adapt to local norms and their desire for contact with the host population. Thus, using Cohen's typology, based on the level of interaction sought (Cohen 1972), it is the drifter who tends to shun contact with the tourist establishment, organizes his or her own itinerary and means of travel, and generally makes the greatest efforts to integrate with and understand the residents of the area he or she is visiting. Contacts are individual and spontaneous and may be a positive agent of cultural exchange, though overall impact tends to be limited on account of the small numbers of such visitors. At the other end of the spectrum, the organized mass tourist is the least adventurous and does not seek contact with the local population, preferring instead the security and familiarity of congregating with fellow tourists in the facilities provided by the tourist establishment, creating what Smith (1977, 6) has termed a "tourist bubble."

In Canada, the mass tourist is most conspicuous at the major destination areas, such as Banff, Niagara Falls, and Quebec City. The experiences sought by the visitors here do not generally require or promote much direct contact with local residents. Even in Quebec City, where the experience is undoubtedly more of a cultural one, most tourists interact mainly with other tourists in a "tourist bubble" centred on the Chateau Frontenac and the rue Saint-Louis. As Gazillo (1981, 117) commented: "It is the image of rue Saint-Louis that is sold to tourists; the stone walls, Victorian houses, extensive restorations, exquisite cuisine, propriety, and all that is redolent of history." This is not the place for the drifter. He or she will more likely be found in rue Saint-Jean, symbolic of Quebec's "culture populaire" and frequented mainly by Quebeckers.

ii) Type of activity: Different activities make different demands on the residents and environment of a destination area. Thus, some forms of ethnic or cultural tourism, such as a visit to the Canadian North to learn about and experience Inuit lifestyle and customs, may involve considerable contact with the indigenous population. Some forms of recreational tourism, on the other hand, may be very much natural-resource-oriented and involve relatively little contact with the local population apart from those members working in the tourist industry and related services. The type of activity thus not only influences the level of contact but also where the contact takes place and, hence, with what members of the host population.

iii) Length of stay: Generally, longer stays in a destination area promote more personal, less superficial contacts between hosts and visitors. Of particular relevance here is the type of tourist. Thus, Cohen (1974, 544) describes the institutionalized or mass tourist as basically a sightseer, visiting several destinations within one trip. The stays are short and the social contacts limited. For example, a study of American visitors to Quebec City (Listfield 1979) found that the average stay was three days and suggested that such a time constraint was partly responsible for most Americans seeing the city as merely a series of symbols and monuments.

iv) Number of visitors: Visitors can exert an impact on a host population simply by virtue of their numbers. As numbers increase so do the pressures on local resources and infrastructure. Facilities become congested and the environment may suffer deterioration through overuse. Contacts between hosts and visitors may become strained. For Smith (1977, 12), a critical point is reached with respect to cultural impact when visitors begin to outnumber hosts.

Destination Area Characteristics

Characteristics of the destination area capable of influencing social impact may be identified as follows: natural environment features, political organization, level of tourist development.

i) Natural environment features: Climate and physical landscape influence the types of activity possible in an area and ultimately the level of use that can be supported before an unacceptable deterioration in quality occurs in either the physical environment or the experience gained by users. Where residents number among the users, increasing visitor levels may therefore create stresses.

Climate also governs the length of the visitor season. Where the season is long, late-season contacts tend to lose their spontaneity and become less social and more economic in nature. However, where the season is short, resident populations tend to show more tolerance to the demands of visitors and the tourist industry, knowing that any disruption to their lives is only short-lived. In Canada, the season for summer outdoor recreation activities is rarely more than three months and is probably a factor contributing to generally positive attitudes in summer resort towns (Keogh 1982, 330). Relatively short visitor seasons also lessen the attraction of an area for large commercial enterprises, with the result that there tends to be a greater degree of local involvement in the tourist industry and hence more positive local attitudes towards visitors.

ii) Political organization: An important consideration here is the level of involvement of the local population in planning and decision-making processes affecting tourism development. If input is solicited from the local population and tourist organizations, attitudes tend to be more favourable. However, tourism development may involve several levels of government and sometimes decisions may appear to be imposed from the outside. As will be shown later, the establishment of several of Canada's parks has encountered a number of problems in this respect. Frequently, regional and national planning authorities approach tourism development with different perspectives from those of local organizations. At the national level, the creation of jobs and a healthy trade balance are of prime concern, while at the regional level, although an attempt is made to take into account the needs, capabilities, and desires of communities within the region, planners are not always aware of the attitudes and aspirations of local inhabitants. As Murphy (1981) has shown, however, this does not mean that the inhabitants of destination areas are necessarily against tourism development. Often, negative attitudes may be dispelled simply by providing more information on proposed developments and giving local inhabitants adequate opportunity to provide input in the planning process.

iii)   Level of tourism development: The level of tourism development is important for a number of reasons. First, it influences the infrastructural demands, and hence impact, on the local community. Second, it is often related to the degree of local involvement in decision-making processes and in the tourist industry. Generally, local involvement decreases as the level of tourism development increases, tending to foster more distant attitudes to both visitors and the tourist industry. Third, the level of development is related to the number and types of tourists attracted to the area.

In an endeavour to facilitate understanding of the changes that occur in a community as tourism development takes place, observers have proposed that destination areas undergo cycles of evolution (Butler 1980) or pass through development stages (Noronha 1979). It has also been suggested by Doxey (1975, 195) that concomitant changes take place in host-visitor relationships, with the host's attitude to the visitor ranging from "euphoria," in the initial stages of development, through "apathy" and "irritation," to "antagonism" in the later stages as more and more visitors and visitor facilities place increasing strain on the local community. Doxey arrived at this hypothesis following research undertaken in Barbados in the West Indies and Niagara-on-the-Lake in Ontario, Canada. His observations in Niagara-on-the-Lake (Doxey 1976), for example, led him to believe that, after twenty-five years of increasing visitor pressure, the community was rapidly approaching and might soon pass the irritation stage unless appropriate planning measures were introduced.

More recent empirical research in Canada has also suggested that destination communities have limits with respect to their tolerance to tourism and that growth beyond such limits may lead to negative social impacts (Cooke 1982). However, as a number of observers have pointed out, threshold levels are dependent upon given sets of conditions and these conditions may change or be changed through planning and management strategies (Getz 1983, Haywood 1986).

Though models of tourism provide useful conceptualizations of trends observed in many areas, Cohen (1979a) has warned against overgeneralization, believing that more research should be conducted into discovering different types of basic dynamics, such as the attitudes of local inhabitants to outsiders, even before the advent of tourism, and the way in which tourism has been introduced into the area. A further factor that may influence host attitudes is the speed of tourism development. When changes are abrupt, the destination area and its inhabitants may have difficulty adapting to increasing visitor flows, a situation that can lead to stress and negative attitudes on the part of both residents and visitors.

Resident Characteristics

The characteristics of the resident population that may have a significant bearing on social impact include religious affiliation, moral conduct, levels of health and safety, strength of local culture including language, traditions, and gastronomic practices, and perceptions of and attitudes towards visitors.

A destination area with a strong and viable local culture is generally more resistant to change when exposed to visitors from different cultural backgrounds. If the area also has its own language (Lundgren 1973, 5), this will act as a barrier to communication for visitors and hence further reduce impact. Within Canada, Quebec has both a strong culture, related in part to the numerical strength of its people, and its own language, so that despite large influxes of tourists from outside the province, it has until now been able to largely maintain its cultural identity.

The situation for the minority cultures of Canada's native peoples, however, is more delicate. The potential for cultural impact from tourism and recreation is considerably greater. Two reasons may be suggested. First, the majority of tourists, within Canada as elsewhere, are from metropolitan regions, relatively affluent and mobile, with urban lifestyles and values. The potential impact of such visitors on the residents of destination areas will therefore increase as they travel farther away from the core areas to regions of less affluence, with more rural values and less dominant cultures or subcultures. The potential for greatest socio-cultural impact will therefore be in Canada's peripheral regions inhabited by minority cultures such as the Inuit, regions referred to by Graburn (1976, 1) as the Fourth World. Second, the "native peoples" cultures are particularly fragile because of their members' lack of numerical strength. Even if many groups inhabit peripheral areas and are therefore at some distance from the tourist-generating regions, communities are so small that the visitor/ resident ratio can easily reach a level that poses a threat to the survival of the culture. From the above observations, it may be suggested that the potential for social impact on host communities increases along a continuum from core areas to peripheral areas (Figure 2). Such a model does not imply, however, that social impact cannot be important in cities. Here the number of visitors may be considerable and activities may be concentrated in a limited district of the city, such as the Old Town in Quebec City or Gastown in Vancouver. In general, however, it is suggested that the cultural gap between city dwellers and visitors (who are also mostly city dwellers) is not as great.

Residents' perceptions and attitudes regarding visitors are in part a product of the area's general culture and of the perceived benefits and costs of tourism in the community. They may also be related to more general attitudes to outsiders, perhaps even before the advent of tourism. Thus, Smith (1977, 70) notes that historic Eskimo contacts with American whalers and gold-seekers had generally been profitable, a situation which facilitated the first contacts with American tourists. Defert (1984) has even suggested quantifying contacts with all outsiders with a view to better understanding host attitudes to tourists.

Infrastructure Development

Visitors to an area must be fed, transported, provided with equipment for certain activities, entertained, and, in the case of tourists, offered accommodation. The infrastructure created for these purposes can have an important effect on the host community. Three main areas of impact may be identified, relating to investment, space, and staffing requirements.

Investment in tourism infrastructure can be considerable and often means opportunities forgone in other sectors. Opportunity costs must therefore be taken into account in the planning and decision-making process and weighed with other anticipated costs against anticipated benefits if a balanced perspective is to be reached. As stated previously, deliberations must involve the participation of the local population.

Benefits accruing to the host community from investment in the tourism industry will arise mainly through the creation of jobs and increased revenues, and the provision of new or

Figure 2: Spatial Aspects of Cultural Impact

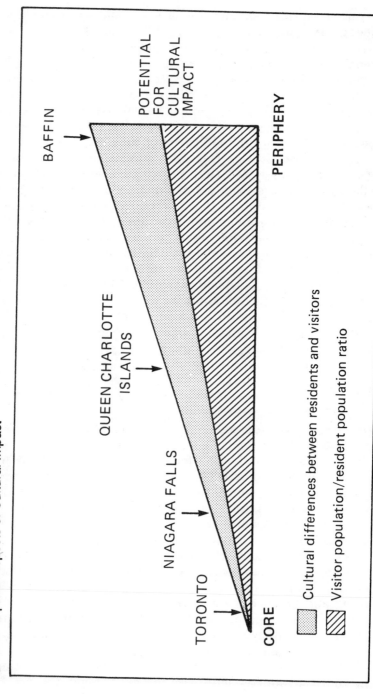

TORONTO   NIAGARA FALLS   QUEEN CHARLOTTE ISLANDS   BAFFIN

CORE   PERIPHERY

POTENTIAL FOR CULTURAL IMPACT

Cultural differences between residents and visitors

Visitor population/resident population ratio

improved facilities and services, such as parks, hospitals, and roads. Investment may also take the form of restoration or renovation of historic buildings within the community, and this too may benefit hosts and visitors alike. Thus, the renovation of Halifax's Historic Properties and waterfront has provided enjoyment for both tourists and many local residents.

Infrastructure development also makes considerable demands on local space. Several implications may be noted. First, depending on the availability of land, infrastructure requirements may cause inflation of land prices, sometimes pricing local bidders out of the market. Conversely, where the infrastructure is perceived as having a negative impact on the local landscape, possibly through increased noise levels or visual pollution, its development may depress land values. This was one of the fears expressed by some residents near the site of Canada's Wonderland, near Toronto, before construction began (Roberts and Wall 1979).

Second, infrastructure demands may lead to some local inhabitants losing property or their rights to use land. In Canada, for example, the creation of many parks has involved expropriation, as with Kouchibouguac, Gros Morne, and Forillon National Parks, and the loss of traditional rights to hunt and fish as in most national parks and many provincial parks.

Third, tourism infrastructure serves as a permanent reminder of the tourist industry and may cause negative feelings among some residents even in the off-season when the tourists are no longer there. However, spatial planning can play an important role, for when infrastructure is physically and visually separated from the local population, attitudes tend to be more favourable. Spatial organization of course, also affects impacts during the season by either encouraging or discouraging contact between visitors and hosts.

Infrastructure development also brings change to the lives of local residents through the jobs and revenues it creates. Some jobs will be filled by local inhabitants, others by imported labour, the relative proportions of each depending on the level of tourism development. Generally, the more developed the industry in an area, the greater the involvement of outside interests, with national and international accommodation and restaurant chains employing a large proportion of imported labour. In this case, much of the profit and the benefits will not go to the local community, and residents may feel left out. However, where tourism remains small-scale, big business is less attracted and most jobs and benefits will go to the local population. The social impact of such a development will therefore tend to be positive, particularly in areas of low revenues and high unemployment. Thus, in Kent County, New Brunswick, where high unemployment had for long been the norm, it is easy to understand why most local residents, though admittedly not all, welcomed the establishment of Kouchibouguac National Park, in the early 1970s.

Whatever a community's role in tourism development, however, it is important to remember that the level of involvement, and the associated benefits and costs, will vary significantly among individuals within the host population. Thus, local business people and individuals who find employment in the tourist industry will often hold more favourable attitudes than others with regard to both the industry and its clients (Kendall and Var 1984). For them, negative aspects will be more than offset by personal gains. It is not unusual, therefore, to find conflicts arising between different elements of the host population. In Quebec City, for example, a citizens' group was formed in 1976 to combat the tourism industry's encroachment into residential districts of the Old Town. More recently, the eviction of tenants in Vancouver's East Side district by property owners wishing to capitalize on providing accommodation for Expo '86 visitors, was another flagrant example of tourism's potential for creating conflict within host communities.

Further conflicts may arise between the local population and imported labour. Although migrant labour may have a positive impact on the local community by bringing in new ideas, energy, and increased spending power, this is rare, and more often than not the overall social impact is negative. The reasons for this are several. First, the indigenous population may resent outsiders filling jobs in preference to locals. Second, it has been noted (Cheng 1980, 78) that transient labour has no responsibilities or obligations to the local community and therefore takes little part in community life. Third, outsiders often have different values, attitudes, and behavioural patterns from those of permanent residents, and this too may be a source of conflict. Moreover, since transient workers generally stay for the season, contacts with residents are often less superficial than those between residents and tourists, so that their impact on the host community, particularly on fellow workers who are residents, can be quite considerable. Outsiders who decide to take up permanent residence may have an even greater impact (Packer 1974, 241).

TYPES OF SOCIAL IMPACT

The consequences of tourism and recreation development for the indigenous population of destination areas are many and varied. The physical, economic, and socio-cultural dimensions of residents' lives may be affected in ways that are tangible or intangible, positive or negative. However, not every individual in a community will be affected in the same way. Some may not perceive any impact at all, while others may perceive several impacts but not necessarily in the same way. Furthermore, as changes occur in interrelationships between residents and visitors, possibly as a result of changes in the number and types of tourists, so too might perceptions of impacts alter over time.

As indicated in the foregoing conceptual framework, social impacts arise basically from interaction between a resident population on the one hand and visitors and infrastructure development on the other. Impacts arising from resident-visitor encounters may be further divided into two groups: those resulting from the physical presence or the number of visitors; those related to visitor characteristics or, more specifically, the differences between resident and visitor characteristics. In the following section, this categorization provides the basis for an analysis of the nature and dimensions of the social impacts of tourism and recreation within Canada. Subsequently, the relationships between impacts and individual and community attitudes will be examined.

Impacts Resulting From Physical Presence of Tourists

Visitor numbers impact on local populations in several ways. On the negative side, they exert pressure on facilities and resources, while on the positive side they are the source of economic benefits and may provide the impetus for the creation of new and improved facilities and services in a community.

i) Pressure on facilities: In destination areas, residents must often share facilities with visitors, resulting in congested roads, amenities, and stores, and overburdened services. Surveys among residents in Prince Edward Island (Abt Associates 1976), Stratford, Ontario (MacFarlane 1979), Manitoulin Island, Ontario (Owens 1981) and Shediac, New Brunswick (Keogh 1982), and observations at Niagara-on-the-Lake, Ontario (Doxey 1974) and Banff, Alberta (Cheng 1982) have all indicated these problems to be among the most frequently cited negative aspects of local tourism development. On the roads, traffic is slowed, parking becomes difficult, manners deteriorate, and there are more accidents. Thus, in a study of the popular east coast beach resort of Shediac, it was observed that the journey across town, which normally takes little more than five minutes, required thirty minutes during the summer season, and accident figures for July were more than 50% higher than for any other month (Keogh 1982, 326). Not surprisingly, 95% of the residents interviewed complained about the summer traffic.

Among resort towns, congestion is perhaps nowhere greater than in Banff. The town's permanent resident population of around four thousand is swamped by summer visitors; at the height of the season, overnight populations may reach thirty thousand. The atmosphere is captured well by Cheng (1982, 77-78):

> Pedestrians saunter along the sidewalks window-shopping, people-watching, eating ice cream, and looking for things to do. They amble across streets at the same speed. Traffic tie-ups become commonplace as oversized vehicles are laboriously maneuvered into narrow side streets. Erratic driving is the norm as "everyone is a tourist" and does not know where he is going or what lane he should be in. Unlike urban rush hour, where participants appear to be in a hurry, tourism congestion features a no-hurry mood which accentuates the frustration for people with errands or time constraints.

In stores and establishments frequented by visitors, queues and long waits are common. Particularly affected are the restaurants, cafes, liquor and food stores, post offices, and banks. The increased demand for goods and services may also result in negative impacts of a socio-economic nature. Thus, seasonal price inflation has been perceived by some residents of destination areas (Prince Edward Island, Stratford, Shediac), while in others (Banff) a double price system has been noted. Although the latter practice may not negatively affect the local population, it does nothing to enhance the area's image to outsiders. The demands of visitors may also lead to greater commercialization in a host community, with the creation of souvenir shops and sales of cheap and shoddy goods. Sometimes such a development may be to the detriment of services for the local population, as stores become geared to serving visitors.

Less tangible effects of increasing visitor numbers are changes in the form of exchanges in public places. Greater demand often leads to greater rush and a poorer quality of service. There is less or no time for socializing and exchanges become impersonal and purely commercial.

Visitors also put pressure on local police, fire, and ambulance departments, as well as on community services such as sewage disposal and health. Police and ambulance departments are called to deal with more accidents, particularly those involving traffic, while the police also have to contend with an increase in some forms of crime. A number of studies have examined the relationship between tourism and crime, and most seem to suggest that tourism does contribute to an increase in crime rates (Mathieson and Wall 1982, 150-1).

Although further research is needed to determine the exact nature of the relationship between tourism and crime, it seems likely that contributing factors are the increased number of targets for criminal activities during the visitor season, an increased potential for lucrative spoils, the decreased likelihood of detection, and a lack of a sense of responsibility or obligation towards the host community on the part of some visitors. This does not mean that holiday-makers are the sole culprits, however, for other outsiders and some locals (D'Amore Associates 1980, 97) may also be involved. In Banff, Cheng (1982, 79) noted that petty theft and vandalism were the most common crimes that police had to deal with, while in Penticton, British Columbia, it has been observed that most crimes, including assault, breaking and entering, and vandalism, increase in the summer (D'Amore Associates 1980, 93-94). In the latter resort, the local R.C.M.P., which takes on auxiliary staff during the summer, has responded with increased vigilance and has introduced stricter patrols to check anti-social behaviour, particularly among young visitors who tend to congregate in the town on summer weekends. Penticton residents believe that such preventive measures have improved the situation in recent years. In Niagara Falls, police estimated recently that seventy-five to one hundred prostitutes were on the streets during the tourist season (Hilts 1986). Prostitution and

associated violence threaten to tarnish the town's image and
have caused several businesses to close early and lose business
(Hilts 1985).

Community services such as sewage disposal and
maintenance (cleaning of streets and amenity areas) may also
become overburdened during the visitor season. Most surveys
conducted in Canada among residents of destination areas
revealed increased litter to be a fairly general problem of the
tourist season. Not only must streets be cleaned more regularly
but amenities such as parks and recreation areas, which in
some cases may include beach areas, must also be adequately
maintained. Visitor pressure on sewage disposal services may
sometimes require important structural changes to the system.
In Shediac, New Brunswick, for example, lack of adequate
sewage disposal facilities for a dense summer cottage
population to the east of the town presented a serious health
hazard and a pollution threat to local beaches in the late 1960s. In
the 1970s the problem was corrected by extending and upgrading
existing facilities.

ii) Pressure on local resources: Visitor pressure on local
resources is expressed in two ways. First, visitors wishing to
buy land for recreational purposes may cause inflation of
prices. Those selling land will of course benefit from such a
situation, but it may cause resentment among local bidders. If
the land, once acquired, then lies idle for much of the year, the
resentment is likely to be even greater, particularly if it is good
agricultural land. Thus, on Prince Edward Island, this problem
led to measures being introduced by the provincial government
to limit access to land ownership by non-residents. Second,
visitors exert considerable pressure on local resources simply
by using them. Where the local population also uses the
resources there is potential for several forms of conflict.
Increasing levels of visitor use of a resource may cause
congestion and a deterioration in resource quality. Although
congestion need not necessarily have a detrimental impact on
the physical quality of a resource, it can have a deleterious effect
on the recreation experience of users. Noise levels increase and
the need for greater sharing means that individual freedom is
restricted. Some activities, such as power boating, are simply
not compatible with high densities of use.

Any form of restriction may prove to be particularly
resented by local residents, who often feel that they should have
some sort of priority over outsiders. This sentiment emerged in

a tourism impact study among residents of several small localities in British Columbia (D'Amore Associates 1980). In Kimberley and Williams Lake, for example, some residents felt that they were being robbed of "their" lakes by summer visitors. Similarly, in Penticton, British Columbia, residents felt alienated from local beaches because of influxes of summer visitors from lakeside motel and campground developments.

Increasing numbers of visitors can also have a detrimental effect on the quality of the resource and, hence, on the quality of the recreation experience. The negative environmental impacts of recreation and tourism are well documented elsewhere (Wall and Wright 1977, Mathieson and Wall 1982). Of particular relevance to the recreation experience of users is resource deterioration resulting from the trampling of vegetation, littering, pollution of water and beaches, and, in the case of fish and wildlife, disturbances to feeding and breeding habits and the depletion of stocks. Residents of small communities, particularly in more remote areas, often attach considerable value to the opportunities they have for fishing and hunting in the local area. Such activities are an integral part of local life, and should residents' enjoyment be impinged upon by outsiders, resentment may develop. Thus, a survey conducted on Manitoulin Island revealed that some residents felt that tourists increased the pressure on local hunting resources (Owens 1981, 113), while in Campbell River, B.C., it was observed that a common complaint among locals was that visitors, often identified as Americans, caught and canned too many salmon (D'Amore 1983, 149).

Serious conflicts have also arisen, and continue to arise, between visitors fishing and hunting for sport and indigenous populations who rely on fishing and hunting for food or as a source of income. In Newfoundland, for example, Overton (1980) has shown that conflicts over the hunting of caribou have a long history. Caribou hunting for food and commerce was important in the traditional fishing economy in many areas in the nineteenth and early twentieth centuries. From the late nineteenth century the caribou also came to be increasingly recognized as an important tourism resource, with sports hunters from outside the region injecting much-needed revenue into the local economy through licence fees and expenditures on accommodation, outfitting, and transport. It was not surprising, therefore, that the tourism industry was a driving force behind the gradual introduction of game laws to protect the caribou in the early twentieth century. Although these laws benefited some elements of the local population, namely sports hunters and those engaged in the tourism industry, they alienated many of the poorer residents or "poor settlers," who relied on caribou for food. The laws are applied uniformly throughout Newfoundland and Labrador, and continue to stir conflict today among both the whites and native populations.

The issue of native peoples' hunting and fishing rights is a particularly sensitive one in Canada, as such activities not only provide food but are also part of a traditional way of life. If these activities are threatened, the lifestyle and culture will be likewise endangered. Thus, in a study of tourism development in the Canadian North, commissioned by the Inuit Tapirisat of Canada, Butler (1975) concluded, among other things, that although Inuit might benefit from jobs and economic gains in several tourist activities, intensive consumptive forms of recreation, such as hunting and fishing, might lead to competition for resources and a consequent decline in traditional activities, unless appropriate development guidelines are followed. The strategy outlined for the development of tourism in the Northwest Territories reflects similar concerns (Government of the Northwest Territories 1983). It proposes to avoid serious conflict and interference with traditional Dene and Inuit land uses by placing special emphasis on community-based, non-consumptive "learn/observe/experience" activities.

Conflicts between commercial and sport fishermen are numerous and often long-standing. In New Brunswick, for example, depleted fish stocks and powerful lobbying on the part of sport fishing interests have resulted in periodic bans on commercial salmon fishing. Such bans allow salmon to escape upriver to spawning grounds and can thereby contribute to greatly improved catches by sport fishermen. Thus, a ban on commercial fishing in 1972 almost doubled the sport fishermen's catch for that year (N.B. Department of Tourism 1973). Other bans have followed, the latest having been in force since 1984. Sport fishing activities are not unrestricted, however, and since 1984 salmon over a certain size, usually females, must be released. Thus, although the ban is the result of overfishing by both commercial and sport fishermen and places restrictions on them both, the former, who are often local residents, are obviously more affected by it and therefore tend to harbour negative attitudes towards the sport fishermen, whom they view as instrumental in the imposition of the ban.

In Ontario, similar conflict exists between commercial and sport fishermen in Lake Erie. It has been suggested, however, that the conflict here may be based on perceptions by each user group that do not correspond to reality. Berkes (1984) found that although each group believes a conflict exists, neither the fishing areas used nor the composition of the respective catches shows any significant overlap.

iii) Economic benefits: Although visitors put pressure on the facilities and resources of host communities, they also represent the source of economic gains. Visitor demands for goods and services provide communities with increased revenues and create seasonal jobs, and can thereby contribute to an improved lifestyle for the beneficiaries. The economic benefits of tourism and outdoor recreation have been extensively documented in numerous reports and for most host communities in Canada, whether towns or cities; they are seen as the most significant advantage of local tourism development.

The impact on a destination area, and the residents' perception of this impact, is particularly important in the smaller communities. A study at Shediac, New Brunswick (Keogh 1982), for example, revealed that the majority of local businesses increased their takings during the summer and took on extra staff. The total number of employees increased by approximately 50%. Moreover, this positive aspect of tourism would appear to be appreciated by most residents: in an attitude survey, 97% of interviewees declared that they thought that the town was better off. Similarly, most respondents in a survey of Prince Edward Island residents saw tourism as a compatible sector of the Island's agriculture- and fishing-based economy and not as a threat to the labour needs of these activities as some critics had claimed (Abt Associates 1976, 43).

Tourism thus, has considerable potential for exerting a positive impact on the quality of life through the generation of income and employment. In some communities such as Niagara and Banff, it is already an economic mainstay, while for others it is seen to offer a viable option for future economic development. In Kimberley, B.C., for example, where the major employer, Sullivan Mine operated by Cominco Ltd., is due to close down in the year 2000, the municipal council, with firm backing from local citizens, has identified a year-round tourism industry as a feasible goal for future economic development (D'Amore 1983, 146).

iv) Improved facilities and services: Although visitors put pressure on a community's facilities and services, and may cause congestion and overloading, the increased demand may also lead to the provision of new and improved facilities and services and thereby contribute to an improved lifestyle for local inhabitants. Some stores, for example, may remain open all year round but rely largely on sales to visitors for their overall economic viability. Other services and amenities may be created primarily to attract and cater to visitors but may also provide enjoyment for residents. Festivals, sporting events, educational courses, and recreational activities are particularly popular. Two of the most successful festivals in Canada have been the Shakespeare and Shaw theatre festivals held every summer respectively at Stratford and Niagara-on-the-Lake in Ontario. These attract thousands of visitors each year but also provide enjoyment for many local residents. Such festivals may also attract new business firms to the area. In a 1972 survey of Stratford, about 40% of firms contacted concerning industrial location stated that social and cultural amenities had been definite factors in their decision to move to the town (MacFarlane 1979, 105).

Tourism development may also have a positive impact on social services and infrastructure in a host community. Fire and ambulance services, medical care, water supply and sewage disposal systems, and even transportation networks may require upgrading and extending to meet the needs of large numbers of visitors. Thus, the needs of tourists and the tourist industry were an important consideration in the decision to construct a new four-lane highway to link the east coast town of Shediac, New Brunswick, to Moncton and the Trans-Canada Highway in 1975.

A recent survey of the views of Alberta residents concerning tourism and its role in provincial development (Tourism Industry Association of Alberta 1985) also illustrates the positive impact it can have on amenities and infrastructure. Over 95% of residents interviewed considered that tourism had a beneficial effect on the quality and upkeep of attractions, and on the variety and quality of cultural activities and facilities, recreational and sports facilities, entertainment, and restaurants. Even in the Banff area, which experiences the heaviest tourist traffic in the province and where the disadvantages of tourism are probably the most apparent, the great majority of residents interviewed shared the views of other Alberta residents.

When tourism opens up areas to which access was previously difficult, such as the Canadian North, a number of other less direct impacts may also be noted. Imported goods and services may supplant or complement local goods and services, and emigration or, alternatively, immigration may be encouraged. As a result, old lifestyles may undergo profound changes. Indeed, as Packer (1974, 241) has pointed out, outsiders taking up residence can have a more profound effect on local values than host-visitor encounters.

Impacts Arising From Differences Between Visitors and Residents

As noted in the conceptual framework, visitors and residents may differ significantly with respect to levels of affluence, values, attitudes, and behaviour, and interaction between the two groups can produce both positive and negative impacts. On the positive side, it is frequently claimed that encounters between different social groups, cultures, and nationalities can lead to an exchange of ideas, promote better understanding, and be both socially enjoyable and educational. In Canada, the socio-cultural and economic differences dividing host communities and the visitors they receive are not generally as great as those in developing countries. This probably facilitates initial contacts, and once the contact has been made, the subcultural social differences that do exist between visitors and residents are often sufficient to make the encounter interesting and positive for both parties. Thus, the opportunities for meeting new people and exchanging ideas have frequently been cited by residents of destination areas in Canada as the most important positive aspect of tourism after the economic advantages (Abt Associates 1976, 42, Owens 1981, 91, Keogh 1982, 326). The social benefits of encounters with visitors can be particularly important for those residents who offer accommodation in their own homes. As Stringer (1981) has observed, the bed-and-breakfast phenomenon can be considerably more than just a commercial transaction. Thus, in Stratford, MacFarlane found that residents accommodating festival visitors in their own homes often perceived them not as tourists or strangers but rather as house guests (MacFarlane 1979, 112). Similarly, in a study of Niagara-on-the-Lake, Doxey (1974) noted that more personal relationships tended to exist between visitors and residents when local homes were used to lodge visitors.

Positive interaction between residents and visitors is also possible with rural tourism. In Canada, and particularly in Quebec (Moulin 1980), Manitoba, Ontario, New Brunswick, and Prince Edward Island, farm vacations have become increasingly popular over the past decade, providing the non-rural dweller with the opportunity to enjoy rural scenery, fresh air, and a certain tranquillity, to participate in rural sports, and to experience a different lifestyle. Since the latter aspect is one of the main aims of the farm vacation program, this type of holiday tends to attract people who are positively motivated towards learning to understand rural values, a situation which predisposes a more positive encounter. A positive impact on the hosts may be further reinforced by the fact that tourism provides the farmer with additional income and sometimes a form of protection from land-use conflicts, particularly in areas near urban centres. It is obviously in the interests of a city to maintain rural recreation areas which are easily accessible to its inhabitants (Ironside 1971, 3). Although little information exists on the impacts of rural tourism on host communities in Canada, it is generally felt that the farm vacation programs are particularly suited to breaking down some of the prejudices and promoting better understanding between rural and urban dwellers (Canadian Council on Rural Development 1975, 29). A survey among the residents of Prince Edward Island also revealed that farm vacationers were regarded as preferred types of tourists on the Island (Abt Associates 1976, 36).

The subcultural differences between residents and visitors, however, are not always a source of positive impact. Conflict can sometimes arise between the rural or small-town values of the indigenous populations of destination areas and the urban or metropolitan values of most visitors. As already observed, such differences can be further reinforced by the difference in attitudes of the two groups relating to the fact that one is away from home and at leisure, while the other is on home territory and not necessarily at leisure. Thus, Owens (1981, 139) noted that many of the problems of local tourism development perceived by residents of Manitoulin Island were related to the urban way of life of most visitors. Visitors' lack of understanding of and respect for the lifestyle of the rural environs of many destination areas can also cause conflicts. Generally, such conflicts are in unplanned situations, the visitors being in the area for reasons other than the enjoyment of the rural way of life. Thus, conflicts over access to land, damage to crops and property, disturbances to livestock, and illegal hunting and fishing are not uncommon occurrences. In Penticton, for example, although visitors provide income for fruit sellers at roadside stands, incidents have also been reported of fruit stealing and damage to trees and property (D'Amore Associates 1980, 92). Sometimes tourism's impact on farming may be more perceived than real. Thus, in the Manitoulin Island study, some residents felt that tourism had a negative impact on Island farming, but it was not a view generally supported by the farmers themselves (Owens 1981, 113).

Although it is probably safe to say that most resident-visitor encounters within Canada are between English-speakers, there is nevertheless a substantial number which involve other language groups and cultures. Perhaps most important from the point of view of tourism's social impact are those which take place in Quebec and in the territories of Canada's native peoples. Since most visitors are English-speaking Canadians or Americans, the cultural gap between host and visitor is significantly greater than elsewhere in Canada. Encounters between widely differing cultures provide considerable potential for intercultural communication as well as commercial transactions, which can be beneficial to both residents and visitors. Unfortunately, it is a potential that is not always realized.

Though there are distinct possibilities for intercultural communication when tourism juxtaposes two culturally different groups, in reality little exchange takes place (Mathieson and Wall 1982, 163). Instead, tourism is more often a disruptive force. Two reasons may be suggested, the first resulting from the visitors' lack of understanding of the culture they are visiting, the second related to the asymmetrical nature of the relationships between the two groups.

When visitors have an insufficient knowledge of the lifestyle and culture of the community they are visiting, they frequently adopt behaviour patterns which are viewed negatively by the indigenous population and may arouse resentment. Thus, in his study of American visitors to Quebec City, Listfield (1979) notes that the typical tourist sees the city as a series of symbols and monuments and does not really understand the visited environment because of his limited cultural horizons and the time constraints of his visit (the average length of stay is three days). His preconceptions of Quebec culture do not enable him to appreciate the values and perceptions of the local population and may be a basic cause of negative behaviour. Instrumental in the formation and reinforcement of a visitor's image of a destination area are the tourist guides and information brochures. Listfield suggests that these should provide a more faithful reflection of the values and perceptions that Quebec residents hold with respect to their environment.

Most contacts between Canada's native peoples and visitors have also tended to reveal the latter's lack of understanding of the visited environment. Although no systematic studies appear to have been carried out to determine native peoples' attitudes towards tourists, recent tourism development plans for the regions in which they live have all recognized the fragile nature of native communities and the need to incorporate the views of the indigenous population. Thus, the preparation of the Regional Tourism Development Strategy and Community Tourism Development Plans for the Baffin Region of the Northwest Territories (Marshall Macklin Monaghan Ltd. 1982) included a community involvement program which encouraged each community to express its opinions and concerns about tourism development. Among the many issues raised was the concern for the possibly intrusive effect of uncontrolled tourism on existing lifestyles, and it was suggested that tourists should know more about the likes and dislikes of the Inuit before they come and that they should not ask so many questions.

Particularly illustrative of tourism's potential to disrupt local lifestyles is the study of Eskimo tourism in Alaska by Smith (1977, 51-70). She observed, for example, that visitors to the small Inuit community of Kozebue were often insensitive to the local inhabitants' need for some privacy. Tired of being photographed and questioned, Inuit women erected barricades to provide a shield against tourists while carrying out their daily activities (Smith 1977, 59). Similar complaints about visitors' lack of understanding of native culture and lifestyle have also been voiced by the Haida Indians of the Queen Charlotte Islands in British Columbia (D'Amore Associates 1980, 122).

Tourism may also be a disruptive force when it exposes a fragile culture to a more dominant one. One result of such an encounter is the so-called demonstration effect by which changes occur in the attitudes, values, and behaviour of the host population as a result of observing tourists or the facilities built to cater to tourists. The tourists represent, in most cases, the dominant culture and are, therefore, considered less susceptible to change. However, it should be pointed out that tourism is not the sole agent of change in such situations and that other "modernizing" forces are also at work, such as the mass media, education, and urbanization.

Through the demonstration effect, tourism may generate or reinforce socio-economic aspirations among members of the host community. The resulting impact may be positive if such aspirations can be met locally and the host population is encouraged to work or adapt to attain them. However, such aspirations often remain beyond the reach of local inhabitants, who as a result may become frustrated and resentful. The demonstration effect may also cause changes in local behaviour patterns, as some residents strive to imitate tourist behaviour. Local patterns of consumption, for example, may become modified.

Although there is little hard evidence available of tourism's demonstration effect at work in the Canadian North, the potential harm of such an effect to local cultures would appear to be a concern of most residents. It is generally recognized that the social structure of small indigenous communities is fragile, in part because of the erosive action of modernizing influences other than tourism, in part because the communities lack numerical strength. Thus, during discussions with tourism planning authorities, residents in the Baffin Region of the Northwest Territories expressed the desire to control the number of tourists visiting communities, and to decide when they should visit, and where they should go on the land (Marshall Macklin Monaghan Ltd. 1982). Accordingly, tourism development plans for the region have stressed the need to minimize tourism's impact on traditional lifestyles by better informing visitors of what is expected of them and by controlling the degree and form of contact.

Where significant differences exist between the culture and lifestyle of visitors and hosts, such differences may form the basis of commercial transactions involving the sale of arts and crafts of the host community. These transactions may be beneficial to both parties. The tourists obtain a souvenir of the culture they have visited (art and craft forms, photographs, and memories of traditional dances, festivals, customs), while the hosts may obtain satisfaction from demonstrating some aspect of their culture and at the same time receive an economic reward. Tourism may therefore be instrumental in the preservation of local culture and, indeed, the demand by tourists may even lead to a rejuvenation of local culture. However, in reality, this happy situation does not always prevail. Often, the cultural aspects "marketed" are not necessarily valued by local inhabitants and, in some cases, may have no roots at all in local culture, be it present-day or traditional. Local cultures become no more than a commodity and frequently lose their distinctiveness, commercialization rendering them increasingly like the majority culture.

The somewhat ambivalent nature of tourism with respect to its effect on the culture of destination areas is evident in Canada. The Inuit, for example, provide a good illustration of the way in which tourism can contribute to a rejuvenation of local traditions. Graburn (1976, 39-55) has shown that the demands of tourists for souvenirs fostered a rebirth of Eskimo carving, especially in soapstone, an activity which previously had not played an important role in Inuit life. Although motives for production were initially economic, Inuit carvers have also derived considerable satisfaction from performing a craft which enables them to express certain aspects of their culture and traditional lifestyle. It would appear possible, therefore, to combine the preservation and strengthening of the culture of indigenous peoples with the provision of authentic experiences for tourists, and, indeed, this is one of the stated goals of the N.W.T. Tourism Strategy. Thus, it is proposed to use award programs to promote the production of high-quality arts and crafts, and to encourage restaurants to serve native foods (Department of Economic Development and Tourism, N.W.T. 1983, 21).

In the province of Quebec, however, tourism's impact on Quebecois culture has been viewed in a less positive way by many residents. Quebec is, of course, so much more accessible than the Canadian North, and its accessibility coupled with its history and distinctive culture have made it a prime target for mass tourism. Nowhere is this more evident than in the provincial capital, Quebec City. Here, the past twenty-five years have seen particularly rapid tourism development, the focal point for which has been the old sector of town, or Vieux Québec, one of North America's oldest cities.

Indicative of tourism development in Old Quebec is the growth of the bar and restaurant business. As Gazillo (1981) has shown, such development has often been at the expense of the residential function and other services, and has had a profound effect on the atmosphere of this sector of town. In 1959, there were already fifty bars and restaurants in the historic sector, and by 1979 the figure had reached eighty. As one elderly resident commented: "It is no longer Notre Dame of Vieux-Quebec here, it is Notre Dame of the brasserie!" (Gazillo 1981, 103).

Functional changes have been accompanied by runaway commercialization, which has contributed to a certain vulgarization of Quebec customs and values. Many residents feel that the town has sold out to tourism, and in doing so has lost its cultural identity, the very thing that first attracted tourists to Quebec City. They complain that all that typified Quebec culture is gradually being removed to make way for what private and public sector developers think that tourists want. The following passage from a report submitted to Quebec City's Conseil du Tourism by two citizens' groups in Old Quebec (Comité pour la protection de la rue d'Auteuil, Comité de citoyens du Vieux Québec 1976, 4) sums up their sentiments:

> A whole way of life which is typically Quebecois is gradually being replaced by images of what we once were, by a caricature of a culture "made in Quebec." The massacre started outside the walls and now it is the Old Town, the very heart of Quebec City, that is under siege. But this time the attack is more subtle, for it's not the bulldozer that is being used -- this would not be allowed in any case -- but rather the eviction of tenants to make way for stores and restaurants similar to those our visitors have left behind at home.

From the above passage, it is evident that visitors have not been the sole agents of tourism impact in Quebec City. Here, as in other destination areas, the tourism industry has played a most significant role. Through the development of infrastructure to attract and serve visitors, the tourism industry has had profound effects on both physical landscapes and social structures. The nature of the social impacts arising in this way will now be examined in greater detail.

Impacts Arising From Infrastructure Development

As indicated in the conceptual framework, tourism and recreation infrastructure development can affect the indigenous population of destination areas through its requirements with respect to investment, space, and employment.

Infrastructure costs may be considerable and this may mean that investment has to be forgone in other sectors. Thus, investment in tourism may be achieved at the expense of the promotion of other economic activities in the area or at the cost of neglecting services for local residents. The fact that tourism and recreation infrastructure is normally used for only part of the year may also heighten resentment among locals. At Stratford, Ontario, for example, MacFarlane (1979, 114) found that some residents thought that the town had placed enough emphasis on tourism and the theatre and that it was time to pay more attention to residents' needs. Improving access to the local library for the handicapped and senior citizens was cited as one such need. Similarly, in a remarkably early criticism of tourism development on Prince Edward Island, Story (1973, 2) drew attention to the growing resentment among some islanders of the fact that well-appointed motel units were being provided for visitors when many residents were not yet adequately housed. It is perhaps not surprising that a study commissioned a little later by the provincial government found that 61% of survey respondents felt that the government was spending too much on tourism (Abt Associates 1976, 43).

Any investment in tourism infrastructure therefore involves opportunity costs. The impact of such costs on the local population are influenced on the one hand by the needs of the community and on the other by the benefits to be derived from the tourism industry. Benefits arise essentially from the creation of jobs and increased revenues and the provision of new and improved facilities. While not every member of the host community can hope to benefit directly from the increase in jobs and revenues, it is important that they should have access to amenities provided by the tourism industry. Where locals perceive themselves to be excluded in favour of visitors, negative attitudes towards tourists and the tourist industry may arise. Thus, at Penticton, British Columbia, a survey revealed that some residents resented the fact that the local convention centre, financed by local money, was used mainly by non-residents and that they, the residents, had to pay a rental charge for using it (D'Amore Associates 1980, xix). Similarly, MacFarlane's study at Stratford found that certain residents felt that the theatre facilities should be made more accessible to local people, possibly with off-season performances at reduced prices (MacFarlane 1979, 114).

Perhaps the most significant and tangible social impact of infrastructure development in Canada has resulted from its demands on local space. The creation of many of the country's national and provincial parks is particularly illuminating in this respect. Such parks are often seen as serving two important purposes. First, they conserve and preserve natural areas to meet the leisure needs of an increasingly urban-based population. Second, they are instrumental in the development of the tourist industry, and, in the context of regional underdevelopment, they may act as a stimulus for small local businesses and provide employment in economically depressed areas. Quite naturally, therefore, parks find support among large segments of the general population, among conservationists as well as among some residents of the areas in which they are established. Unknown to most visitors, however, is the fact that the creation of some of Canada's parks has caused considerable social upheaval to local communities.

Conflict has arisen over both the acquisition of land by government authorities and the rights to use the land set aside for park purposes. In the early 1970s, Parks Canada policy stated that the Government of Canada was to own all land and resources in national parks. Thus, before a park could be established, private lands and interests in designated areas had to be acquired (usually by the provincial government) through negotiated settlement or, failing this, by expropriation.

Perhaps nowhere has the application of this policy given rise to greater controversy than in New Brunswick with the creation of Kouchibouguac National Park. The agreement to establish the Park, located on the province's eastern shore, was signed in 1969. In 1970, there were still 228 households living in eight communities in the designated area, with a total population of 1,211. Some residents accepted compensation payments and moved out of the park area; others had their lands and property expropriated by the provincial government. Although it may be argued that compensation was adequate in market terms, it was certainly not in human and social terms. The financial settlement and social support received was not sufficient for many to adapt to their new situation. It is ironic that one of the underlying reasons for creating the park was to improve living conditions for the area's residents, many of whom lived in poverty. Kent County, where the park is situated, was the poorest county in the province and one of the poorest in Canada. In the early 1960s, 81% of the families in the park area had incomes under $3,000 per year, compared with 24% for Canada as a whole (La Forest and Roy 1981, 10).

There was thus widespread criticism of the manner in which the land was acquired and residents were relocated. There was very little pre-planning by the government and the various operations such as counselling, land acquisition, resettlement, and social planning were extremely badly coordinated. Following periodic demonstrations and bouts of violence in which most landmarks of human presence in the park were burned, the government took remedial measures to right some of the wrongs. The whole episode, however, has left a bitter taste in the mouths of many former residents and has split communities. According to the report of a special inquiry into the problems at Kouchibouguac (La Forest and Roy 1981), the vast majority of former residents are now in favour of the park, despite their continued criticism of the manner in which expropriation was carried out. Many have better homes than before and have found employment in the park. In 1980, the park employed 113 people, of which 79 were former residents and 22 were from the local area. Local merchants and small businesses catering to tourists also hold generally positive attitudes with regard to the park. However, some expropriates still claim their former lands and rights, and for them the battle is not yet over. As the report of the special inquiry concludes, "Time and patience will be major components of an ultimate settlement" (La Forest and Roy 1981, 117-18).

The trials and tribulations of the people at Kouchibouguac may not have been entirely in vain, for the federal government now appears to have modified its policy with respect to land acquisition for park purposes. The removal of inhabitants is no longer a prerequisite to the creation of a national park and more serious pre-planning is now undertaken to examine ways of helping residents to adapt to and benefit from the establishment of a park. Thus, in 1973, with the creation of Gros Morne National Park in Newfoundland, 175 families were originally to be moved from small settlements within the park area but, following objections to the move by local people, the government relented and allowed residents to stay in their homes, and even let their children inherit them. However, residents were encouraged to move out with the promise of new houses for old, an offer several families found difficult to refuse. As Overton (1979, 42) observes in a critical analysis of the creation of national parks in underdeveloped areas, this represents the first step in the disintegration of communities, as before long the dwindling population is no longer able to support the same level of services. Such a situation occurred in the Forillon National Park in Quebec, where fishermen, who were allowed to stay on in the park in special enclaves, were eventually forced to leave as they were unable to get services in the winter months (Overton 1979, 42).

Conflict has also arisen between indigenous populations and park authorities over the rights to use land set aside for park purposes. Resource exploitation within national park areas is not consistent with park uses, so that hunting, fishing, and trapping are not generally permitted in park confines. However, there is some flexibility in the application of these rules in the Northwest Territories and the Yukon. Here, the lifestyles and livelihood of the native peoples are based upon such activities and parks policy provides for negotiations with the local population over rights within national parks. Indigenous populations in the provinces, however, have no such legal claim, and this has been a source of resentment among many residents in areas where parks have been created or are proposed. In Gros Morne, Newfoundland, for example, park residents claimed that the park was destroying their way of life by the restrictions it imposed on hunting (Overton 1979, 40). At Kouchibouguac, many of the park's former residents and some residents of the surrounding areas used the park area for fishing, hunting, trapping, wood-cutting, and even farming. These activities conflicted with stated park policy and were therefore originally forbidden in the confines of the park. Later, however, the government relented and allowed fishing, which had been the residents' main activity before the park was established.

In northern Labrador, land being considered for a national park in the Torngat Mountains is traditional hunting ground for the Labrador Inuit. There is also the issue of mineral rights in the proposed park area. For these reasons, the Inuit are generally opposed to the creation of a national park until a lands-claim settlement has been made. According to the present wording of parks policies of the Department of Environment, guarantees are to be provided in new national parks to allow certain traditional subsistence resource uses by local people for one or more generations when such uses are an essential part of the local way of life. As Stix (1982, 352-53) has pointed out, however, phrases such as "certain traditional subsistence resource uses" and "essential part of the local way of life" must be carefully defined if future conflicts are to be avoided in this area. He also underlines the need to incorporate local, and specifically Inuit, input into planning policies and, at a later stage, to ensure Inuit involvement in park management.

Tourism and recreation have also had profound effects on urban landscapes. Restoration, renovation, and beautification programs endeavour to create more attractive environments to be enjoyed by both visitors and residents alike. Vancouver's Gastown and Old Montreal are examples of such developments. These areas have been given a new lease on life, and this is undoubtedly positive. However, changes to the physical structure of an area often involve modifications to its social structure, modifications which are not welcomed by all. Thus, in Old Montreal some of the older buildings have been converted into trendy condominiums, attracting more affluent residents, and pressure has been put on certain port facilities with blue-collar jobs to relocate elsewhere, as they are not compatible with the district's new image (Allaby 1983).

In Quebec City, the social impact of tourism infrastructure development has been particularly marked. In Old Quebec, the tourist industry has gradually taken over numerous houses and properties, creating tourist accommodation, bars, restaurants, and souvenir shops, much to the dismay of many long-time residents. Some residents complain that much of what was old, vibrant with life, and typically Quebecois, such as the St. Jean Baptiste district, has been sacrificed to make way for high-rise hotels not at all in keeping with the surrounding architecture. They claim that restoration of the place Royale has meant replacing something authentic, an old residential district, with something artificial, a recreated historical setting. A report prepared by two citizens' action groups (Comité pour la protection de la rue d'Auteuil et Comité de citoyens du Vieux Québec 1976, 3) sums up the situation:

> What they visitors come to see is something which is authentically different. However, what we are in the process of preparing for them is a vulgar city centre with high-rise hotels (Concorde, Hilton, Auberge des Gouverneurs, Holiday Inn) no different from any other North American city centre, next to an Old Quebec looking more and more like a picture postcard.

As tourist functions have gradually encroached upon the residential function in Old Quebec, the dwindling resident population has found it increasingly difficult to sustain the same level of services. Several small businesses serving the local population have closed, while many of those that remain cater mainly to tourists and are often open only part of the year. This confers a marked seasonal character to life in some districts of Old Quebec, much to the regret of many older residents.

Tourism development also affects local populations through the generation of jobs and income. The economic impacts of tourism are well documented elsewhere (for example, Mathieson and Wall 1982, 35-92). As pointed out in the conceptual framework of this chapter, however, while increased revenues and job opportunities may be considered beneficial to a community, such benefits are not shared equally among the population. Those members of the population who do benefit will generally hold more positive attitudes towards tourists and the tourist industry (Owens 1981: 109, Keogh 1982, 329). Moreover, depending on the scale of development, the tourist industry may be partly controlled by outsiders, and there may be a certain amount of imported labour, both of which factors may be a source of resentment among the indigenous population. Mings (1978, 342), for example, found that 41.2% of jobs in tourist lodges along the Alaska Highway in the Yukon were filled by outsiders travelling great distances in search of employment.

Itinerant workers may therefore form a sizable proportion of the total population in the tourist season. In addition, other outsiders, mostly young people, may stay in tourist areas in the hope of finding employment or simply to be in a pleasant environment with other people like themselves. Such transient populations place increased pressure on community services, take little or no part in community life (Cheng 1980, 78), and may even have a disruptive influence on it. Thus, in a study of tourism development in a number of small communities in British Columbia, it was noted that in the popular summer resort of Penticton, the Provincial Human Resources Branch devoted considerable time to dealing with problems associated with young transients (D'Amore Associates 1980, 93).

SOCIAL IMPACTS AND RESIDENTS' ATTITUDES TOWARDS TOURISM AND RECREATION

From the foregoing section it can be seen that the social impacts of tourism and recreation are many and varied. On the positive side, catering to visitors' needs creates jobs and increased revenues and may lead to new and improved services and amenities for the community, all of which can have a beneficial effect on the standard of living of the local population. Visitors from different cultural or subcultural backgrounds also bring with them values, ideas, and attitudes different from those of destination area residents, and these differences may provide a basis for mutually beneficial interaction between the two groups. On the negative side, however, such differences between visitors and residents may also be a source of friction and conflict. In addition, visitors must frequently share facilities and resources with the indigenous population of destination areas and this too may produce a number of conflict situations.

Having identified the various types of social impact, it is important to examine the relationship between such impacts and residents' attitudes towards tourism and recreation. Attitudes determine the way in which visitors and the tourist industry are accepted by a community and its residents and thereby constitute an important ingredient of the experience offered to visitors. If overall attitudes towards visitors are not favourable, they may be expressed in unfriendly if not hostile resident-visitor interaction which detracts from the quality of the visitor's experience. Indeed, in such a situation both residents and visitors are losers. It is clear then that residents' attitudes can have a profound effect on the success of tourism and recreation development.

Individuals' attitudes towards visitors are influenced by both their general socio-cultural characteristics and the impacts they perceive to arise from tourism and recreation. Thus, in any community some individuals may actively search for new experiences and be more open to outsiders, while others, often older members, may be more content with their present situation and less amenable to change of any kind. With regard to impacts, as already mentioned, these are not shared equally among the population of host communities. This situation is largely a reflection of differing resident characteristics. Within any community, some residents may live near zones of intense visitor activity, others may be relatively isolated, some members are young, others are old, some work, others do not. Among those who work, some have jobs related to the tourism industry.

It therefore follows that certain members of the population are better placed than others to benefit from the positive social aspects of tourism and recreation. Similarly, some residents may be more exposed to the negative aspects of tourism and recreation. For example, in his study of tourism impact at Shediac, Keogh found that the younger adult members of the population (16-25 years) and those looking for employment generally held the most positive attitudes towards visitors (Keogh 1982, 327-29). Those groups less likely to benefit from the economic and social aspects of tourism, such as retired people or those at home with young families, were found to hold less positive overall attitudes. Among the working population, not surprisingly those residents employed in hotels and restaurants held the most positive attitudes.

The relationship between impacts and overall attitudes, however, is not always a simple one. Often community members who benefit most from tourism and recreation also perceive negative impacts. To obtain benefits, interaction with the visitors is often necessary, and this interaction may also be a source of some negative impacts. It is, therefore, clear that the level of interaction or contact between residents and visitors is not necessarily correlated with residents' overall attitudes. An important factor in the relationship is the context of the encounter. Where the encounter is sought by residents, with a view to a commercial transaction or social exchange, higher levels of contact may result in increased benefits. On the other hand, where contact is imposed on residents, as is the case when facilities and services become congested, increased contact is likely to lead to greater inconvenience for residents.

The influence of social impacts on residents' general attitudes towards tourists and the tourist industry will therefore depend on the relative weights that each attributes to the different perceived impacts. Thus, residents employed in the tourist industry at Shediac mentioned a number of negative aspects of the tourist season but, since their overall attitudes were positive, one can deduce that perceived disadvantages were more than compensated for by perceived benefits. Similarly, the non-rural population of Manitoulin Island perceived more disadvantages than the rural population but, nevertheless, looked forward more to the arrival of visitors than did the rural population (Owens 1981, 131-3).

Community attitudes towards tourists and the tourist industry reflect individual attitudes. Within any community, some people will hold positive attitudes, while others may think that the community would be better off without tourism. Still others may not have any opinion at all or be indifferent to tourism's effects. In the survey of Manitoulin Island residents, for example, most respondents fell into this last category (Owens 1981, 90).

If tourism development is to succeed in a community, it is most important that overall attitudes are positive. Ideally, such development should have the overwhelming support of the community, for even a few individuals with negative opinions can have a deleterious effect on visitors' experiences and, ultimately, on the development of tourism. In most situations, however, some negative impacts are inevitable. They should therefore be carefully monitored and prevented from reaching a point where they outweigh the advantages of tourism. If this happens, overall attitudes become negative, friendly interaction between residents and visitors diminishes, and both parties are losers.

Since many of the negative social aspects of tourism and recreation are related to the number of visitors, the term *social carrying capacity* has often been used to determine the limits of acceptable tourism development in a given community. D'Amore (1983, 144) used this concept in his study of tourism development in British Columbia and defines it as "that point in the growth of tourism where local residents perceive on balance an unacceptable level of social disbenefits from tourism development."

If the number of visitors represented the only factor in determining social carrying capacity, it could be used, possibly in conjunction with the number of residents and the capacities of local facilities, to determine critical levels for each community. Unfortunately, as indicated in the conceptual framework, social impacts result from the interaction of numerous and complex variables relating to the characteristics of visitors and of the destination area and its residents. For this reason, it would be difficult, if not impossible, to calculate absolute values for social carrying capacities (Wall 1983). However, the identification of general attitudes and perceptions among host communities can indicate where the community is situated with respect to critical tolerance levels and whether management controls should be introduced. If such controls are deemed necessary, their nature will depend on an assessment of the social impacts in the community. The general implications of social impact studies for planning and management are considered below.

IMPLICATIONS FOR PLANNING AND MANAGEMENT

Residents' overall attitudes towards visitors and the tourist industry reflect the real significance of social impacts and hence indicate where the community stands with respect to a tolerance level to visitors. An assessment of the various negative and positive effects of tourism and recreation development in a community provides indispensable input for sound planning, the aim of which should be to maintain generally positive attitudes well within the critical limits. Simply put, planning and management should endeavour to eliminate the negative and accentuate the positive. This is not as simple as it sounds, however, as inevitably the two are linked. Eliminating or mitigating negative aspects may involve a concomitant reduction in positive aspects. Thus, on the one hand, limiting the number of visitors to a destination area may relieve the congestion of local services and facilities and reduce environmental impact, thereby permitting a higher-quality environment for the enjoyment of local users. On the other hand, it may also mean less visitor revenue for local businesses and, possibly, fewer jobs for the community.

The above example serves to underline the fact that planning and management strategies for tourism and recreation development invariably require trade-offs and that such trade-offs can involve all three impact components -- social, economic, and environmental. Decisions on trade-offs may have far-reaching effects for the whole community and should not therefore be taken without adequately consulting all its members. Overall goals and priorities should be identified by residents and used as a base for assessing alternative development options. In this way, community members will feel they have some voice in and control over tourism development and that their needs are not subordinated to those of visitors. Numerous studies have concluded that such conditions are a necessary prerequisite to community support in tourism development programs (for example, Stix 1982, 353, N.W.T. Department of Economic Development and Tourism 1983, 9-10, D'Amore 1983, 153). Thus, in a study of the social sensitivity to tourism in several small communities in British Columbia, D'Amore (1983) observed that at Kimberley there was considerable local involvement in tourism development, which, as a result, had widely-based community support. At Lillooet, on the other hand, tourism was seen as a future economic development possibility by a number of public and private groups, but this view was not shared by most residents. The latter felt that they had no real control over future tourism and were, therefore, not widely supportive of it.

If community involvement in planning and management decisions is to succeed, it is important that information is made available to residents to enable them to reach informed opinions. Where a community is already receiving visitors, the local population should be made aware of the associated impacts. In this way, negative opinions can sometimes be dispelled as perceptions are brought more in line with reality. When there are obvious positive impacts for a community, the negative impacts can be tolerated more easily. In Penticton, for example, heavy visitor traffic each summer brings with it a certain number of problems. Most citizens, however, are aware of the economic benefits that tourism bestows on the town and, as a consequence, overall attitudes are positive (D'Amore 1983, 147).

With respect to future development, impact statements must be prepared which will provide the information necessary for an assessment of the different alternatives. In the past, such information has often been lacking among local populations. Surveys of Prince Edward Island residents, for example, showed that over 30% of respondents could not decide whether the Island way of life was positively or negatively affected by tourism (Abt Associates 1976, 46). Benefits and costs (including opportunity costs) associated with different development options should therefore be identified and a clear indication given of how such benefits and costs will be shared among the local community. Host populations should also be informed of the wider impacts of each alternative, and in particular the enjoyment that their community can provide for visitors. A better understanding among residents of the role of tourism in general and the realization that they, too, are sometimes tourists can help them reach a more balanced perspective and thereby can promote more positive attitudes.

More positive attitudes can also be obtained through planning and management policies designed to reduce the negative impacts and enhance the positive impacts of tourism and recreation in the host community. Among the positive aspects of tourism development, the most significant have been shown to be those related to the economic benefits. As far as possible, such benefits should go to the local population. If the indigenous population perceives it has been excluded in favour of outsiders, negative feelings may arise. Local investment, ownership, and employment in the tourist industry must therefore be encouraged. Incentives could be provided in the form of financing and job-training schemes within the community. For many communities embarking upon tourism and recreation development, small-scale operations will probably provide the best option, since this form of development generally enables the local population to become more involved and to retain control of their own affairs.

It was also noted that positive impacts can arise from the provision of new and improved facilities and services.

Although these may be created primarily to cater to visitors, it is most important that local inhabitants have at least equal access if favourable community attitudes are to be maintained.

Among the negative social impacts of tourism and recreation development in Canada, perhaps the most evident have arisen from the demands made by tourism infrastructure on local space. As the tourism function has encroached on other functions, in both urban and non-urban settings, local lifestyles have been severely disrupted if not completely replaced. Planning which is insensitive to local identity and values has little chance of success in the long term and, as has already been pointed out, may even be destroying the very thing that attracted visitors in the first place. Every effort must therefore be made to respect the rights, needs, and priorities of indigenous populations and to preserve their lifestyles. In cases where some negative impacts are unavoidable, those who are adversely affected must be identified and adequately compensated. It is important that they do not feel that they are worse off as a result of tourism and recreation development. Sound pre-planning based on carefully prepared impact statements can obviate later remedial planning. As noted in the conflicts over Kouchibouguac National Park, remedial planning is often not only more costly but also leaves scars among the local population which are slow to heal.

Other negative impacts are related to the type and number of visitors. The type of visitors attracted to an area can be influenced by the type of attractions offered. To reduce negative impacts, the type of development promoted should be compatible with local lifestyles and should receive wide community support. A survey among Prince Edward Island residents, for example, suggested that family groups and farm vacationers were the preferred types of visitor (Abt Associates 1976, 36). Events and themes should, as far as possible, be rooted in local culture. This inspires greater local involvement and facilitates positive contacts between residents and visitors.

Conflicts arising from differences between visitors and residents can also be reduced by efforts to educate visitors with respect to local customs, values, and lifestyles. This may be done through promotional material or through intermediaries such as tour guides and travel agents. In Canada, this is particularly important for Quebec and the areas inhabited by native peoples, where tourism brings widely differing cultural groups into contact with one another. A basic understanding of the culture and lifestyle of the indigenous population of destination areas enables visitors to have more realistic trip expectations and to adapt their behaviour so as to conform with local standards. In short, better-informed visitors mean fewer negative social impacts.

Finally, visitor numbers must not reach levels which the host community cannot adequately absorb. It has been shown that many of the negative social impacts of tourism and recreation development arise from too much visitor pressure on local populations, facilities, and resources. In planning to avoid or mitigate such impacts, authorities can establish various capacity levels. As Getz (1983, 260) has pointed out, however, these should not be seen as formulas for determining inherent or optimal limits on growth and change but rather as means of identifying thresholds under given sets of conditions, to be used as guidelines for planning and management. Threshold or capacity levels are a function of a number of complex and interrelated factors, namely the type of visitors and experiences sought, the characteristics and spatial organization of resources and facilities, and the receptivity of residents to visitors. All these factors are subject to change and must, therefore, be regularly monitored if impacts are to be understood and planned for. Alternatively, planning and management strategies can be used to effect changes in these factors and thereby increase the carrying capacity of destination areas.

CONCLUSIONS

In Canada, tourism and outdoor recreation, both as activities and industries, have experienced unprecedented growth over the past quarter century. Since participants in these activities spend considerable sums of money on equipment, user fees, accommodation, and travel, tourism and recreation development has been recognized by both corporate and government planners as a way of stimulating economic activity. Given that many existing and potential visitor destination areas lie within the more peripheral and poorer regions of the country, such development has also be seen at regional and national planning levels as a means of reducing regional economic disparities.

While the economic impacts of tourism and recreation development on destination areas are undoubtedly real, and in many cases largely beneficial, they are not the only impacts of such development. There are also important environmental and social effects. Thus, research into the latter over the past fifteen years has revealed a variety of ways in which the lifestyles of resident populations of destination areas have been affected by both visitors and the infrastructures created to cater to their needs. Unlike the economic impacts, the social impacts appear, on the whole, to be mostly negative. It is, therefore, regrettable that most tourism and recreation planning has, until recently, tended to ignore such impacts, concentrating instead mainly on satisfying visitor needs and on the associated economic impacts.

Although it could probably be said that economic benefits appear to outweigh social disadvantages at most destination areas in Canada, this situation should in no way be seen as a mandate for no change in planning and management policies. There is, without doubt, room for improvement. This chapter has identified the types of social impact arising from tourism and recreation in Canada and has assessed their implications for planning and management. It has also underlined the complex and dynamic nature of social impacts. Generally positive resident attitudes today are no guarantee of such attitudes tomorrow.

Though it has been late coming, there now appears to be a growing recognition among planners of the need to incorporate local attitudes, aspirations, and needs into the decision-making process. The studies by Abt Associates (1976) for Prince Edward Island and D'Amore Associates (1980) for British Columbia, the N.W.T. Tourism Strategy (N.W.T. Department of Economic Development and Tourism 1983) and the more flexible planning procedures employed recently by the federal government all bear witness to this welcome change in thinking.

It is increasingly realized that the attitudes of local populations towards visitors and the industry that caters to them are not determined by economic impacts alone. Undesirable social impacts can cause resentment and even overtly negative attitudes, and this in spite of economic benefits. If this happens, visitors may perceive their experience to be less enjoyable. They will be less likely to return and may discourage others from coming, so that in the long run everybody is the loser. Planning and management of tourism and recreation resources should therefore seek to satisfy visitors and host populations alike, thereby ensuring that these resources are truly renewable. This can only be achieved if carefully prepared statements on the social impacts of tourism and recreation development are incorporated into the decision-making process.

Chapter 9

The Future

Richard Butler
Department of Geography
University of Western Ontario

The Future

INTRODUCTION

The task of predicting the future is something which has fascinated mankind since time immemorial. To forecast trends and patterns in even stable and well-documented phenomena is still difficult and prone to error. To forecast trends and changes in something as esoteric and dynamic as recreation is almost pointless if one wishes to be accurate. As Smith has pointed out in chapter 3 of this volume, such forecasting is complicated by the facts that, first, we are not entirely sure of causal agents, and second, most projections assume stable and continued relationships between dependent and independent variables. However, we know many of the variables are not truly independent, and as Jackson argues in chapter 4, predicting on the basis of activity participation alone is rarely accurate beyond the very short term. Rather, we need to understand behaviour and the related perceptions, attitudes, values, and motivational forces, before we can hope to predict the future. One way of doing this would be to identify clear indicators of change, but as Paine *et al.* point out, "despite the collection of an immense amount of data over the last two decades, there is no clearly defined set of indicators in the outdoor recreation field" (Paine, Marans, and Harris 1980, 7).

There are several ways of examining the future, and considerable work has been carried out in describing and evaluating various approaches (see, for example, Lehteniemi 1976, Fritz, Brandon, and Xander 1984, Clawson 1985, Uysal and Compton 1985, and Ng 1988). In general, the results of predictions have been disappointing (Smith 1980). This perhaps explains why people keep trying, coupled with the fact, as Smith points out, that few researchers or readers go back to verify if the projections came true.

Statistically-oriented methods tend to give reliable short-term forecasts for stable recreation activities for which considerable longitudinal data exist, but are poor for forecasting patterns of new, rapidly growing activities or those characterized by instability. Qualitative predictions may be more suited for longer-term projections and for speculation on activities not yet participated in, but are at best inspired guesswork (for example, Ehricke 1968). Even the most experienced researchers do not have high levels of accuracy when it comes to predictions. Of fourteen items related to tourism anticipated to be in place by 1990 or before, based on predictions made in 1980, only six were even partially happening by 1988 (Hawkins, Shafer, and Rovelstad 1980).

It seemed pointless, therefore, to attempt in this chapter to predict in detail, participation rates in outdoor recreation in Canada, or to speculate at length on new activities which may appear or new areas which may be developed. Rather, it was decided to discuss potential changes at a more general level and to take a broader field than outdoor recreation alone. The approach is, therefore, to discuss factors which affect Canadians and their outdoor recreation behaviour now, and which are likely to affect them in the future, although not necessarily in the same way, and to anticipate the likely changes, if any, in the Canadian outdoor recreation scene.

A major consideration to bear in mind is that in the short term or even medium term future, massive change is unlikely, barring a major catastrophe such as global war. People do not abandon lifetime preferences and behaviour lightly, especially when they may have considerable amounts of money and time invested in equipment, property, and skills. Change is, therefore, likely to be incremental and gradual at an aggregate level. In a study of national surveys of outdoor recreation participation in the United States over a nineteen-year period, Bevins and Wilcox (1980) showed that there were few changes in participation levels in individual activities of more than 5%, and the most common activities remained relatively constant in popularity over almost two decades. Those activities which did decline in popularity included hunting, boating, and fishing, while those which increased in popularity included camping, swimming, and hiking. Whether similar trends exist in Canada is impossible to confirm, as there are no comparable national surveys over such a period of time. Indeed, there are, unfortunately, few reliable comprehensive national surveys of outdoor recreation participation in Canada, and fewer still which are comparable and consistent. One of the few sources of comparable data over time, albeit a short period, is the Alberta Public Opinion Survey on Recreation (1981, 1984). Increases in participation in such activities as walking, jogging, swimming, electronic recreation, and certain sports were mirrored by declines in participation in dancing, bowling, reading, and camping (Alberta 1988). But before we can conclude from these data that people are becoming more active and outdoor recreation-oriented, it must be noted that this report also suggested the home was becoming increasingly the centre of leisure activity. The Alberta study also noted what other researchers such as Gold (1985) have commented on: that there is a blurring of boundaries between work and leisure, and that most new activities cannot be predicted.

The decreasing distinction between work and leisure is mirrored in the increasing irrelevance of separating leisure, recreation, and tourism, or indoor and outdoor recreation. People are selecting leisure opportunities and participating in activities from a wide range of possibilities, and as many authors from Clawson and Knetsch (1966) onwards have noted, they are participating in a recreation experience rather than a single activity. Accordingly, the following discussion covers leisure and recreation generally, rather than simply outdoor recreation, because so much of what happens in the indoor urban recreation scene, for example, has relevance for outdoor recreation patterns. If large numbers of urban residents purchase private swimming pools, they may reduce travel to beach areas, or if pollution closes beaches for swimming, attendance at indoor urban public pools may increase.

Attention is paid first to societal trends and potential changes in some of the demand shifters referred to by Smith in chapter 3, including the supply of opportunity discussed by Kreutzwiser in chapter 2. Secondly, there is discussion of the anticipated effects of technology and the rate of change of attitudes and behaviour in Canada. Finally, there is a brief examination of the impacts of the anticipated changes in recreation patterns in Canada upon the environment and upon communities. A short conclusion attempts to pull together major threads and implications.

SOCIETAL TRENDS

Population

Perhaps the most definite trend in Canadian society in terms of the certainty of its continuing is the ageing of the population. Although forecasts may not be entirely accurate, the number of people in Canada over the age of sixty-five at the end of the century is likely to be double what it was in 1971, and the only age cohort anticipated to show an absolute decline is the youngest (Table 1). Some implications of this trend are already apparent, which may give some indications of the way recreation patterns may change in the future.

This elderly population is not, and will not be, like previous older generations. While it can be expected to retain some of the same traditional and conservative values, the present older generation has more money, better health, is better educated, and has travelled more extensively than elderly generations before it. Its recreational preferences and behaviour have been modified by the Great Depression, the Second World War, the Korean War, the postwar boom, the 1960s, the jet aircraft, and terrorism. Those who will be sixty-five in the year 2000, however, will not have experienced the Depression, will probably barely remember the Second World War and will have spent their adolescence during the postwar boom of the 1950s. The cohort turning sixty-five in the year 2010 and thereafter will be of the baby boom generation.

We can expect, therefore, that the increasingly large elderly population will be more like current forty- to fifty-year-olds than current seventy- to eighty-year-olds. Like the latter group, but probably much more effectively, many of them will reject the limitations of old age and continue to travel and to engage in many activities which they engage in now, such as camping, hiking, skiing, swimming, and travelling. They will conform less to society's preconceived and stereotyped roles for them and will have the numbers and financial power to act as an influential force in society. While some will seek out retirement pastures in Victoria, in semi-rural areas, and in the southern United States, many will choose to remain where they are, perhaps in condominiums or apartments, possibly travelling for long breaks during the winter, and taking other vacations and recreation trips during the late spring and early fall.

Table 1

Canadian Population by Age Group, 1971-2001
(In Thousands)

	Population	%	Population	%
Age 0 -- 24	10,395.9	48.2	9,532.2	33.6
25 -- 44	5,413.6	25.1	8,794.6	31.0
45 -- 64	4,011.7	18.6	6,695.2	23.6
65 -- 74	1,078.4	5.0	1,872.4	6.6
75+	668.6	3.1	1,475.2	5.2
	21,568.2	100%	28,369.6	100%

Source: Statistics Canada, 1975.

One effect of this pattern would be to increase the shoulder season accommodation occupancy rates and the use levels at many recreational sites, and possibly slightly reduce peaking. However, because this large elderly population can be expected to remain active for more years than previous generations, many recreation areas will be busier in the future than at present . The impact is likely to be particularly great in many highly scenic areas, in heritage areas such as national parks and historic sites, and in northern and wilderness areas. This group has both time and money to spend on longer trips to remote areas, and many have the health and ability to accept considerable physical challenge. This population has enough experience not to want or to accept the ordinary on every occasion. While not for all members of that group by any means, but certainly attractive to some are exploration trips to the Canadian Arctic, heritage excursions to Quebec and the East Coast, mountain hikes in the Rockies, and natural history excursions throughout Canada.

This group, as it grows and continues to be active, could pose considerable problems in the outdoor recreation scene. While many of its members may be extremely environmentally conscious and interested in heritage and natural history, that very interest may draw them in increasing numbers to the wilderness and protected areas such as national parks. They, or those catering for them, may demand additional developments and facilities such as roads, trails, and lifts to allow them access to many parts of such areas. They are less likely to want campgrounds in these areas than they are to want good hotels. As they gain more and more political influence, if only because of sheer numbers, policies may have to change to accommodate them. There is nothing inherently wrong in this, but additional conflicts may arise as a result in many areas over the degree and nature of development.

This population also appears likely to be much more interested than its predecessors in continuing education in the widest sense of the word. The Elderhostel concept is one example of this, a non-profit organization for people over sixty, offering non-credit academic and travel programs and courses in Canada and in other countries, with destinations from the Mackenzie Delta to Australia. In the future the discounts currently available as inducements to encourage the elderly to travel may not be necessary nor economic, given the numbers who may be travelling. They may be levelled at the young instead to encourage them to begin travelling.

The figures in Table 1 also reveal that while the oldest age cohorts are growing most rapidly, only the youngest shows an absolute decline in numbers and a relative decline in proportion of the total. Major absolute growth (over 50%) is forecast for both of the next two cohorts, and in proportional terms the cohort of people aged twenty-five to forty-four will have the largest increase, that is, the people who are teenagers and in their twenties now. It is not likely that this youngest group, in the next decade or so, will radically alter their behaviour patterns from those which they have now and which their parents have. By the end of the century, they will either have no children yet or only young children, and much if any change in behaviour outside already established patterns will be slow to develop and incremental rather than major and rapid in nature.

Supply

Research has shown the importance of supply in shaping participation (Beaman, Kim, and Smith 1979), and Kreutzwiser in chapter 2 has discussed the nature of the supply of outdoor recreation in Canada. It is difficult to foresee major changes in the overall pattern of the provision of outdoor recreation opportunity by the public sector in Canada in the short to mid-term future. At the federal level, new initiatives by the Canadian Parks Service can be expected to result in some candidate park areas becoming national parks, especially in the North, Quebec, and British Columbia, and additional national historic sites are likely in all areas in small numbers. However, budget limitations, continued reluctance by provincial governments to allow the creation of new national parks when required to release all rights to resources, reluctance by some local populations to have national parks established close to their permanent homes, and the fact that there is a foreseeable finite limit to the number of national parks in Canada -- all these suggest new parks will be few in number in the next few decades.

Many provincial governments have similar problems with expanding their provincial park systems, as well as the added major problem of overcoming opposition to new park establishment from other resource users, especially the logging industry. Some provinces, such as Ontario, have expanded their park systems in recent years to levels unanticipated twenty or thirty years ago -- Ontario's system has grown from eight parks in 1954 to over three hundred in 1988 -- and future major expansion is not likely. Changes in policy and classifications at both federal and provincial levels may well occur, however, which could have significance for the way parks are managed, but probably less significance for the overall use made of the parks. As long ago as the early 1960s, Wolfe (1964) demonstrated clearly that location of a provincial park is much more important in shaping the use patterns that park receives than the category in which it is classified.

If recent trends continue, conflict over the degree of protection and range of uses in both national and provincial parks is likely in the future. Disagreements over multiple use in several provincial park systems will continue, as will arguments over what are acceptable recreational uses in national parks in particular. The proceedings of the National Parks Centennial Conference in Banff (Scace and Nelson 1986) contain provincial caucus reports and transcripts of the conference meetings, and a perusal of these reveals that sentiments are markedly similar to those expressed at the National Parks Today and Tomorrow Conference in Banff in 1968 (Nelson and Scace 1968). While protection is now identified as the first priority in national parks, the emphasis in the Canadian Parks Service appears to have shifted to include a wider range of recreational developments. This may be a reflection of changing demands -- related to special user groups, for example, the aged and handicapped as noted above -- and of political factors, including pressure from the government to stimulate tourism in Canada, a view supported by many provincial governments. The creation of a marketing position in the Canadian Parks Service suggests also that tourism may be promoted more in the national parks in the future.

This is not a new process, and part of it can be explained by the need and desire of park agencies at all levels to safeguard their budgets in a period of public sector spending cutbacks. The ill-fated privatization scheme in Ontario provincial parks is another example of a budget-induced change in philosophy. If present trends continue in the future, national and provincial parks may have to be shown to be commercially valuable to continue to receive public sector support. This could be translated into additional and more varied developments in accommodation, services, and recreation activities than previously allowed, with possibly some expansion of the system as compensation. To the wilderness purist such developments would be anathema, but to politicians probably highly attractive.

Alternatives to national and provincial parks are not likely to appear, and could not be expected to provide the degree of protection to the environment afforded by these areas. Over the years there have been attempts and suggestions to adopt variations of European strategies to secure public access to private land for recreation (Butler and Troughton 1985). With the exception of hunting and fishing, two activities traditionally carried out on public and private property, and trails, for example, the Bruce Trail and snowmobile trails in Quebec and Ontario, such efforts have met with relatively little success. Legal liability and problems of damage to and loss of property of landowners have proved the main obstacles, and changes in legislation have failed to resolve all of these problems. Without the creation of special agencies and funding, probably at the provincial level, there appears little chance of significantly changing the situation. Legal liability of landowners to users of their property would still remain a serious problem, and given North American trends, one which could become even greater in the future. Landowners in some rural areas have become less sympathetic to recreational use of their land by hunters and fishermen (Kreutzwiser and Pietraszko 1986). This tendency is more prevalent among exurbanites moving to the countryside to live, or owning recreational properties in rural areas, than among long-time rural residents.

Private commercial recreation, such as campgrounds, theme parks, and ski areas, on the other hand, can be expected to continue to expand as market opportunities are perceived. Large-scale theme parks like Canada's Wonderland are not likely to appear in more than one or two additional locations, if at all, given market requirements and climatic conditions. However, smaller amusement and leisure facilities will be developed. One innovation which has been developed in some numbers in Europe has been climate-controlled aquatic leisure centres, featuring wave pools, artificial beaches, and other water-based attractions under domes or in indoor settings. While the Canadian summer climate makes such developments less necessary, economic imperatives would require this type of controlled environment to operate year-round. Hotels in several cities have this type of facility on a smaller scale, and at the other end of the scale there is the West Edmonton Mall. Intermediate facilities in urban locations may well begin to appear, possibly on a joint public-private basis, incorporating other public and private facilities also.

Cultural Mosaic

There is little doubt that Canadian outdoor recreation patterns
are different from those of the nineteenth century, although
remnants of that pattern still exist. As Lundgren has shown in
chapter 5, some patterns remain relatively constant, even if
activities change. One of the factors which has caused and can
be expected to continue to cause changes in the outdoor recreation
patterns of Canadians is the cultural composition of the country.
Immigration, especially in the past hundred years, has seen
significant numbers of many different ethnic groups settle in
Canada, often giving clear and distinctive cultural identity to
specific parts of the country or different cities, for example,
Mennonites in Ontario, Chinese in Vancouver, and Italians in
Toronto.

Such groups bring with them very different and distinctive
cultures and forms of recreation. At one level such differences
are highly visible -- the proportion of Europeans on soccer teams,
or of West and East Indians on cricket teams, for instance, or
cultural festivals such as Carnival in Toronto. The celebration
of Italian Canadians when Italy won the World Cup in soccer in
1986 could hardly have been less boisterous than celebrations in
Italy itself. Yet we know little about how long it takes an
immigrant to become "Canadianized" as far as outdoor
recreation behaviour is concerned, if such a process ever, in
fact, takes place.

We need to determine, for example, if there is speedy
acceptance of and participation in traditionally Canadian
recreation activities, such as hockey, fishing, and camping, by
immigrants, or by their children, or whether absorption does not
take place to any significant degree for several generations, if
at all. Certain groups, especially those with strong religious
convictions, such as Mennonites, do not participate to the same
extent in traditionally Canadian recreation activities. Other
groups appear to participate quickly and fully.

It would appear that, as in times past, the immigration mix
will continue to change, with fewer new Canadians coming
from Europe and the traditional countries of origin, and more
coming from Asia and the Third World generally. In the short
term these immigrants are likely to display lower participation
levels in recreation than current residents of Canada, in part
because of economic, linguistic, and social constraints, and in
part because of unfamiliarity with and, perhaps, dislike of

Canadian activities and opportunities. The long-term situation is much less certain. It would be surprising if such groups did not succeed in introducing new patterns of recreation behaviour into the Canadian scene, and thus indirectly bring about a decrease or decline in growth of participation in more traditional activities. At the same time, as the economic and other constraints are reduced, these new Canadians can be expected to take advantage of opportunities becoming available to them.

The precise mix of the immigrant population is probably less important than the size and location of that population. If it is spread throughout the country, the effects are likely to be minimal, and newcomers are more likely to adapt to Canadian recreation patterns or not participate at all. On the other hand, if considerable numbers from one place of origin locate in one community, then they may have sufficient numbers to make it feasible to provide their own facilities and continue some, at least, of their traditional recreation activities. One example of the latter development is the number of ethnic clubs which exist in most large Canadian cities, and which provide opportunities for both cultural interaction and recreation participation (Sousa 1988). It would be naive and inappropriate, however, to expect these ethnic groups to continue to provide their own facilities on a private basis in the long term, and the public sector will inevitably have to make some efforts to provide more than the traditional arenas, swimming pools, and conventional parks in Canadian cities in the future.

Employment

Employment has been regarded as one of the major factors shaping recreation behaviour, and virtually every survey of recreation activities from the Outdoor Recreation Resources Review Commission (1962) onwards has substantiated this view. Its importance is felt in several ways, including through providing income, part of which can be utilized for recreational activities; through structuring social patterns by defined hours of work and, as a corollary, hours of potential leisure; and through the networks of contacts and opportunities provided within the work environment and because of work obligations.

Employment in Canada, while having some distinctive features reflecting the nature of the country's economy and geography, has followed the same broad trends which have affected employment in developed countries generally.   In particular, it has experienced a decline in primary sector employment with major increases in the service sector.   In recent years, too, there have been attempts to contain or reduce the public sector component.   Regional variations in employment and unemployment have been persistent features of Canada's economic scene for many decades and are not likely to change in the foreseeable future.   Indeed, it is not unlikely that regional differences may be even greater in the future if current trends continue, and if government policies are maintained.   The future may see Canada resemble older industrial countries such as Britain, with growth, inflation, and low unemployment in one area (the south in Britain, the Windsor-Quebec axis in Canada), and stagnation or decline, high unemployment, and depression in peripheral areas. While this scenario already exists in Canada, it may become even more marked in the future.

One major implication of such a development is the creation of a much larger group of unemployed individuals who may well be permanently unemployed.   Only in a very few places in Canada have steps been taken in the recreation field to deal with such a group, and such actions have been tentative and untested (Ministry of Tourism and Recreation 1987).   In European countries, such as Britain, where unemployment has remained in excess of 10% in many areas of the country for almost a decade, numerous attempts have been made by recreation agencies to provide leisure opportunities to these groups.   Such steps include reduced admissions to sporting events, special recreation programs at community centres, and major efforts to involve the unemployed in leisure-related projects, including volunteering services.   A major obstacle is still the stigma associated with unemployment, but in areas of long-term unemployment this appears to be declining, and among the young unemployed it is often not present. As public sector financing becomes harder and harder to obtain, it is likely that recreation agencies, especially at the municipal and provincial level, will have to become more involved with other social agencies to help meet social needs from a more integrated viewpoint, or face a relative, if not an absolute, decline in their financial support. In Ontario, the provincial government's decision in 1987 to reallocate some of the revenue generated from lotteries from purely recreation projects to other areas, including health care, roused strong, if narrow-minded, opposition from recreation agencies, which probably correctly saw this action as the thin end of a wedge. Clearer justification of the role of recreation and its benefits compared to costs and, particularly, its relevance in helping solve social problems such as unemployment may be required in the future to ensure continued public sector support.

Leisure Time

Some changes in employment-related factors have not all materialized as anticipated (Campbell 1976). The work week for most Canadians has not declined to twenty-five or even thirty hours but remains around the thirty-five-hour level, and there are even signs that significant numbers are working longer hours than a decade ago. The normal work week is still five days long, and for many people any minor gains in non-work time on a daily basis have been lost to increased travel time, especially for those living in metropolitan areas. This situation is not likely to improve at all for most people in the near future, and as people in major cities locate farther away from their place of employment to escape urban problems, including high accommodation prices, their travel times are likely to increase and their potential leisure time decrease.

Anticipated widespread use of computer technology, which would allow considerable numbers of employees to remain at home to work, has not occurred, although in certain occupations and locations this has happened for limited numbers of people. Neither has flextime or job sharing been accepted by employers or employees as eagerly and on as large a scale as once thought. While these innovations may see more participants in the years ahead, major changes in the working patterns and habits of most Canadians are not anticipated in the next two decades at least.

The weekend, and all the inevitable problems of peaking and crowding it creates, is likely to remain the major block of leisure time available for recreation to most Canadians on a regular basis. What may alter this more than changes in the working habits of most people are changes in laws restricting commercial and other activities on Sundays. Sunday shopping, already flirted with in some provinces, may see large numbers of retail employees having to work one or both weekend days with subsequent changes in their families' behaviour patterns. While Sunday shopping is common in tourist and recreation areas, it is not widespread elsewhere in Canada. If it should become the norm, with associated demands being placed on transportation and other services, some fundamental shifts in the temporal pattern of recreation may occur. Any phenomenon which reduces the problems associated with weekend peaking would be welcomed by many in the supply side of recreation, who would appreciate a spreading of demand over seven rather than two days of the week. Without subsequent adjustments elsewhere, however, for example, in education and industry, many of the people required to work on Sundays would be forced to recreate alone, or at least apart from their families, from Monday to Friday on whichever day off replaced Sunday. One alternative result could therefore be an overall decline in current Sunday, and perhaps weekend, recreation participation.

Family Structure

A major social change which has taken place throughout Canada and the developed world is the decline in the traditional nuclear family, consisting of two adults of opposite sexes and two or more children, normally living close to other family members. In a more mobile population, the contact and support provided by the extended family members are becoming less common. Frequent job and location changes among many upwardly mobile baby-boomers have disrupted stable family groups. The increasing incidence of single-parent families has also changed what was the normal lifestyle of Canadian families of the 1950s and 1960s.

The impacts of the single-parent phenomenon on recreation and leisure are not known and have not been studied. Single-parent families are more likely to be headed by women, and incomes are usually considerably lower than for two-parent families. As the single parent is usually working full- or part-time, babysitters for small children are often a necessity, and there is not a parent at home to play with young children or to do what once were traditional functions, such as taking children to neighbourhood parks and playgrounds. Less time is available in most cases to parents for participating in recreation outside conventional working hours, both with children and by themselves.

The single-parent family may not result in significant changes in Canadian recreation behaviour, however, for the model of the conventional nuclear family is striven for by many single parents, attempting to not deprive their offspring of participation in activities other children may engage in. Organizations such as Big Brothers and Big Sisters aid in this process. The financial limitations, however, may preclude full participation even if time and other constraints can be overcome. The current lack of research makes conclusions on the likely implications of the decline of the nuclear family too tentative to draw. Compensatory organizations are being developed, as noted above, and in many communities, particularly new resource communities which face large numbers of new resident families each year and high turnover rates, clubs, church, and other groups help fill the void left by absent extended family members (Holman 1982).

In the long term, smaller family size is likely to have a more significant effect upon Canadian recreation patterns by the implied reduction in the younger age cohorts at which many recreation facilities and programs are currently aimed. This will mean a larger proportion of young Canadians will be immigrants or first-generation immigrants, who may have equally legitimate but different recreational desires and needs from those of young people in the 1960s and 1970s.

Special Events

In the past few years major spectacles, hallmark events as they have now become known, may have been capable of producing long-term as well as short-term changes in leisure behaviour patterns. In the relatively recent past Canada has hosted several of these events, including the summer and winter Olympic Games, the Commonwealth and World Student Games, two World Fairs, and several motor-racing Grand Prix, as well as the 1988 Economic Summit. Such events serve two main purposes. They attract immense media coverage on a global scale and thus focus attention on the host country and city. Secondly, they expose local residents to activities with which they were previously unfamiliar but may find attractive and may desire to participate in, and to performers they may wish to emulate. Some of these effects may be short-lived, even briefly anticipatory -- as, for example, in different driving habits immediately before and after a Grand Prix Motor Race (Fischer, Hatch, and Paise 1986) -- while others may leave a legacy of permanent facilities, such as the two Olympic sites, which may create induced demand or tap latent demand, as discussed by Smith in chapter 3.

In the coming years Canadian cities are bidding for two hallmark events, the summer Olympics for Toronto in 1996, and the Commonwealth Games for Victoria in 1994. If either or both cities are successful, the legacy of facilities can be expected to stimulate increased participation in related activities in these cities, at least, as well as to increase international tourism to Canada and probably mildly affecting Canadian travel patterns in those years. A successful Canadian challenge for the Americas Cup in 1990 would almost certainly result in increased interest and participation in sailing, while renewed Canadian success on the World Cup ski circuit could stimulate further growth in skiing. A Canadian team in the World Series might have similar effects in baseball. However, the absence of Canada from the 1990 World Cup (soccer) may prove a near fatal blow to the existence of professional soccer in Canada.

The demonstration effect of successful Canadian participants in other activities, such as tennis, golf, bowling, or swimming, may have similar if smaller results on levels of participation in those recreational activities. However, there is a great deal of difference between a child emulating a media sports hero briefly, and a long-term commitment to participation in a specialized and often expensive competitive activity. It is the media coverage, especially on television, which is almost certainly the key factor in terms of initiating a change in recreation behaviour, coupled with the availability of facilities as a result of the hosting of specific events, rather than the fact that a Canadian won a specific event. At a regional or local level, the creation of new facilities, as in Kananaskis in Alberta, may have significant effects on previously established patterns of certain activities. If the ski developments at Mount Allan receive good snow and suitable weather, Calgarians and other Albertans, at least, may travel there rather than to sites in Banff National Park, for example. Since 1976 serious competitive cyclists have travelled to Montreal to use the velodrome built for the summer Olympics. In the long term it is changes in regional travel patterns and participation levels which may be the real legacy of hallmark events, not nation-wide changes in participation patterns.

Special Groups

One of the social movements of the past decade has been the push for equal rights of access to all areas for the disabled in Canada.

This movement concentrated on employment, transport, and social services other than recreation in its first years of activity, but has increasingly broadened its scope; recreation facilities from private commercial operations such as movie theatres, to public places such as national parks have had to make efforts to provide equal opportunity for access to the disabled. This is an area in which considerable change can be expected in the years ahead. The handicapped lobby is becoming highly effective and has considerable public support behind its efforts to improve opportunities and access for its constituency.

The future, however, may see a reduction in support in some instances, and at the very least some controversies are likely to emerge. Two areas seem likely to be contentious in the public sector. The first is financial. All public recreation agencies are facing, and are likely to continue to face, some underfunding in their budgets, and the costs of improving access for the disabled and other special populations are high and increasing. Difficult decisions are having to be made over trade-offs between, for example, improving access and continuing interpretive programs. This is not a new situation, for opportunity costs have for long been a problem to recreation facility managers, and access for special populations is basically just one more, albeit an expensive, item to be placed in the budget equation. As with other items, limits will eventually be reached, when other items assume greater importance.

A more serious issue in the long-term is the potential clash of perceptions and values between proponents of improved and increased access in heritage areas, and proponents of the preservationist/wilderness viewpoint, who regard almost any intrusion of people into protected areas as unacceptable. Coupled with this group are those concerned about the authenticity and aesthetics of heritage properties when they are modified to provide improved access and ease of movement for special populations. This potential problem is likely to be exacerbated by the needs of the increasing proportion of the population which is entering the over-sixty age cohort. While this group can still be highly active, fewer members of it are active primitive campers or long-distance hikers, and their preferences and abilities may exhibit similarities to the needs of special populations such as the disabled. Conferences focusing on the place and needs of the disabled in heritage areas have considered some of these problems, but have not yet suggested solutions (Heritage Resources Centre 1986).

Other Factors

There are, of course, likely to be many other changes in Canadian society which affect recreation patterns. The women's movement and feminism have certainly changed the level of participation in many outdoor recreation activities, particularly sports, in the past decade. Perhaps more important, attitudes towards "appropriate" gender-based recreation behaviour are changing. Old stereotypes and shibboleths can be expected to continue to decline in relevance and significance in the future, and fuller participation by women in all recreation activities, especially outdoor ones, will occur.

No specific comments have been made on increasing affluence, although income has long been accepted as a major determinant of recreation participation. This is not because such a relationship is expected to change in the future; in fact, it may become more significant if Canada moves towards becoming a more economically divided nation. Beyond a certain minimum level, however, income does not so much alter the activities engaged in as it does the nature, location, duration, and frequency of the participation. More affluent skiers may go to the Rockies for a week rather than to the local ski slope for a day, for example, but the key is obtaining the minimum amount of disposable income needed to participate in the activity and the desire to participate. It is not unreasonable to assume that levels of affluence may continue to rise in Canada at an aggregate level in the future, but the process of the democratization of leisure may not continue for all groups or for the more expensive activities in the same manner as it has for the past half century or more. While two-income families are increasing in Canada, there is a finite limit to the growth of such a phenomenon. Such growth is also dependent on job creation, and for many lower-income Canadians may be driven as much by necessity as by desire for material goods. Inflation in the price of essentials, such as housing in large cities, may more than account for increases in gross income and leave little extra, if any, for additional recreational participation.

Finally, for more than two decades there has been a growing concern for the environment and signs, in the 1980s, that such feelings may have finally registered with political and corporate decision-makers. Whether such indications will translate into major action to reduce environmental degradation and even to restore environmental quality remains to be seen. Initially, such action would have little direct impact on recreation patterns, but if additional areas became suitable for outdoor recreation, especially polluted water bodies, then spatial patterns may change, resulting in increased recreational activity in, or closer to, metropolitan centres, reducing pressure on access routes and more remote areas. A further result of increased environmental concern would be additions to the list of protected areas, although a political response may be that increased expenditures on environmental improvement may reduce the need for formally protected areas. Irrespective of these possibilities, increased participation in outdoor recreation in scenic, resource-based areas is likely to continue in Canada in the future. Without significant improvements in access, the patterns are not likely to change significantly from those discussed by Lundgren earlier in this volume, but use levels towards the fringe can be expected to increase. Additional pressure will continue to be felt on national parks, exacerbated by increasing numbers of foreign tourists.

TECHNOLOGY AND RATES OF CHANGE

One major factor which has typified modern Canadian society is the rate of change of many once traditional attitudes and values, and patterns of behaviour. The speed at which information is disseminated throughout the world has increased exponentially and, with respect to communications and travel, the past two centuries have seen the increasing development of a "shrinking world" (Abler, Janelle, Philbrick, and Sommer 1975). The developments in these areas have been of crucial significance to recreation and will continue to be so in the future. The ability to access information almost immediately has allowed the development of a wide range of services by recreation/tourism agencies, especially those in the transportation and accommodation fields, and has enabled travel agents and others to confirm travel and other requirements of would-be recreationists almost instantly. Reports on road conditions, space available in parks, weather conditions, facility opening hours, and skiing conditions are just a few of the information services a telephone call away from most Canadians.

The availability of this information has increased, and will continue to increase, the ease of substitution of various elements of the recreation experience. The combination of the personalized mobility afforded by the automobile, increased leisure time, improved transportation facilities, increased affluence, and increased supply of opportunities have given the recreationist of the 1980s a wide range of options to select from. Whereas, in earlier times, decisions to book accommodation and make travel arrangements would have to be made days or even months in advance, and plans were difficult if not impossible to change, now decisions can often be made the day of departure, or even during travel. While it is true that some commercial transportation carriers offer inducements for early booking and allow few if any changes, such constraints are optional and tend to apply primarily to long-distance, vacation travel.

In the context of day and weekend recreation, participants can exercise an increasing number and combination of options, relating to time at which the recreational experience is taken, location visited, and activity engaged in. As facilities tend to become more multi-functional rather than designated for a single activity, the precise activity pattern and behaviour of individuals becomes even harder to predict. Jackson and Dunn (1988) have demonstrated the high annual turnover rate in participation in specific recreational activities and the difficulty of explaining and predicting such changes. As the choice of recreational activities grows, the turnover rate is likely to increase. In the past two decades alone, a number of activities not only have witnessed increases and declines in popularity, such as cycling and cross-country skiing, but also have run the full course from appearance to virtual extinction, for example, hula hoops. Several other activities are in too early a stage for one to be sure of their widespread adoption, but would appear likely to retain a significant number of adherents in Canada; these include skateboarding, wind surfing, hang gliding, and most recently, snow boarding.

All of the four latter activities have certain elements in common, which may provide some guide to directions of future new activities. They all utilize "new" technology in terms of materials (fibreglass, resins, plastics); they all appeal to a young audience (primarily ten years to thirty years of age); they are all individual activities; they all require physical activity, agility, and practice; and they all allow the demonstration of talent and performance. Snowmobiling, surfing, yachting (in one- or two-person boats such as Lasers), scuba diving, jet skiing, downhill skiing, para sailing and sky diving are somewhat similar, and recent interest in four-wheel-drive and other off-road vehicles is also related. These activities offer challenge and excitement to a bored society. As well, they are glamorous, they possess a positive image -- hence the role they play as the backdrop in many lifestyle commercials -- and, perhaps of some importance to participants, they are activities the preceding generation did not participate in to any great degree, if at all. In those activities in which there was participation, such as downhill skiing, at least one new form, free-style skiing, has developed, and equipment, especially dress, has changed dramatically from the conservative forms of two decades ago.

One can speculate, therefore, that activities which may appear on the Canadian scene in the future will be those which offer the following features: challenge and excitement at a personal level, the opportunity to improve and to display that improvement, the opportunity to engage in the activity in conjunction with others and alone in an outdoor setting, the opportunity to make a personal statement through participation -- for example, by personalizing equipment or technique, and the utilization of new technology in the form of equipment and means of access to use areas.

Further developments in small boats can be expected which will allow rapid and extensive exploration of hitherto inaccessible water bodies. Other forms of over-snow and on-snow recreation may also appear. Jet or motorized snow skis are probably as unlikely as personal gyrocopters were unsuccessful, but the combination of skiing and para-sailing may reappear. In the 1960s this activity appeared briefly in Europe, especially Scotland, where parachutes were used in conjunction with favourable winds to allow participants to ski up slopes without lifts, and then to ski down in a conventional manner -- a poor man's version of heli-skiing! One adaptation of heli-skiing which has appeared in the Rockies in recent years is heli-hiking, where walkers are transported to an initial high-level location by helicopter. Underwater activities are likely to grow in popularity, although Canadian waters do not hold the appeal of warmer areas such as the Caribbean. Submarines are now appearing in tropical waters in a variety of locations for tourist excursions, following their success for years at Disneyland and Disney World, and may be attractive in some locations. The Great Lakes, especially the shipwreck-rich area in the new national park off the tip of the Bruce Peninsula where clear water exists, would be a likely candidate site in Canada.

Diving under the ice in the Arctic, which has been engaged in by such personalities as the Prince of Wales, may also appeal to a limited number of participants.

To speculate on entirely new activities belongs more in the realm of science fiction than academia, and the speed with which new equipment and activities can appear and become popular (and unpopular) is one of the major characteristics of twentieth century recreation. One of the few really new activities, and probably the only form of recreation created in Canada in this century is snowmobiling. While with hindsight it seems its adoption and adaptation should have been easily anticipated, its popularity, its economic, environmental, social, and legal implications, and its permanence were not appreciated nor successfully managed until almost a decade and a half after the first appearance of the machine in something resembling its present form in 1959 (Butler 1982). The appearance of new activities and new equipment and the spread of new forms of recreation into areas previously not exposed to such activities can be expected to duplicate many of the problems which resulted from the popularity of snowmobiling in its first decade. These include conflict between participants in the new forms of recreation and in those more traditional forms over use of resources and incompatibility; conflicts between participants in the new forms of recreation and non-recreational users of the same areas, including indigenous people in some areas; philosophical conflicts over the acceptability of the new activities, both under any circumstances, and in specific areas; safety concerns, both for users and non-users; legal problems stemming primarily from liability and trespass issues; and licensing and operating regulations where appropriate.

These are not new problems and have been present in some form since fire and the wheel were invented, but as noted above, where the rate of introduction and acceptance of innovations is so rapid, the ability of users and non-users to adapt to the innovations is often overtaken by events. Hopefully some of the lessons learned from innovations such as the snowmobile can be applied to new situations to avoid a repetition of mistakes and omissions in the future. Over the years, however, there seems to have been a hardening or polarization of attitudes in many groups over such issues as environmental protection, native peoples' and others' rights to areas and resources, and increasing use of the legal system to acquire or prohibit access to areas. There is, unfortunately, little reason to expect this trend to change significantly, at least in the near future, and thus we will almost certainly be faced with continued problems to resolve relating to compatibility and acceptability of new forms of recreation in the areas in which they will be used and with non-users.

The one area in which such conflicts are less prevalent is the field of electronic recreation and leisure. Canadians, like many others, have acquired a wide variety of electronic leisure goods, beginning with radio, television, and record players and in the last decade, portable cassette players, video recorders, CB radios, cellular telephones, compact disc players, micro-portable televisions, personal and portable computers, and video games. The results for recreation participation have been somewhat contradictory. Many of the above items, for example, television, computer games, and videocassette recorders, encourage owners of the equipment to stay at home, or at least indoors, to utilize the equipment. On the other hand, many are designed specifically to be taken out of the home so that people may enjoy the outdoors without being denied their exposure to urban-oriented entertainment. Thus, not only can one listen to tapes while jogging or even canoeing, or listen to a compact disc and talk on the telephone while driving to recreation, one can also experience the wonders of a northern sunset while watching the World Series on a three-inch television screen, listening to U2 on a portable cassette player, and cooking the evening meal on a portable, battery-operated microwave oven. With increasing use of solar power cells in calculators and other items, it may not be long before most other portable electronic appliances are available with solar power sources. Ongoing improvements in operational efficiency and power-to-weight ratio will allow a far larger variety of items to become truly completely portable and capable of being carried on many excursions and into many areas not currently accessible. It is not too far removed from reality to envisage super-light engines and other power units, and water transport -- for example, inflatable boats -- which could revolutionize back-country travel.

In urban areas, the improvements to television hardware have not made great differences, if any, in television viewing habits, nor have compact disc players changed listening habits in terms of time allocated to the activities. VCRs, however, have undoubtedly had a major impact, both on television watching patterns (increasing time spent in front of the television set but decreasing the time spent watching television programs) and, to a lesser but still significant extent, on viewing movies at conventional movie theatres. While going to movies is still popular, movie theatres have become smaller, tending to be found in complexes with several screens, and increasingly often being located in shopping malls rather than individual sites in downtown locations. The past decade has seen the virtual disappearance in Canada of the drive-in movie theatre, which has been unable to compete on grounds either of quality or economy with newer movie complexes.

The development of shopping malls beyond a simple collection of stores to multi-functional developments with major leisure components has also been a feature of the past two decades, culminating in the late 1980s in the West Edmonton Mall, complete with hotel, ice rink, submarines, pools, and roller coasters, as well as several hundred stores and services. While many more developments on a similar scale cannot be expected in Canada, the diversification, remodelling, and enlarging of existing malls is likely to continue. The grouping of retail and service facilities with leisure facilities makes a great deal of sense from a social as well as an economic point of view. In some northern towns and isolated communities, too, the creation of a community centre which includes not only the above facilities but also educational, medical, and public sector services is one attempt to overcome some climatic handicaps. It also provides a definite nucleus for an isolated community where quality of life depends on social cohesion and contact.

The home can be expected to remain the principal location for leisure for almost all Canadians into the future, despite longer and increasing numbers of recreation-related trips out of the city. The home has always been the leisure centre for most people, and other developments have encouraged this situation. Apart from the items mentioned above, a vast array of labour-saving devices from microwave ovens to motorized lawn mowers and mini-tractors have reduced the amount of time required to do a large number of tasks around the home, allowing potentially more time in which to perform such newer duties as cleaning the backyard swimming pool. The acquisition of major leisure items, such as private swimming pools, has become a practical possibility for many Canadian families, with commensurate changes in recreational travel habits and visits to other locations (Wright 1981). The early 1980s may have seen an expansion in the number of private pools and tennis courts which may not be duplicated in the future. In many urban centres the price and lack of availability of land have combined to reduce the average lot size for new houses, and many new yards are barely large enough for a swimming pool. If a pool is added, then the remaining space is very limited, and a real choice has to be made between a garden or other facilities. Other amenities, such as gas barbecues and hot tubs, also make the home more attractive as a leisure focus to those fortunate enough to be able to afford them. Additional facilities can be expected to become available in the future to allow reasonably affluent Canadians to be able to undertake an even wider range of activities, or pseudo-activities, without leaving their own property. Playing golf (on a video machine), rowing or cross-country skiing (on an exercise machine), having a cook-out (on a barbecue) or a beach party (in a private pool with a wave-making machine), and watching a movie (on a VCR) are all possible now, and developments are certainly not going to cease.

At the other end of the economic scale, some 20% of Canadian households do not own a car, a higher proportion still in some large urban centres, and even more do not own their own homes, and are thus much more dependent upon private, commercial, and public leisure opportunities than private, personal ones. Public urban recreation facilities have not changed or widened in scope significantly in several decades, consisting primarily of urban parks, arenas, swimming pools, community centres, and libraries. Fortunately, programming and opportunities offered at these facilities have broadened considerably and can be expected, within financial limits, to become even wider. The combination of education and recreational facilities, with the addition of social services such as day-care and senior citizen centres, is a trend which will likely continue. To serve adequately in a future probably typified by financial cutbacks, a combination of functions is a cost-effective action, as is increasing reliance upon volunteers. Early retirement and the larger elderly population offer a potentially large force of volunteers with a tremendous range of skills. Interest in education in a multiplicity of forms, allied with the lifelong-learning concept, provides another outlet for volunteers and a way of filling leisure time without great demands for money or equipment. There have also been some indications of recognition of the need to provide other opportunities in urban areas than the traditional ones noted above. Some examples include the use of the Rideau Canal in Ottawa in winter for public skating, the use of Nathan Phillips Square in Toronto for public recreation, Gastown in Vancouver, and the Man and his World site in Montreal (Burton 1973). In terms of formal recreation facilities and public facilities which are heavily used for leisure purposes, Ontario Place and the Science Centre in Toronto, Science North in Sudbury, and the Olympic Village in Montreal stand out as examples for future developments if and when large amounts of funding are available.

Some of the major developments taking place in Canadian urban centres now require a mix of public and private funding and management. One example is the Skydome in Toronto. Domed stadiums, such as the Olympic Stadium in Montreal or the Skydome, require the combination of all sectors to develop and operate. That many of these facilities will appear in Canadian cities in the future is unlikely, for a large population base is necessary to sustain them, along with one or more major league sports franchises, and few Canadian cities meet those criteria. Smaller versions of climate-controlled leisure centres, noted elsewhere in this chapter, may be a substitute in smaller but still relatively large urban communities.

The private, commercial sector has expanded and broadened its leisure offerings in Canada on a major scale in the past two decades and can be expected to go on expanding in existing and new areas in the future, as it continues to capitalize on the apparently ever-continuing increase in leisure-related expenditures. Health spas/fitness clubs, private golf, ski, and racquet sport facilities, theme parks, multi-purpose campsites, and video arcades are perhaps the most visible, and some of the most successful, forms of private involvement in recreation. However, the private sector has also made significant developments in accommodation in recreation areas, particularly in the form of condominiums, both conventional and in the time-sharing format. Ownership of the conventional cottage has stabilized in Canada over the past two decades, and this may be an indication that the amount of investment of time and money in this type of facility is greater than many Canadians can or want to make. A shared property, or part of a shared property, has certain attractions to the present generation. While time-sharing is not a major feature in most of Canada, it has appeared at several major recreation areas such as Whistler in British Columbia, Banff in Alberta, Collingwood in Ontario, and the Laurentians in Quebec (Butler 1985), and can be expected to spread to other areas.

The conventional, private, commercial urban forms of recreation not hitherto discussed, especially bars, bowling alleys, bingo halls, and dance halls are still popular, but many have changed and will continue to change. Bars have become much more varied in their nature and offer a wider range of facilities, including dancing and video screens, and bowling alleys are rarely without video games. Again, many of these facilities can be expected to broaden still further in terms of the opportunities they will provide in order to attract customers in an increasingly competitive market. The principal difficulty faced by some urban facilities is the quality of the surrounding environment and, in particular, the safety of the city in the evening, the principal recreation time. While Canadian cities do not currently face the problems or have the negative image of their counterparts in the United States, the situation is more likely to deteriorate than it is to improve as Canadian cities become larger and more like American cities in many aspects. To reverse this trend and ensure a safe and attractive recreational environment in Canadian cities will be a major task facing public agencies in the future.

FUTURE EFFECTS OF RECREATION

While the extent and dimensions of impacts do not necessarily increase in direct proportion to increases in numbers of participants, it would be naive not to anticipate an increase in both positive and negative effects of recreation in the future, if participation continues to grow as it is expected to do. The important questions relate to the nature of the impacts and possible mitigation measures where desirable, and accurate assessment and prediction of new impacts not currently experienced.

In the economic field, expenditures on leisure have been increasing on an aggregate basis for several decades and can be expected to continue to do so in the future. While depressions, such as in the early 1980s, and other major economic upheavals, such as that brought on in the 1970s by sharp and sudden increases in oil prices, have noticeable effects on expenditures, their overall effects on recreation behaviour have been short in duration. Evidence in the 1970s suggested people would reduce travel for all other activities before reducing travel for leisure, and reduce expenditures on other items, if possible, before curtailing recreation partipation. Barring changes in the world's or Canada's economy on a catastrophic scale, expenditure on leisure, recreation, and tourism in Canada will continue to increase.

Canada's future in world tourism, as a destination for foreign tourists, can also be expected to be reasonably secure. While recent attempts to change and broaden Canada's image of moose, mountains, and Mounties have met with some slight success, Canada's attraction on a global scale still remains its geographical heritage. The major physical features -- the Rockies, the West Coast, the Arctic and the Canadian Shield -- are the most important attractions for tourists who are neither American, nor relatives of Canadians, and can be expected to increase in importance as wild and scenic places become scarcer in the world at large. Some inevitable conflicts between tourism and other uses of these areas are noted below. Canada's other tourism and recreation attractions will also continue to attract visitors internationally as well as nationally, and inter-provincial tourism can be expected to continue to increase (Smale and Butler 1986). The development of international resorts has already occurred in places such as Whistler in British Columbia, Banff in Alberta (despite national park limitations), Muskoka in Ontario, and the Laurentians in Quebec, as well as considerable upgrading of facilities in other locations such as Niagara-on-the-Lake in Ontario and Halifax in Nova Scotia. While large-scale investment in recreation and tourism projects may proceed much more slowly, if at all, in some other locations, expansion of facilities and subsequent income and employment is likely throughout Canada. One trend already visible is the move, where possible, towards year-round recreation use, rather than a summer-only season. The spectacular growth in skiing and snowmobiling in the 1960s and 1970s laid the basis for this trend, which will almost certainly continue in all suitable locations.

The environmental effects of recreational activities have been well documented by Wall elsewhere (Wall and Wright 1977, Mathieson and Wall 1982), and there is likely to be little change in the nature of the impacts in the future, based on the use of similar technology. (Should Canadians use personal nuclear power sources or should new disposable toxic containers appear, then a new set of problems would emerge.) Of more significance will be the extent of impacts, both spatially and temporally, and their effect upon ecosystem diversity and uniqueness. A model by Speight (1973) is useful in this respect, and focuses on extent, scarcity, and diversity. If, as suggested, technology allows Canadians to venture more frequently and more widely into the outdoors, to even the most remote regions, then areas currently free from significant use are liable to be exposed to potential damage and change.

Problems arise when use is not anticipated and methods of control or mitigation are not in place before use occurs, when the level of use far exceeds that anticipated, and when the nature of the impact is new and unforeseen. All three conditions are likely to take place in many parts of Canada in the future. Parks and other protected areas may be spared impacts of many of the new forms of recreation, but cannot expect to avoid increased use, particularly if the more attractive and well-known ones are marketed for tourism, as appears possible. Thus, there will be continued and more serious problems relating to loss of vegetation and soil in areas exposed to walkers and hikers, which include not only footpaths and trails, but also areas adjoining popular facilities such as campsites, picnic sites, car parks, and scenic viewpoints. Disturbance of wildlife will increase because of greater numbers of visitors desiring to see wildlife, especially if the growing interest in natural history continues.

It is less likely that hunting will increase in popularity, given the trends discussed earlier, and thus the consumptive use of wildlife may decrease. The future pattern of fishing in most of Canada is less clear, but angling in northern waters is likely to increase as tourism is marketed more strongly in the territories. Also, changes in ethnic composition may contribute to a re-evaluation of desirability of particular species. The ironic fact remains that much, if not most, of the environmental impacts resulting from recreation-related activity will be caused unintentionally by individuals who appreciate the Canadian natural heritage, but who, by their increasing numbers, are threatening its integrity in many areas. It is not the car-borne, hotel-staying urbanite who poses the greatest problems to managers of protected areas and others responsible for the environment, but users of the back-country, who travel on foot, by canoe, plane, and ski and who are the strongest supporters of the preservation of wild areas. This paradox can be expected to become a more serious problem in the future.

The anticipated increase in numbers of recreationists and tourists in Canada's recreation areas will also mean the near certainty of increased social impacts and conflicts between users and permanent and semi-permanent residents of these areas. D'Amore's studies (1982, 1986) of Canadian tourism futures support this view. The occurrence of problems between visitors and the visited population has been discussed in chapter 8 by Keogh, and the concerns recorded in specific locations in Canada (Doxey 1975, Cheng 1980) over the last few years are likely to become greater in number and severity. A shift towards "alternative tourism" or "culturally sympathetic" tourism and recreation, while resulting in an increase in the proportion of visitors desiring authentic experiences and symbiotic relationships with local residents and their environment, may only aggravate the situation. This could result in the number of visitors growing, and direct contact between visitors and visited -- and with it the possibility of change and conflict -- increasing.

The transformation of communities into resorts over time, while perhaps not inevitable, is certainly the norm in Canada as elsewhere (Butler 1980), and such a process does not always meet the approval and support of local residents. The creation of new facilities which attract visitors, for example, national parks, has met with considerable opposition in several areas in Canada from Nova Scotia (Ship Harbour proposed national park) to Ontario (Lindsay township adjoining the Bruce Peninsula National Park) to British Columbia (Tofino and Ucluelet adjoining Pacific Rim National Park) as noted by Harris (1986). While good planning, to some extent, can reduce the negative effects of and opposition to recreation developments, increased numbers of recreationists and tourists can only be expected to increase potential problems in the human sphere.

CONCLUSIONS

The picture that has been drawn of future recreation patterns in Canada is perhaps not an overwhelmingly positive one. Growth in almost all aspects of leisure and recreation is anticipated, but such growth is expected to be incremental and in similar directions to what is witnessed today. This is because many of the current recreationists will still be in Canada and active in recreation for several decades into the future, and will be exposing their children to many of the same recreational activities they themselves have been engaging in for many years. Expansion into new areas, in a spatial sense, is almost inevitable, both because of crowding, reduction in environmental quality, and lack of opportunity for new development, and because technological innovations will allow and encourage such expansion.

Some suggestions have been made about the nature of these innovations, particularly in the context of types of recreation activities which may appear. Most of the innovations are likely to be variations on activities engaged in now, as are most of the innovations in equipment and transportation, such as the increasing portability of many items, electric automobiles and, increasingly, computerized information dissemination and recording systems for users and managers of recreation areas.

The discussion in this chapter has been based on the assumption of no catastrophic change in the Canadian or global situation, such as nuclear war, a major economic depression as in 1929, or massive medical or environmental tragedies. Such events would, in varying degrees, clearly render much, if not all, of the previous discussion meaningless. There is, however, at least one other factor which may also cause some change in Canadian (and global) patterns of recreation behaviour, and that is climatic change brought about by what is known as the "greenhouse effect." Global change, with predicted effects including rising sea levels, declining inland lake levels, declining rainfall in some areas, changes in vegetation and hence wildlife distribution and regeneration, all resulting from a warming of the planet, could have major effects in Canada as elsewhere. The increases in temperature, while not major from a human perceptive point of view in southern Canada, could have major effects on both summer and winter recreation patterns, especially winter recreation in currently near-marginal areas. Wall (1988) has shown the serious consequences of rising temperatures for skiing in Ontario, as have Lamothe and Périard (1988) in Quebec, and also the more positive effects upon summer camping. The predictions are much more negative for winter recreation than they are positive for summer recreation, and while they are only possible scenarios, the implications are extremely serious. In addition, while beaches may increase in area in the Great Lakes and other inland water bodies, rivers and streams may have reduced flow, possibly to a level prohibiting many forms of water-based recreation, such as sailing and fishing. Oceans are expected to rise if global warming occurs, and many beaches will disappear beneath the waves, along with parts of many communities including Charlottetown and Vancouver. The social and particularly the economic upheaval and the necessary readjustments could result in even greater change in recreational and tourist behaviour in Canada and the world at large.

Global change may not be inevitable and may prove not to be a reality but rather a short-term misinterpretation of the climatic record. However, the very possibility serves to remind mankind of the fragility and interdependence of the earth's physical and human systems. Much of Canadian recreation activity is tied closely to the environment and requires a clean and healthy environment if participants are to derive enjoyment and satisfaction from their recreation experiences, now and in the future, whatever that may be.

References

Abler, R., Janelle, D.G., Philbrick, A.K., and Sommer, J. 1975. *Human geography in a shrinking world*. (Scituate, Mass.: Duxbury Press).

Abt Associates. 1976. *Tourism impact study for Prince Edward Island*. (Cambridge, Mass.).

Alberta Recreation and Parks. 1981. *Public Opinion Survey on Recreation*. (Edmonton).

_____. 1984. *Public Opinion Survey on Recreation*. (Edmonton).

_____. 1988. *Recreation trends: A Look at leisure, no. 20*. (Edmonton).

_____. 1982. *Recreational activity preferences, reasons for participating, and the satisfaction of needs*. (Edmonton).

Allaby, I. 1983. "Old Montreal: Its old self again" *Canadian Geographic*. 103(1), 36-45.

Allen, L.R. and Buchanan, T. 1982. "Techniques for comparing leisure classification systems" *Journal of Leisure Research*. 14, 307-22.

Allen, L.R., Donnelly, M.A., and Warder, D.S. 1984. "The stability of leisure factor structures across time" *Leisure Sciences*. 6, 221-37.

Anderson, D.H. and Brown, P.J. 1984. "The displacement process in recreation" *Journal of Leisure Research*. 16, 61-73.

Backerman, S. 1983. *Arts mean business: An economic impact survey of Vancouver's non-profit cultural industry.* (Vancouver: City of Vancouver, Social Planning Department).

Bainbridge, S. 1979. *Restrictions at Stonehenge: The reactions of visitors to limitations in access.* (London: HMSO).

Balmer, K.R. 1979. "Canadian societal futures: Implications for the leisure research community" in E.M. Avedon, M. LeLièvre, and T.O. Stewart eds. *Contemporary leisure research: Proceedings of the Second Canadian Congress on Leisure Research.* (Waterloo: Ontario Research Council on Leisure) 545-58.

Barker, M.L. 1971. "Beach pollution in the Toronto region" in W.R.D. Sewell and I. Burton eds. *Perceptions and attitudes in resources management.* (Ottawa: Department of Energy, Mines and Resources) 37-47.

_____. 1982. "Traditional landscape and mass tourism in the Alps" *Geographical Review.* 72, 395-415.

Barrett, J.A. 1958. *The seaside resort towns of England and Wales.* Ph.D. thesis, London University.

Barton, M.M. 1969. "Water pollution in remote recreational areas" *Journal of Soil and Water Conservation.* 24, 132-34.

Bates, G.H. 1935. "The vegetation of footpaths, sidewalks, cart-tracks and gateways" *Journal of Ecology.* 25, 470-87.

_____. 1938. "Life forms of pasture plants in relation to treading" *Journal of Ecology.* 26, 452-54.

_____. 1950. "Track making by man and domestic animals" *Journal of Animal Ecology.* 19, 21-28.

Battin, J.G. and Nelson, J.G. 1982. "Recreation and conservation: the struggle for balance in Point Pelee National Park" in G. Wall and J.S. Marsh eds. *Recreational land use: Perspectives on its evolution in Canada.* (Ottawa: Carleton University Press) 77-101.

Bayfield, N.G. 1974. "Burial of vegetation by erosion material near chairlifts on Cairngorm" *Biological Conservation.* 6, 246-51.

_____. 1979. "Recovery of four montane heath communities on Cairngorm, Scotland, from disturbance by trampling" *Biological Conservation.* 15, 165-79.

B.C. Central Credit Union. 1983. "What makes B.C. tick?" *Economic Analysis of British Columbia.* 3(2), 1-4.

Beaman, J., Kim, Y., and Smith, S.L.J. 1979. "The effects of supply on participation" *Leisure Sciences.* 2(2), 71-88.

Beard, J.G. and Ragheb, M.G. 1980. "Measuring leisure satisfaction" *Journal of Leisure Research.* 12, 20-33.

_____. 1983. "Measuring leisure motivation" *Journal of Leisure Research.* 15, 219-28.

Becker, R.H. 1981. "Displacement of recreational users between the Lower St. Croix and the Upper Mississippi" *Journal of Environmental Management.* 13, 259-67.

Becker, R.H., Jubenville, A., and Burnett, G.W. 1984. "Fact and judgment in the search for a social carrying capacity" *Leisure Sciences.* 6, 475-86.

Bella, L. 1987. *Parks for profit.* (Montreal: Harvest House).

Berger, E., and Associates. 1983. *Recreation ... A changing society's economic giant,* volume 1. (Toronto: Ontario Ministry of Tourism and Recreation).

Berkes, F. 1984. Competition between commercial and sport fishermen: An ecological analysis" *Human Ecology.* 12, 413-29.

Bevins, M.I. and Wilcox, D.P. 1980. *Outdoor recreation participation -- analysis of national surveys, 1959-1978.* Vermont Agricultural Experimental Station Bulletin 686. (Vermont: University of Vermont).

Binkley, C. 1977. *Estimating recreation benefits: A critical review and bibliography.* Council of Planning Librarians, Exchange Bibliography no. 1219. (Monticello, Ill.: Vance Bibliographies).

Bishop, D.W. 1970. "Stability of the factor structure of leisure behavior: Analyses of four communities" *Journal of Leisure Research.* 2, 160-70.

Blackorby, C., Donaldson, G., and Slade, M. 1984. *Expo 86: An economic impact analysis.* (Vancouver: B.C. Economic Policy Institute, University of British Columbia).

Boggs, P. and Wall, G. 1984. "Economic impacts of a recreational facility: Perspectives from Canada's Wonderland" *Operational Geographer.* 5, 42-46.

Boxall, P.C. 1986. "The use of fish and wildlife resources by non-Albertans: Sport hunting and fishing" Paper presented at "Tourism and the Environment: Conflict or Harmony?" Symposium sponsored by the Alberta Chapter of the Canadian Society of Environmental Biologists, Calgary.

British Columbia. 1985a. *Tourism highlights, 1984.* (Victoria: Ministry of Tourism).

British Columbia. 1985b. *The economic significance of recreation in British Columbia.* (Victoria: Ministry of Provincial Secretary and Government Services, Recreation and Sport Branch; and Ministry of Industry and Small Business Development).

Britton, R. 1979. "Some notes on the geography of tourism" *Canadian Geographer.* 23, 276-82.

Brown, T.C. 1984. "The concept of value in resource allocation" *Land Economics.* 60, 231-46.

Bryan, H. 1979. *Conflict in the great outdoors: Toward understanding and managing for diverse sportsmen preferences.* (Birmingham: University of Alabama, Bureau of Public Administration).

Buchanan, T. and Buchanan, J.P. 1981. "Some initial observations on conflict research" *Recreation Research Review*. 8, 36-42.

Buckley, P. and Girling, S. 1979. "Defining outdoor recreational interests" in G. Wall ed. *Recreational land use in Southern Ontario*. (Waterloo: University of Waterloo, Department of Geography,) 81-96.

Bultena, G.L. and Klessig, L.L. 1969. "Satisfaction in camping: A conceptualization and guide to social research" *Journal of Leisure Research*. 1, 348-54.

Burch, W.R. 1984. "Much ado about nothing: Some reflections on the wider and wilder implications of social carrying capacity" *Leisure Sciences*. 6, 487-96.

Burton, T.L. 1967. *The cassification of recreation demands and supplies*. (University of Birmingham, Centre for Urban and Regional Studies).

_____. 1973. *Leisure*. (Toronto: Van Nostrand Reinhold).

_____. 1981. "You can't get there from here: A personal perspective on recreation forecasting in Canada" *Recreation Research Review*. 9, 38-43.

_____. 1984. *The economic significance of recreation in Alberta*. (Edmonton: University of Alberta, Department of Recreation and Leisure Studies).

Busack, S.D. and Bury, R.B. 1974. "Some effects of off-road vehicles and sheep grazing on lizard populations in the Mojave Desert" *Biological Conservation*. 6, 179-83.

Butler, R.W. 1975. *The development of tourism in the North and implications for the Inuit*. Renewable Resources Project volume 9. (Ottawa: Inuit Tapirisat of Canada).

_____. 1979. "The social impact of tourism and recreation" in E.M. Avedon, M. LeLièvre and T.O. Stewart eds. *Contemporary leisure research: Proceedings of the Second Canadian Congress on Leisure Research*. (Waterloo: Ontario Research Council on Leisure) 371-77.

_____. 1980. "The concept of a tourist area cycle of evolution: Implications for management of resources" *Canadian Geographer.* 24, 5-12.

_____. 1981. "Geographical research on leisure: Reflections and anticipations on Accrington Stanley and fire hydrants" in D. Ng and S. Smith eds. *Perspectives on the nature of leisure research.* (Waterloo: University of Waterloo Press) 43-68.

_____. 1982. "The development of snowmobiles in Canada" in G. Wall and J.S. Marsh eds. *Recreational land use: Perspectives on its evolution in Canada.* (Ottawa: Carleton University Press) 365-92.

_____. 1985. "Timesharing: the implications of an alternative to the conventional cottage" *Loisir et Société.* 8, 769-80.

Butler, R.W. and Troughton, M.J. 1985. *Public access to private land.* (London: University of Western Ontario).

Butler, R.W., Elder, P.S., Janisch, H.N., and Petrie, B.M. eds. 1971. *Proceedings: Conference on Snowmobiles and All-Terrain Vehicles.* (London: University of Western Ontario).

Cameron, J.M. and Bordessa, R. 1981. *Wonderland: Through the looking glass.* (Maple, Ont.: Belsten Publishing).

Campbell, C.K. 1976. "Future symptoms" in Canadian Outdoor Recreation Research Committee ed. *Park and recreation futures in Canada: Issues and options.* (Toronto: Ontario Research Council on Leisure) 83-147.

Canada, Federal Environmental Assessment Review Office. 1979. *Banff highway project (East Gate to km 13): Report of the Environmental Assessment Panel.* (Hull: Minister of Supply and Services).

_____. 1982a. *Banff highway project (km 13 to km 27): Report of the Environmental Assessment Panel.* (Hull: Minister of Supply and Services).

_____. 1982b. *CP Rail Rogers Pass Development, Glacier National Park: Preliminary report of the Environmental Assessment Panel.* (Hull: Minister of Supply and Services).

_____. 1983. *Banff highway project: Final report of the Environment Assessment Panel.* (Hull: Minister of Supply and Services).

Canadian Climate Centre. 1986. *Understanding CO_2 and Climate. Annual Report 1985.* (Downsview: Environment Canada, Atmospheric Environment Service).

Canadian Council on Rural Development. 1975. *Tourism and outdoor recreation in rural development.* (Ottawa).

Canadian Society of Environmental Biologists. 1986. *Tourism and environment: Conflict or harmony?* (Edmonton: Alberta Chapter).

Canadian Wildlife Service. 1983. *The Importance of wildlife to Canadians.* See Filion, F.L. et al.

Carbyn, L.N. 1974. "Wolf population fluctuations in Jasper National Park, Alberta, Canada" *Biological Conservation.* 6, 94-101.

Chadwick, R.A. 1981. "Some notes on the geography of tourism: A comment" *Canadian Geographer.* 25, 191-97.

Chappelle, D.E. 1973. "The need for outdoor recreation: An economic conundrum?" *Journal of Leisure Research.* 5, 47-53.

Chase, D.R. and Cheek, N.H., Jr. 1979. "Activity preferences and participation: Conclusions from a factor analytic study" *Journal of Leisure Research.* 11, 92-101.

Chase, D.R., Kasulis, J.J., and Lusch, R.F. 1980. "Factor invariance of nonwork activities" *Journal of Leisure Research.* 12, 55-68.

Cheng, J. 1980. "Tourism: How much is too much? Lessons for Canmore from Banff" *Canadian Geographer*. 24, 72-80.

Cheron, E.J. and Ritchie, J.R.B. 1982. "Leisure activities and perceived risk" *Journal of Leisure Research*. 14, 139-54.

Christaller, W. 1964. "Some considerations of tourism location in Europe" *Papers and Proceedings of the Regional Science Association*. 12, 95-105.

Christensen, H.H. and Clark, R.R. 1983. "Increasing public involvement to reduce depreciative behavior in recreation settings" *Leisure Sciences*. 5, 359-79.

Chubb, M. ed. 1971. *Proceedings of the 1971 Snowmobile and Off the Road Vehicle Research Symposium*. (East Lansing: Michigan State University).

Cicchetti, C.J. 1971. "Some economic issues in planning urban recreation facilities" *Land Economics*. 47, 14-23.

Clark, R.N. and Stankey, G.H. 1979. *The recreation opportunity spectrum: A framework for planning, management, and research*. General Technical Report PNW-98. (Portland, Oreg.: Pacific Northwest Forest and Range Experiment Station).

Clark, R.N., Hendee, J.C., and Campbell, F.L. 1971. "Values, behavior and conflict in modern camping culture" *Journal of Leisure Research*. 3, 143-59.

Clarke, J. and Chritcher, C. 1985. *The devil makes work: Leisure in capitalist Britain*. (Basingstoke: Macmillan).

Clawson, M. 1959. *Methods of measuring demand for and value of outdoor recreation*. (Washington, D.C.: Resources for the Future).

_____. 1985. "Outdoor recreation: Twenty-five years of history, twenty-five years of projection" *Leisure Sciences*. 7, 73-99.

Clawson, M. and J.L. Knetsch. 1971. *Economics of outdoor recreation*. (Baltimore: Johns Hopkins Press).

Cohen, E. 1972. "Towards a sociology of international tourism" *Social Research*. 39, 164-82.

_____. 1974. "Who is a tourist? A conceptual clarification" *Sociological Review*. 22, 527-53.

_____. 1979a. "Rethinking the sociology of tourism" *Annals of Tourism Research*. 6, 18-35.

_____. 1979b. "A phenomenology of tourist experiences" *Sociology*. 13, 179-202.

Comité pour la protection de la rue d'Auteuil et Comité de citoyens du Vieux Québec. 1976. *Mémoire*. submitted to the Conseil du Tourisme, Ville de Québec, Québec.

Cooke, K. 1982. "Guidelines for socially appropriate tourism development in British Columbia" *Journal of Travel Research*. 21, 22-8.

Crandall, R. 1980. "Motivations for leisure" *Journal of Leisure Research*. 12, 45-54.

Crowe, R.B., McKay, G.A., and Baker, W.M. 1977. *The tourist and outdoor recreation climate of Ontario*. Publications in Applied Meteorology REC-1-73 (Toronto: Fisheries and Environment Canada, Atmospheric Environment Service, Meteorological Applications Branch).

D'Amore, L.J. 1975. *Tourism in Canada -- 1986*. (Montreal: L.J. D'Amore and Associates).

_____. 1983. "Guidelines to planning in harmony with the host community" in P.E. Murphy ed. *Tourism in Canada: Selected issues and options*. Western Geographical Series, volume 21. (Victoria: University of Victoria) 135-39.

_____. 1988. *Delphi study: Tourism in Canada -- 2001*. (Montreal: L.J. D'Amore and Associates).

D'Amore, L.J., and Associates Ltd. 1980. *Guidelines for socially appropriate tourism development in British Columbia*. (Victoria: Ministry of Industry and Small Business Development).

Dearden, P. 1980. "Landscape assessment: The last decade" *Canadian Geographer*. 24, 316-25.

De Burlo, C. 1980. *Tourism in developing countries: Complementary approaches in geography and anthropology*. Discussion Paper no.64. (Syracuse: Syracuse University, Department of Geography).

Defert, P. 1984. "Recherche sur une méthode d'évaluation d'un impact culturel entre touristes et population d'accueil" *Revue de Tourisme*. 3, 2-4.

De Kadt, E. 1979. *Tourism -- Passport to development?* (New York: Oxford University Press).

Department of Regional Economic Expansion. 1970. *The Canada Land Inventory Land Capability Classification for outdoor recreation*. Report no 6. (Ottawa: Queen's Printer for Canada).

Désy, J. 1967. *Quelques aspects de la géographie des Petites Laurentides de St.-Raymond*. Thèse de maitrise en géographie, Université Laval, Québec.

Devall, B. and Harry, J. 1981. "Who hates whom in the great outdoors: The impact of recreational specialization and technologies of play" *Leisure Sciences*. 4, 399-418.

Ditton, R.B., Goodale, T.L., and Johnsen, P.K. 1975. "A cluster analysis of activity, frequency, and environmental variables to identify water-based recreation types" *Journal of Leisure Research*. 7, 282-95.

Donnelly, M.P., Vaske, J.J., and Graefe, A.R. 1986. "Degree and range of recreation specialization: Toward a typology of boating related activities" *Journal of Leisure Research*. 18, 81-95.

Dorrance, M.J., Savage, P.J., and Huff, D.E. 1975. "Effects of snowmobiles on white-tailed deer" *Journal of Wildlife Management.* 39, 563-69.

Downie, B. and Peart, B. 1982. *Parks and tourism: Progress or prostitution?* (Victoria: National and Provincial Parks Association of Canada).

Doxey, G.V. 1974. *Tourism in Niagara-on-the-Lake, Ontario: A case study of resident-visitor interaction.* (Toronto: G.V. Doxey and Associates, York University).

_____. 1975. "A causation theory of visitor-resident irritants: Methodology and research inferences" in *Proceedings of the Travel Research Association.* 6th Annual Conference. (San Diego, Calif.) 195-98.

_____. 1976. "When enough's enough: The natives are restless in old Niagara" *Heritage Canada.* 2(2), 26-27.

DPA Group, Inc. 1985. *Economic impacts of the XV Olympic Winter Games.* (Calgary: City of Calgary and Edmonton; Alberta Ministry of Tourism and Small Business).

Driver, B.L. and Brown, P.J. 1978. "The opportunity spectrum concept and behavioral information in outdoor recreation resource supply inventories: A rationale" in *Integrated inventories of renewable natural resources: Proceedings of the workshop.* General Technical Report RM-55. (Fort Collins, Colo.: Rocky Mountain Forest and Range Experiment Station) 24-31.

Driver, B.L. and Tocher, S.R. 1970. "Toward a behavioral interpretation of recreational engagements, with implications for planning" in Driver, B.L. ed. *Elements of outdoor recreation planning.* (Ann Arbor: University of Michigan Press) 9-31.

Driver, B.L., Brown, P.J., Stankey G.H., and Gregoire, T.G. 1987. "The ROS planning system: Evolution, basic concepts, and research needs" *Leisure Sciences.* 9, 201-12.

Duncan, J.S. 1978. "The social construction of unreality: An interactionist approach to the tourist's cognition of environment" in D. Ley, and M. Samuels eds. *Humanistic geography: Prospects and problems.* (Chicago: Maaroufa Press) 269-82.

Dunlap, R.E. and Heffernan, R.B. 1975. "Outdoor recreation and environmental concern: An empirical examination" *Rural Sociology.* 40, 18-30.

Dunlap, R.E. and Van Liere, K.D. 1978. "The 'new environmental paradigm': A proposed measuring instrument and preliminary results" *Journal of Environmental Education.* 9, 10-19.

_____. 1984. "Commitment to the dominant social paradigm and concern for environmental quality" *Social Science Quarterly.* 65, 1013-28.

Eagles, P.F.J. 1984. *The planning and management of environmentally sensitive areas.* (London: Longman).

Eckstein, R.G., O'Brien, T.F., Rongstad, O.J., and Bollinger, J.G. 1979. "Snowmobile effects on movements of white-tailed deer: A case-study" *Environmental Conservation.* 6, 45-51.

Ehricke, K.A. 1968. "Astrapolis -- the first space resort" *Playboy.* 15(11), 96-99.

Ellis, J.B. 1982. *Economic impacts of sport, recreation and fitness activities in Ontario: A preliminary view.* (Toronto: Ministry of Tourism and Recreation).

Ellis, M.J. 1971. "Play and its theories re-examined" *Parks and Recreation.* 6, 51-55.

English Tourist Board. 1979. *English Cathedrals and Tourism: Problems and Opportunities.* (London: English Tourist Board).

Environment Canada. 1978. *The Canada Land Inventory Land Capability for Recreation summary report.* Canada Land Inventory Report no. 14. (Ottawa: Supply and Services Canada).

Environment Canada, Parks. 1988. *Public use of the Parks Service 1986-87.* (Ottawa: Environment Canada).

Filion, F.L., Jacquemot, A., and Reid, R. 1985. *The importance of wildlife to Canadians.* (Ottawa: Canadian Wildlife Service, Environment Canada).

Fischer, A., Hatch, J., and Paise, B. 1986. "Road accidents and the Grand Prix" in J.P.A. Burns, J.M. Hatch, and T.J. Mules eds. *The Adelaide Grand Prix -- The impact of a special event.* (Adelaide: Centre for South Australian Economic Studies) 151-68.

Fischer, D.W. 1975. Willingness to pay as a behavioral criterion for environmental decision-making" *Journal of Environmental Management.* 3, 29-41.

Fitness Canada. 1981. The Canada Fitness Survey. Data tapes available through Leisure Studies Data Bank, University of Waterloo, Waterloo, Ontario.

Foster, H.D. 1986. "Risk-taking and recreation" in *Current research by Western Canadian geographers: The University of Victoria papers 1985.* B.C. Geographical Series no. 42. (Vancouver: Tantalus) 87-101.

Foster, L.T. and Kuhn, R.G. 1983. "The energy/leisure interface: A review and empirical exploration" *Recreation Research Review.* 10, 49-61.

Foster, R.J. and Jackson, E.L. 1979. "Factors associated with camping satisfaction in Alberta provincial park campgrounds" *Journal of Leisure Research.* 11, 292-306.

Francken, D.A. and Van Raiij, W.F. 1981. "Satisfaction with leisure time activities" *Journal of Leisure Research.* 13, 337-52.

Frissell, S.S. and Stankey, G.H. 1977. "Wilderness environmental quality: Search for social and ecological harmony" *Proceedings of the Society of American Foresters Annual Meeting.* (Hot Springs, Ark.) 170-83.

Fritz, R.G., Brandon, C., and Xander, J. 1984. "Combining time-series and econometric forecast of tourism activity" *Annals of Tourism Research.* 11, 219-29.

Gates, A.D. 1975. *The tourism and outdoor recreation climate of the Maritime Provinces.* Publications in Applied Meteorology REC-3-73. (Toronto: Environment Canada, Atmospheric Environment Service, Meteorological Applications Branch).

Gazillo, S. 1981. "The evolution of restaurants and bars in Vieux-Québec since 1900" *Cahiers de Géographie du Québec.* 25, 101-18.

Geddert, R.L. and Semple, A.K. 1985. "Locating a major hockey franchise: Regional considerations" *Regional Science Perspectives.* 15, 13-29.

Geisler, G.C., Martinson, O.B., and Wilkening, E.A. 1977. "Outdoor recreation and environmental concern: A restudy" *Rural Sociology.* 42, 241-49.

Getz, D. 1983. "Capacity to absorb tourism: Concepts and implications for strategic planning" *Annals of Tourism Research.* 10, 239-63.

Gilbert, C., Peterson, G., and Lime, D. 1972. "Toward a model of travel behavior on the Boundary Waters Canoe Area" *Environment and Behavior.* 4, 131-57.

Gilbert, E.W. 1939. "The growth of inland and seaside health resorts in England" *Scottish Geographical Magazine.* 55, 16-35.

————. 1954. *Brighton: Old ocean's bauble.* (London: Methuen).

Godbey, G. 1985. "Nonuse of public leisure services: A model" *Journal of Park and Recreation Administration.* 3, 1-12.

Gold, S. 1988. "Future leisure environments in cities" in T.L. Goodale and P.A. Witt eds. *Recreation and leisure: Issues in an era of change.* (State College, Pa.: Venture Publishing) 135-51.

Graburn, N.H. ed. 1976. *Ethnic and tourist arts: Cultural expressions from the Fourth World.* (Berkeley: University of California Press).

Graefe, A.R. 1980. *The relationship between level of participation and selected aspects of specialization in recreational fishing.* Ph.D. thesis, Texas A and M University, College Station.

Graefe, A.R., Kuss, F.R., and Loomis, L. 1985. "Visitor impact management in wildland settings" in *Proceedings -- National Wilderness Research Conference: Current Research.* (Ogden, Utah: USDA Forest Service, Intermountain Research Station) 424-31.

Graefe, A.R., Vaske, J.R., and Kuss, F.R. 1984. "Social carrying capacity: An integration and synthesis of twenty years of research" *Leisure Sciences.* 6, 395-431.

Graham, R., Nilsen, P.W., and Payne, R.J. 1987. "Visitor activity planning and management in Canadian national parks: Marketing within a context of integration" in M.L. Miller, R.P. Gale, and P.J. Brown eds. *Social science in natural resource management systems.* (Boulder, Colo.: Westview) 146-49.

Gramman, J.H. and Burdge, R. 1981. "The effect of recreational goals on conflict perception: The case of water skiers and fishermen" *Journal of Leisure Research.* 13, 15-27.

Grant, J.L. and Wall, G. 1979. "Visitors to Point Pelee National Park: Characteristics, behaviour and perceptions" in G. Wall ed. *Recreational land use in Southern Ontario.* (Waterloo: University of Waterloo) 117-26.

Gratton, C. and Taylor, P. 1985. *Sport and recreation: An economic analysis.* (London: Spon).

Grimm, S. 1987. *Recreational specialization among river users: The case of Nahanni National Park Reserve.* M.A. thesis, University of Waterloo, Department of Geography.

Gudykunst, W.B., Morra, J.A., Kentor, W.I., and Parker, H.A. 1981. "Dimensions of leisure activities: A factor analytic study in New England" *Journal of Leisure Research.* 13, 28-42.

Gunn, C.A. 1976. "Tourism-recreation-conservation synergism" *Contact.* 8, 130-38.

Hammitt, W.E. and Cole, D.N. 1987. *Wildland recreation: Ecology and management.* (New York: Wiley).

Harris, C.M. 1986. The effects of national parks on local populations. M.A. thesis, University of Western Ontario, Department of Geography.

Hawes, D.K. 1978. "Satisfactions derived from leisure-time pursuits: An exploratory nationwide survey" *Journal of Leisure Research.* 10, 247-64.

Hawkins, D.E., Shafer, E.L., and Rovelstad, J.M. 1980. *International Symposium of Tourism and the Next Decade: Summary and recommendation.* (Washington, D.C.: George Washington University).

Haywood, K.M. 1986. "Can the tourist-area cycle be made operational?" *Tourism Management.* 7, 154-67.

Heberlein, T.A. 1977. "Density, crowding, and satisfaction: Sociological studies for determining carrying capacities" in *Proceedings: River Recreation Management and Research Symposium.* General Technical Report NC-28 (St. Paul, Minn.: North Central Forest Experiment Station) 67-76.

Helleiner, F. 1983. "Loon Lake: The evolution and decline of a cottage community in northwestern Ontario" *Recreation Research Review.* 10(3), 34-44.

Hendee, J.C., Gale, R.P., and Catton, W.R., Jr. 1971. "A typology of outdoor recreation activity preferences" *Journal of Environmental Education.* 3, 28-34.

Hendee, J.C., Stankey, G.H., and Lucas, R.C. 1978. *Wilderness management.* (Washington, D.C.: USDA Forest Service).

Herbert, D.T. 1988. "Work and leisure: Exploring a relationship" *Area.* 20, 241-52.

Hilts, D. 1985. *Globe and Mail.* August 31.

_____. 1986. *Globe and Mail.* January 7.

Holman, G.A. 1982. *Ethnic clubs in London, Ontario: Purposes and opportunities.* M.A. thesis, University of Western Ontario, Department of Geography.

Howard, D.R. and Crompton, J.L. 1984. "Who are the consumers of public park and recreation services?" *Journal of Park and Recreation Administration.* 2, 33-48.

Howard, G.E. and Stanley-Saunders, B.A. 1979. *Impacts of recreation activities associated with streams: A problem analysis.* (Clemson, S.C.: Clemson University, Department of Recreation and Park Administration).

Ironside, G. 1971. "Agricultural and recreational land use in Canada: Potential for conflict or benefit" *Canadian Journal of Agricultural Economics.* 19, 1-12.

Ittner, R., Potter, D.R., Agee, J.K., and Anschell, S. 1979. *Recreational impact on wildlands.* (Seattle: USDA Forest Service and National Park Service, Pacific Northwest Region).

Jaakson, R. 1970. "Planning for the capacity of lakes to accommodate water-oriented recreation" *Plan Canada.* 10, 29-40.

_____. 1974. "A mosaic pattern of balanced land-water planning for cottage development and lake planning" *Plan Canada.* 14, 40-45.

Jackson, E.L. 1980. "Socio-demographic variables, recreational resource use, and attitudes towards development in Camrose, Alberta" *Leisure Sciences.* 3, 189-211.

_____. 1985. "Recreation, energy, and the environment: A survey of Albertans' preferences and behaviour" Report to the Recreation, Parks and Wildlife Foundation and Alberta Recreation and Parks (mimeo).

_____. 1986. "Outdoor recreation participation and attitudes to the environment" *Leisure Studies.* 5, 1-23.

_____. 1987. "Outdoor recreation participation and views on resource development and preservation" *Leisure Sciences.* 9, 235-50.

_____. 1988. "Leisure constraints: a survey of past research" *Leisure Sciences.* 10, 203-15.

_____. In press. "Recreation in Edmonton and Calgary" in P.J. Smith ed. *Essays in honour of William C. Wonders.* (Edmonton: University of Alberta, Department of Geography).

Jackson, E.L. and Dunn, E. 1988. "Integrating ceasing participation with other aspects of leisure behaviour" *Journal of Leisure Research.* 20, 31-45.

Jackson, E.L. and Schinkel, D.R. 1981. "Recreational activity preferences of resident and tourist campers in the Yellowknife region" *Canadian Geographer.* 25, 350-64.

Jackson, E.L. and Wong, R.A.G. 1982. "Perceived conflict between urban cross-country skiers and snowmobilers in Alberta" *Journal of Leisure Research.* 14, 47-62.

Jacob, G.R. and Schreyer, R. 1980. "Conflict in outdoor recreation: A theoretical perspective" *Journal of Leisure Research.* 12, 368-80.

James, T.D.W., Smith, D.W., Mackintosh, E.E., Hoffman, M.K., and Monti, P. 1979. "Effects of camping on soil, jack pine, and understory vegetation in a northwestern Ontario park" *Forest Science.* 25, 333-49.

Johnston, R.J. 1968. "Choice in classification: The subjectivity of objective methods" *Annals of the Association of American Geographers.* 58, 575-89.

Kahn, H. 1976. *The next 200 years.* (New York: Morrow).

Kariel, H.G. 1973. "Rating of noises in campgrounds: Some preliminary findings" *Great Plains -- Rocky Mountain Geographical Journal.* 2, 64-70.

_____. 1980a. "Evaluation of campground sounds in Canadian Rocky Mountain National Parks" *Great Plains -- Rocky Mountain Geographical Journal.* 9, 72-84.

_____. 1980b. "Mountaineers and the general public: A comparison of their evaluation of sounds in a recreational environment" *Leisure Sciences.* 3, 155-67.

Kariel, H.G. and Jacks, J.E. 1980. "Rehabilitation of meadow and trails adjacent to Elizabeth Park hut, Lake O'Hara area, Yoho National Park" *Canadian Alpine Journal.* 63, 44-45.

Kauffman, R.B. and Graefe, A.R. 1984. "Canoeing specialization, expected rewards and resource related attitudes" in J.S. Popadic, D.I. Butterfield, D.H. Anderson and M.R. Popadic eds. *National River Recreation Symposium Proceedings.* (Baton Rouge: Louisiana State University) 629-41.

Keddy, P.A., Spavold, A.V., and Keddy, C.J. 1979. "Snowmobile impact on old field and marsh vegetation in Nova Scotia, Canada: An experimental study" *Environmental Management.* 3, 409-15.

Kelly, J.R. 1980. "Outdoor recreation participation: A comparative analysis" *Leisure Sciences.* 3, 129-54.

Kendall, K.W. and Var, T. 1984. *The perceived impacts of tourism: The state of the art.* Discussion Paper 83-03-02. (Burnaby, B.C.: Simon Fraser University, Faculty of Business Administration).

Keogh, B. 1982. "L'impact social du tourisme: Le cas de Shédiac, Nouveau-Brunswick" *Canadian Geographer*. 26, 318-31.

Kirkpatrick, L.W. and Reeser, W.K., Jr. 1976. "The air pollution carrying capacities of selected Colorado mountain valley ski communities" *Journal of the Air Pollution Control Association*. 26, 992-94.

Knetsch, J.L. 1970. "Assessing the demand for outdoor recreation" in B.L. Driver ed. *Elements of outdoor recreation planning*. (Ann Arbor: University of Michigan Press) 131-36.

Knopp, T.B. and Tyger, J.D. 1973. "A study of conflict in recreational land use: Snowmobiling versus ski-touring" *Journal of Leisure Research*. 5, 6-17.

Knopp, T.B., Ballman, G., and Merriam, L.C., Jr. 1979. "Toward a more direct measure of river user preferences" *Journal of Leisure Research*. 11, 317-26.

Kolson, J. 1988. "The Calgary Olympic visitor study" *Operational Geographer*. 16, 15-17.

Kraus, R. 1971. *Recreation and leisure in modern society*. (New York: Meredith).

Kreutzwiser, R.D. 1986. "Ontario cottager associations and shoreline management" *Coastal Zone Management Journal*. 14, 93-111.

Kreutzwiser, R.D. and Pietraszko, L.J. 1986. "Wetland values and protection strategies: A study of landowner attitudes in Southern Ontario" *Journal of Environmental Management*. 22, 13-23.

Kroening, L.L. 1979. Motivations of wilderness canoeists. M.A. thesis, University of Alberta, Department of Geography.

Kroening, L.L. and Jackson, E.L. 1983. "Motivations of wilderness canoeists" in *Proceedings of the Third Canadian Congress on Leisure Research*. (Edmonton: Canadian Association for Leisure Studies) 85-111.

Kuss, F.R. and Graefe, A.R. 1985. "Effects of recreation trampling on natural area vegetation" *Journal of Leisure Research*. 17, 165-83.

La Forest, G.V. and Roy, M.K. 1981. *The Kouchibouguac affair - - Report of the special inquiry on Kouchibouguac National Park*. (Ottawa: Environment Canada).

Lamothe and Périard. 1988. Implications of climate change for downhill skiing in Quebec. *Climate Change Digest 88-03*. (Ottawa: Environment Canada, Ministry of Supply and Services).

Lanken, D. 1987. "Summer places down the St. Lawrence" *Canadian Geographic*. 107(2), 54-63

LaPage, W.F. 1967. *Some observations on campground trampling and ground cover response*. (Upper Darby, Pa.: USDA Forest Service, Northeastern Forest Experiment Station).

Lavery, P. 1971. "Resorts and recreation" in P. Lavery ed. *Recreation Geography*. (Newton Abbot: David and Charles) 167-96.

Lawrence, H.W. 1983. "Southern spas: Source of the American resort tradition" *Landscape*. 27, 1-12.

Lee, J. and Yates, B. 1984. *Capitalizing on sport events*. (Victoria: British Columbia Recreation and Sport Branch).

Lehteniemi, L. 1976. "Futures forecasting techniques" in Canadian Outdoor Recreation Research Committee ed. *Park and recreation futures in Canada: Issues and options*. (Toronto: Ontario Research Council on Leisure) 11-52.

Leighton, D. 1985. "Banff is where it all began" *Canadian Geographic*. 105, 8-15.

_____. 1988. "Helping animals cross the road" *Canadian Geographic*. 108(4), 22-28.

Leiper, N. 1979. "The framework of tourism: Towards a definition of tourism, tourist and the tourist industry" *Annals of Tourism Research.* 6, 390-407.

Liddle, M.J. 1975. "A selective review of the ecological effects of human trampling on natural ecosystems" *Biological Conservation.* 7, 17-36.

_____. 1988. *Recreation and the environment: The ecology of recreation impacts, Vegetation and wear.* (Brisbane: Griffith University, Division of Australian Environmental Studies).

Liddle, M.J. and Scorgie, H.R.A. 1980. "The effects of recreation on freshwater plants and animals: A review" *Biological Conservation.* 17, 183-206.

Liddle, M.J. and Tothill, J.C. 1984. *The ecological basis of the interactions between organisms.* (Brisbane: Griffith University, School of Australian Environmental Studies).

Lime, D.W. and Stankey, G.H. 1971. "Carrying capacity: Maintaining outdoor recreation quality" in *Forest Research Symposium Proceedings.* (Upper Darby, Pa.: Northeast Forest Experiment Station) 174-84.

Listfield, A.D. 1979. The Anglo-American tourist and Quebec City: The determinants of negative behavior in a visited Environment. M.A. thesis, Université Laval, Québec, Département de Géographie.

Lucas, R.C. 1964. "Wilderness perception and use: The example of the Boundary Waters Canoe Area" *Natural Resources Journal.* 3, 394-411.

Lucas, R.C. and Stankey, G.H. 1974. "Social carrying capacity for backcountry recreation" in *Outdoor recreation research: Applying the results.* General Technical Report NC-9. (St. Paul, Minn.: USDA Forest Service, North Central Forest Experiment Station).

Lucky, S., Nelson, J.G., and Carruthers, J. eds. 1986. *Physically disabled persons and Heritage Areas Workshop Proceedings.* Occasional paper 6. (Waterloo: University of Waterloo, Heritage Resources Centre).

Lundgren, J. 1973. "The development of the tourist travel systems" *Tourist Review.* 1, 2-14.

_____. 1983. "Development patterns and lessons in the Montreal Laurentians" in P. Murphy ed. *Tourism in Canada: Selected issues and options.* Western Geographical Series (Victoria: University of Victoria) 95-126.

_____. 1985. "Circumpolar tourist space: A geographic comparison of Northern Canada and Northern Sweden" in L. Deshaies and R. Pelletier eds. *Proceedings of the Canadian Association of Geographers.* (Trois-Rivières: Université du Quebec) 228-45.

MacFarlane, R.N. 1979. Social impact of tourism: Resident attitudes in Stratford. M.A. thesis, University of Western Ontario, Department of Geography.

Mackintosh, E.E. 1979. *Impact of recreation on vegetation and soils in Rushing River Provincial Park, Ontario.* (Sault Ste. Marie and Toronto: Canadian Forestry Service and Ontario Ministry of Natural Resources).

Macleans Magazine. 1986. "Selling a new Canada" January 13, p. 33.

Manning, R.E. 1979. "Impacts of recreation on riparian soils and vegetation" *Water Resources Bulletin.* 15, 30-43.

Manson-Blair, D. 1984. The role of gender, motivation and clubhouse access on the total sports experience. M.A. thesis, University of Victoria, Department of Geography.

Marsh, J. 1983. "Canada's parks and tourism: A problematic relationship" in P.E. Murphy ed. *Tourism in Canada: Selected issues and options.* Western Geographical Series. (Victoria: University of Victoria) 271-307.

Marsh, J.S. 1970. "Bears -- their biology and management" in *Proceedings of the International Conference held at Calgary, Alberta, Canada 6-9 November 1970.* (Morges, Switzerland: International Union for Conservation of Nature and Natural Resources) 289-96.

_____. 1984. "The economic impact of a small city annual sporting event: An initial case study of the Peterborough church league atom hockey tournament" *Recreation Research Review.* 11, 48-55.

Marshall Macklin Monaghan Ltd. 1982. *Baffin regional tourism planning project: Executive summary.* Prepared for Department of Economic Development and Tourism, Government of Northwest Territories, Yellowknife.

Maslow, A. 1954. *Motivation and personality.* (New York: Harper and Row).

Masterton, J.M., Crowe, R.B., and Baker, W.M. 1976. *The tourism and outdoor recreation climate of the Prairie Provinces.* Publications in Applied Meteorology REC-1-75 (Toronto: Environment Canada, Atmospheric Environment Service, Meteorological Applications Branch).

Mathieson, A. and Wall, G. 1982. *Tourism: Economic, physical and social impacts.* (London: Longman).

McCool, S.F. 1978. "Recreational activity packages at waterbased resources" *Leisure Sciences.* 1, 163-73.

McKay, G. 1985. Skiing and regional tourism development in British Columbia. M.A. thesis, University of Victoria, Department of Geography.

McKechnie, G.E. 1977. "The environmental response inventory in application" *Environment and Behavior.* 9, 255-76

McPherson, B.D. and Curtis, J.E. 1986. *Regional and community-type differences in the physical activity patterns of Canadian adults.* (Ottawa: Fitness Canada).

Meyer-Arendt, K.A. 1985. "The Grand Isle, Louisiana resort cycle" *Annals of Tourism Research*. 12, 449-65.

Michaud, J.L. 1967. *La zone récréative de la région des Lacs Beauport et Saint-Charles: Étude d'utilisation du sol* (Québec: Memoire présenté à l'Institut de Géographie de l'Université Laval).

Mieczkowski, Z.T. 1981. "Some notes on the geography of tourism: A comment" *Canadian Geographer*. 25, 186-91.

Mings, R.C. 1978. "The importance of more research on the impacts of tourism" *Annals of Tourism Research*. 5, 340-44.

Mitchell, B. 1979. *Geography and resource analysis*. (London: Longman).

Mitchell, B. and Turkheim, R. 1977. "Environmental impact assessment: Principles, practices and Canadian experiences" in R.R. Krueger and B. Mitchell eds. *Managing Canada's renewable resources*. (Toronto: Methuen) 47-66.

Montgomery, G. and Murphy, P.E. 1983. "Government involvement in tourism development: A case study of TIDSA: Implementation in British Columbia" in P.E. Murphy ed. *Tourism in Canada: Selected issues and options*. Western Geographical Series. (Victoria: University of Victoria) 183-209.

Monti, P.W. and Mackintosh, E.E. 1979. "Effect of camping on surface soil properties in the boreal forest region of northwestern Ontario, Canada" *Journal of the Soil Science Society of America*. 43, 1024-29.

Mosimann, T. 1985. "Geo-ecological impacts of ski piste construction in the Swiss Alps" *Applied Geography*. 5, 29-37.

Moulin, C.L. 1980. "Plan for ecological and cultural tourism involving participation of local population and associations" in D.F. Hawkins, E.L. Shafer, and J.M. Rovelstad eds. *Tourism planning and development issues.* Washington, D.C.: George Washington University) 199-211.

Mundy, K.R.D. and Flook, D.R. 1973. *Background for managing grizzly bears in the national parks of Canada.* (Ottawa: Canadian Wildlife Service).

Murphy, P.E. 1981. "Community attitudes to tourism: A comparative analysis" *International Journal of Tourism Management.* 2, 189-95.

_____. ed. 1983a. *Tourism in Canada: Selected issues and options.* Western Geographical Series. (Victoria: University of Victoria, Department of Geography).

_____. 1983b. "Tourism as a community industry: An ecological model of tourism development" *Tourism Management.* 4, 180-93.

_____. 1985. *Tourism: A community approach.* (London: Methuen).

Murry, D., Consulting Associates Ltd. 1985. *A study to determine the impact of events on local economies: Executive summary.* (Regina: Saskatchewan Tourism and Small Business).

Nelson, J.G. 1973. "Canada's national parks: Past, present, future" *Canadian Geographical Journal.* 86(3), 68-89.

Nelson, J.G. and Butler, R.W. 1974. "Recreation and the environment" in I.R. Manners and M.W. Mikesell eds. *Perspectives on environment.* (Washington, D.C.: Association of American Geographers) 290-310.

Nelson, J.G. and Scace, R.C. 1968. "Canadian national parks: Today and tomorrow" *Studies in land use history and landscape change, no. 3.* (Calgary: University of Calgary).

Nelson, R. and Wall, G. 1986. "Transportation and accommodation: Changing interrelationships on Vancouver Island" *Annals of Tourism Research.* 13, 239-60.

Neulinger, J. 1983. "Introduction" in *The academy of leisure sciences values and leisure and trends in leisure services.* (State College, Pa.: Venture Publishing) 1-5.

Neumann, P.W. and Merriam, H.G. 1972. "Ecological effects of snowmobiles" *Canadian Field Naturalist.* 86, 207-12.

New Brunswick, Department of Tourism. 1973. *Hospitality.* (Fredericton).

Ng, D. 1988. "Forecasting leisure futures" *Recreation Research Review.* 13(4), 32-38.

Noronha, R. 1975. *Review of the sociological literature on tourism.* (Washington, D.C.: World Bank).

_____. 1979. *Social and cultural dimensions of tourism: A review of the literature in English.* (Washington, D.C.: World Bank).

Northwest Territories, Department of Economic Development and Tourism. 1983. *Community based tourism: A strategy for the Northwest Territories tourism industry.* (Yellowknife).

Ohmann, L.F. 1974. *Ecological carrying capacity.* General Technical Report NC-9. (St. Paul, Minn.: USDA Forest Service, North Central Forest Experiment Station) 24-28.

O'Neill-Mayer, P. 1985. *Planning for visitor use of marine parks: A study of specialization and preferences among scuba divers.* M.A. thesis, University of Waterloo, Department of Urban and Regional Planning.

Ontario, Ministry of Natural Resources. 1978. *Ontario provincial parks planning and management policies.* (Toronto).

Ontario, Ministry of Tourism and Recreation. 1987. *The changing patterns of work and leisure.* (Toronto: Queens Park).

Ontario, Parks and Recreational Areas Branch. 1984. *Ontario provincial parks economic impact model.* (Toronto).

Orfald, D. and Gibson, R. 1985. "The conserver society idea: A history with questions" *Alternatives.* 12, 37-45.

O'Riordan, T. 1977. "Sharing waterspace: How coarse fish anglers and boat users react to one another" in *Proceedings of the Recreational Freshwater Fisheries Conference.* (U.K. Water Research Centre).

Outdoor Recreation Resources Review Commission. 1962. *Outdoor recreation for America.* (Washington, D.C.: Government Printing Office).

Overton, J. 1979. "A critical examination of the establishment of national parks and tourism in underdeveloped areas: Gros Morne National Park in Newfoundland" *Antipode.* 11(2), 34-47.

_____. 1980. "Tourism development, conservation and conflict: Game laws for caribou protection in Newfoundland" *Canadian Geographer.* 24, 40-49.

Owens, L. 1981. Resident reaction to tourism on Manitoulin Island. M.A. thesis, University of Western Ontario, Department of Geography.

Owens, P.L. 1977. "Recreational conflict: the interaction of Norfolk Broads coarse anglers and boat users" in J. Alabaster ed. *Recreational freshwater fisheries: Their conservation, management and development* (Stevenage Herts.: Water Research Centre) 136-52.

_____. 1985. "Conflict as a social interaction process in environment and behaviour research: The example of leisure and recreation research" *Journal of Environmental Psychology.* 5, 243-59.

Packer, L.V. 1974. Tourism in the small community: A cross-cultural analysis of developmental change. Ph.D. thesis, University of Oregon.

Paine, J.D., Marans, R.N., and Harris, C.C. 1980. "Social indicators and outdoor recreation: The forgotten sector" in W. LaPage *Proceedings 1980 National Outdoor Recreation Trends Symposium*. USDA Technical Reference NE-57. (Broomall, Pa.: Northeast Forest Experiment Station).

Papson, S. 1981. "Spuriousness and tourism: Politics of two Canadian provincial governments" *Annals of Tourism Research*. 8, 220-35.

Parker, S. 1973. "Relations between work and leisure" in M. Smith, S. Parker, and C. Smith. *Leisure and society in Britain*. (Allen Lane: London) 75-85.

_____. 1983. *Leisure and work*. (London: Allen and Unwin).

Parks Canada. 1979. *Parks Canada Policy*. (Ottawa).

_____. 1982. *Point Pelee National Park management plan*. (Cornwall: Parks Canada, Ontario Region).

_____. 1985. *Economic assessment of the Parks Canada Program, 1982-83*. (Ottawa: Parks Canada, Socio-Economic Branch).

_____. 1986. *In trust for tomorrow: A management framework for four mountain parks*. (Ottawa: Supply and Services Canada).

Patmore, J.A. 1968. "Spa towns in Britain" in R.P. Beckinsale and J.M. Houston eds. *Urbanization and its problems* (Oxford: Blackwell) 47-69.

Payne, N.F. 1978. "Hunting and management of the Newfoundland black bear" *Wildlife Society Bulletin*. 6, 206-11.

Peterson, G.L. 1974. "A comparison of the sentiments and perceptions of wilderness managers and canoeists in the Boundary Waters Canoe Area" *Journal of Leisure Research*. 6, 194-206.

_____. 1983. "Rationing and redistribution of recreational use of scarce resources with limited carrying capacity" in S.R. Leiber and D.R. Fesenmaier eds. *Recreation planning and management*. (State College, Pa.: Venture Publishing) 286-302.

Phillips, A.A.C. 1970. *Research into planning for recreation*. (London: Countryside Commission).

Pinhey, T.K. and Grimes, M.D. 1979. "Outdoor recreation and environmental concern: A re-examination of the Dunlap-Heffernan thesis" *Leisure Sciences*. 2, 1-11.

Plog, S.C. 1972. "Why destination areas rise and fall in popularity." Paper presented at Southern California Chapter of the Travel Research Association. (Los Angeles)

Priddle, G. and Wall, G. 1978. "Anti-social behaviour in Ontario provincial parks" *Recreation Research Review*. 2, 13-23.

Priddle, G.B., Clark, C.D., and Douglas, L.A. n.d. "The behavioural carrying capacity of primitive area for wilderness travel"(Waterloo) (mimeo.)

Rajotte, F. 1975. 'The different travel patterns and spatial framework of recreation and tourism" in F. Helleiner ed. *Tourism as a factor in national and regional development*. Occasional paper 4. (Peterborough: Trent University, Department of Geography).

Reed, A. and Boyd. H. 1984. "The impact of opening weekend hunting on local black ducks breeding in the St. Lawrence estuary and on transient ducks" in H. Boyd ed. *Waterfowl Studies*. (Ottawa: Canadian Wildlife Service) 84-91.

Rees, R. 1988. "St. Andrews, N.B.: A chosen place" *Canadian Geographic*. 108(1), 58-65.

Reid, R. 1985a. *The value and characteristics of resident hunting.* Victoria: Ministry of Environment.

_____. 1985b. *The value and characteristics of non-resident hunting.* (Victoria: Ministry of Environment).

Revelle, R. 1967. "Outdoor recreation in a hyper-productive society" *Daedalus.* 96: 1172-92.

Richens, V.B. and Lavigne, G.R. 1978. "Response of white-tailed deer to snowmobiles and snowmobile trails in Maine" *Canadian Field Naturalist.* 92, 334-44.

Ritchie, J.R.B. and Claxton, J.D. 1983. "Leisure lifestyles and energy use" in *Proceedings of the Third Canadian Congress on Leisure Research.* (Edmonton: Canadian Association for Leisure Studies) 871-96.

Roark, C.S. 1974. "Historic Yellow Springs: The restoration of an American spa" *Pennsylvania Folklife.* 24, 28-38.

Roberts, C. and Wall, G. 1979. "Possible impacts of Vaughan theme park" in G. Wall ed. *Recreational land use in Southern Ontario.* (Waterloo: University of Waterloo).

Roggenbuck, J.W., Smith, A.C., and Wellman, J.D. 1980. *Specialization, displacement and definition of depreciative behavior among Virginia canoeists.* (St. Paul, Minn.: USDA Forest Service, North Central Forest Experiment Station).

Romsa, G.H. 1973. "A method of deriving outdoor recreation activity packages" *Journal of Leisure Research.* 5, 34-46.

Romsa, G.H. and Girling, S. 1976. "The identification of outdoor recreation market segments on the basis of frequency of participation" *Journal of Leisure Research.* 8, 247-55.

Romsa, G. and Hoffman, W. 1980. "An application of non-participation data in recreation research: Testing the opportunity theory" *Journal of Leisure Research.* 12, 321-28.

Root, J.D. and Knapik, L.J. 1972. *Trail conditions along a portion of the Great Divide Trail Route, Alberta and British Columbia Rocky Mountains.* (Edmonton: Research Council of Alberta).

Rousseau, S., Beaman, J., Renoux, M., and Hendry, J. 1976. "Analysis of variance as a tool for estimating participation in outdoor recreation activities" in *Canadian outdoor recreation demand study, The technical notes.* (Toronto: Ontario Research Council on Leisure) 240-69.

Rutherford, G.K. and Scott, D.C. 1979. "The impact of recreational land use on soil chemistry in a provincial park" *Park News.* 15(1), 22-25.

Rutledge, A.J. 1971. *Anatomy of a park: The essentials of recreation area planning and design.* (New York: McGraw-Hill).

Satchell, J.E. and Marren, P.R. 1976. *The effects of recreation on the ecology of natural landscapes.* (Strasbourg: Council of Europe).

Scace, R.C. 1969. "Banff townsite: An historical-geographical view of urban development in a Canadian national park" in J.G. Nelson and R.C. Scace eds. *The Canadian national parks: Today and tomorrow.* Studies in Landscape History and Landscape Change no.3. (University of Calgary) 770-93.

Scace, R.C. and Nelson, J.G. 1986. *Heritage tomorrow.* Proceedings of the Canadian Assembly on National Parks and Protected Areas, vol. 1-5. (Ottawa: Ministry of Supply and Services).

Schiff, M.R. 1971. "The definition of perceptions and attitudes" in W.R.D. Sewell and I. Burton eds. *Perceptions and attitudes in resources management.* (Ottawa: Department of Energy, Mines and Resources) 7-12.

Schreyer, R. 1979. *Succession and displacement in river recreation -- problem definition and analysis.* (St. Paul, Minn.: USDA Forest Service, North Central Forest Experiment Station).

_____. 1984. "Social dimensions of carrying capacity: An overview" *Leisure Sciences.* 6, 387-93.

Science Council of Canada. 1977. *Canada as a conserver society: Resource Uuncertainties and the need for new technologies.* Report no. 27 (Ottawa).

Seabrooke, A.K. 1981. "The environmental impacts of water-based recreation" *East Lakes Geographer.* 16, 11-19.

Searle, M.S. and Jackson, E.L. 1985a. "Recreation non-participation and barriers to participation: Considerations for the management of recreation delivery systems" *Journal of Park and Recreation Administration.* 3, 23-35.

_____. 1985b. "Socioeconomic variations in perceived barriers to recreation participation among would-be participants" *Leisure Sciences.* 7, 227-49.

Segger, M. 1986. "Economic state of the arts in Victoria" Paper given to Business and the Arts Conference, Victoria, B.C.

Sewell, W.R.D. and Mitchell, B. 1981. "The way ahead" in B. Mitchell, and W.R.D. Sewell eds. *Canadian resource policies: Problems and prospects.* (Toronto: Methuen) 262-84.

Shaffer, M., and Associates. 1985. *The economic impact of annual parks expenditures in British Columbia.* (Victoria: British Columbia Ministry of Lands, Parks and Housing).

Shaffer, M., Hale, R., and Lyle, J. 1977. *The economic impact of recreational boating in British Columbia.* (Ottawa: Environment Canada).

Shelby, B, and Heberlein, T.A. 1984. "A conceptual framework for carrying capacity determination" *Leisure Sciences.* 6, 433-51.

_____. 1986. *Carrying capacity in recreation settings.* (Corvallis: Oregon State University Press).

Simpson-Lewis, W., Moore, J.E., Pocock, N.J., Taylor, M.C., and Swan, H. 1979. *Canada's special resource lands: A national perspective of selected land uses.* Map folio no. 4 (Ottawa: Environment Canada, Lands Directorate).

Smale, B.J.A. and Butler, R.W. 1985. "Domestic tourism in Canada: Regional and provincial patterns" *Ontario Geography.* 26, 37-56.

Smith, S.L.J. 1977. "Room for rooms: A procedure for the estimation of potential expansion of tourist accommodations" *Journal of Travel Research.* 25(4), 26-29.

_____. 1980. "The poverty of futurology" *Recreation Research Review.* 8, 9-11.

_____. 1983. *Recreation geography.* (London: Longman).

_____. 1985. "Location patterns of urban restaurants" *Annals of Tourism Research.* 12, 581-602.

_____. 1988. "Defining tourism: A supply-side view" *Annals of Tourism Research.* 15, 179-90.

Smith, S.L.J. and Stewart, T.O. 1980. "Estimation of the effects of regional variation of supply on participation in cultural activities" *Ontario Geographer.* 15, 3-16.

Smith, V. ed. 1977. *Hosts and guests: The anthropology of tourism.* (Philadelphia: University of Pennsylvania Press).

Sousa, P.M. 1988. The effect of last place of residence on recreation and leisure in a resource based community: A case study of Fort McMurray, Alberta. B.A. Senior Report, University of Western Ontario, Department of Geography.

Speight, M.C.D. 1973. *Outdoor recreation and its ecological effects: A bibliography and review.* (London: University College).

Spry, I.M. 1980. "The prospects for leisure in a conserver society" in T.L. Goodale and P.A. Witt eds. *Recreation and leisure: Issues in an era of change.* (State College, Pa.: Venture Publishing) 141-53

Stankey, G.H. 1972. "A strategy for the definition and management of wilderness quality" in Krutilla, J. ed. *Natural environments: Studies in theoretical and applied analysis.* (Baltimore: Johns Hopkins University Press) 88-114.

_____. 1973. *Visitor perception of wilderness recreation carrying capacity.* Research paper INT-142. (Ogden, Utah: USDA Forest Service, Intermountain Forest and Range Experiment Station).

_____. 1982. "Recreational carrying capacity research review" *Ontario Geography.* 19, 57-72.

Stankey, G.H. and McCool, S.F. 1984. "Carrying capacity in recreational settings: Evolution, appraisal and application" *Leisure Sciences.* 6, 453-74.

Stansfield, C.A. 1972. "The development of modern seaside resorts" *Parks and Recreation.* 5, 43-46.

Stansfield, C.A. and Rickert, J.E. 1970. "The recreation business district" *Journal of Leisure Research.* 2, 213-25.

Statistics Canada. 1975. *Technical report on population projections for Canada and the provinces, 1972-2001.* 91-5-16. (Ottawa).

_____. 1976. *Travel, tourism, and outdoor recreation: A statistical digest.* Cat. 66-202. (Ottawa: Ministry of Industry, Trade, and Commerce).

_____. 1984. *Tourism and recreation: A statistical Ddigest.* Cat. 86-401. (Ottawa: Department of Supply and Services).

_____. 1986. *Tourism and recreation: A statistical digest.* (Ottawa: Supply and Services Canada).

————. 1987. *Canada Year Book 1988*. (Ottawa: Supply and Services Canada).

————. 1988. *Touriscope 1988 tourism in Canada: A statistical digest* . (Ottawa: Supply and Services Canada).

Stix, J. 1982. "National parks and Inuit rights in northern Labrador" *Canadian Geographer*. 26, 349-54.

Story, A. 1973. "The place to be in '73: The development of tourism on P.E.I." *Round One*. 1, 1-8.

Stringer, P.F. 1981. "Hosts and guests: The bed and breakfast phenomenon" *Annals of Tourism Research*. 8, 357-76.

Tanner, M.F. 1969. *Coastal recreation and holidays: Coastal preservation and development special study report*. (London: HMSO).

Tatham, R.L. and Dornoff, R.J. 1971. "Market segmentation for outdoor recreation" *Journal of Leisure Research*. 3, 5-16.

Taylor, G.D. 1983. "Canada's tourism trends for the 1980's" in P.E. Murphy ed. *Tourism in Canada: Selected issues and options*. Western Geographical Series (Victoria: University of Victoria) 29-55.

Thompson, D. 1982. "A conserver society: Grounds for optimism" *Alternatives*. 11, 3-9.

Thurot, J-M. 1975. *Impact of tourism on socio-cultural values*. (Aix-en-Provence: Centre d'Etudes du Tourisme).

Tourism and Outdoor Recreation Planning Study. 1975. *Ontario recreation supply inventory users manual*. (Toronto: Tourism and Outdoor Recreation Planning Study Committee).

Tourism and Outdoor Recreation Planning Study. 1977. *Ontario recreation survey tourism and recreational behaviour of Ontario residents, Profiles of participants.* (Toronto: Tourism and Outdoor Recreation Planning Study Committee).

Tourism Canada. 1985. *Tourism tomorrow: Towards a Canadian tourism strategy.* (Ottawa).

Tourism Industry Association of Alberta. 1985. *Tourpulse 1: A survey of the views of Alberta residents concerning tourism and its role in provincial development.* (Calgary).

Travel Alberta. n.d. *1976 ski industry evaluation study.* (Edmonton).

Trottier, G., Holland, W.D., Kivett, K.W., and Wells, R.E. 1976. *Environmental impact study. Mt. Kerkeslin campground, Jasper National Park.* (Edmonton: Environment Canada).

Trowell, A. 1987. "Too many feet are spoiling the Grand Bend sand dunes" *Canadian Geographic.* 107(2), 38-45.

Uysal, M. and Crompton, J.L. 1985. "An overview of approaches used to forecast tourism demand" *Journal of Travel Research.* 18(4), 7-15.

Van Liere, K.D. and Dunlap, R.E. 1980. "The social bases of environmental concern: A review of hypotheses, explanations, and empirical evidence" *Public Opinion Quarterly.* 44, 181-97.

_____. 1981. "Environmental concern: Does it make a difference how it's measured?" *Environment and Behavior.* 13, 651-76.

_____. 1983. "Cognitive integration of social and environmental beliefs" *Sociological Inquiry.* 53, 333-41.

Van Liere, K.D. and Noe, F.P. 1981. "Outdoor recreation and environmental attitudes: Further examination of the Dunlap-Heffernan thesis" *Rural Sociology.* 46, 501-13.

Vancouver Sun. 1986. "Next the Charlottes" September 27, B4.

Vaske, J.J., Donnelly, M.P., Heberlein, T.A., and Shelby, B. 1982. "Differences in reported satisfaction ratings by consumptive and nonconsumptive recreationists" *Journal of Leisure Research.* 14, 195-206.

Vaske, J.J., Fedler, A.J., and Graefe, A.R. 1986. "Multiple determinants of satisfaction from a specific waterfowl hunting trip" *Leisure Sciences.* 8, 149-66.

Vaske, J.J., Graefe, A.R., and Kuss, F.R. 1983 "Recreation impacts: A synthesis of ecological and social research" in *Transactions of the 48th North American Wildlife and Natural Resources Conference.* (Washington, D.C.: Wildlife Management Institute) 96-107.

Wagar, J.A. 1974. "Recreational carrying capacity reconsidered" *Journal of Forestry.* 72, 274-78.

_____. 1977a. "Recreational carrying capacity" in *Proceedings of the Wildland Recreation Conference.* (Edmonton: University of Alberta, Department of Forest Science and Faculty of Extension) 168-75.

_____. 1977b. "Resolving user conflicts" in *Proceedings of the Wildland Recreation Conference.* (Edmonton: University of Alberta, Department of Forest Science and Faculty of Extension) 133-45.

Walejko, R.N., Pendleton, J.W., Paulsun, W.H., Rand, R.E., Tenpas, G.H., and Schlough, D.A. 1973. "Effect of snowmobile traffic on alfalfa" *Journal of Soil and Water Conservation.* 28, 272-73.

Wall, G. 1979a. "The demand for outdoor recreation in Ontario" in G. Wall ed. *Recreational land use in Southern Ontario.* Department of Geography Publication Series 14 (Waterloo: University of Waterloo) 63-80.

_____. ed. 1979b. *Recreational land use in Southern Ontario.* (Waterloo: University of Waterloo, Department of Geography).

_____. 1981. "Research in Canadian recreational planning and management" in B. Mitchell and W.R.D. Sewell, eds. *Canadian Resource policies: Problems and prospects.* (Toronto: Methuen) 233-61.

_____. 1982a. "Changing views of the land as a recreational resource" in G. Wall and J.S. Marsh eds. *Recreational land use: Perspectives on its evolution in Canada.* (Ottawa: Carleton University Press) 15-25.

_____. 1982b. "Cycles and capacity: Incipient theory or conceptual contradiction?" *Tourism Management.* 3, 188-92.

_____. 1982c. "The fluctuating fortunes of water-based recreational places" in G. Wall and J.S. Marsh eds. *Recreational land use perspectives on its evolution in Canada.* (Ottawa: Carleton University Press) 239-54.

_____. 1983a. "Cycles and capacity: A contradiction in terms?" *Annals of Tourism Research.* 10, 268-70.

_____. 1983b. "Health and pleasure at Preston Springs" *Recreation Research Review.* 10(3), 57-61.

_____. 1988. Implications of climatic change for tourism and recreation in Ontario. *Climate Change Digest 88-05.* (Downsview: Environment Canada, Atmospheric Environment Service).

Wall, G. and Knapper, C. 1981. *Impacts of the Tutankhamun exhibition on Metropolitan Toronto.* (Waterloo: University of Waterloo, Department of Geography).

Wall, G. and Sinnott, J. 1980. "Urban recreational and cultural facilities as tourist attractions" *Canadian Geographer* 24, 50-59.

Wall, G. and Wright, C. 1977. *The environmental impact of outdoor recreation.* (Waterloo: University of Waterloo, Department of Geography).

Wall, G., Dudycha, D., and Hutchinson J. 1985. "Point pattern analyses of accommodation in Toronto" *Annals of Tourism Research.* 12, 603-18.

Walsh, R.G. 1977. "Effects of improved research methods on the evaluation of recreational benefits" in *Outdoor recreation: Advances in applications of economics.* General Technical Report WO-2. (Washington, D.C.: U.S. Forest Service).

Weaver, T. and Dale, D. 1978. "Trampling effects of hikers, motorcycles and horses in meadows and forests" *Journal of Applied Ecology.* 15, 451-57.

Webster's II new Riverside dictionary. (Boston: Hughton Mifflin Company).

Wennergren, E.G. and Johnston, W.E. 1977. "Economic concepts relevant to the study of outdoor recreation" in *Outdoor recreation: Advances in applications of economics.* General Technical Report WO-2. (Washington, D.C.: U.S. Forest Service).

White, G.F. 1966. "Formation and role of public sttitudes" in H. Jarrett ed. *Environmental quality in a growing economy.* (Baltimore: Johns Hopkins Press) 105-27.

White, T.H. 1975. "The relative importance of education and income as predictors of outdoor recreation participation" *Journal of Leisure Research.* 7, 191-99.

Wightman, D. and Wall, G. 1985. "The spa experience at Radium Hot Springs" *Annals of Tourism Research.* 12, 393-416.

Wilder, R.L. n.d. *Parks and recreation -- An economic justification.* (Washington, D.C.: National Recreation and Park Association).

Willard, D.E. and Marr, J.W. 1970. "Effects of human activities on alpine tundra ecosystems in Rocky Mountain National Park, Colorado" *Biological Conservation.* 2, 257-65.

_____. 1971. "Recovery of alpine tundra under protection after damage by human activities in the Rocky Mountains of Colorado" *Biological Conservation.* 3, 181-90.

Williams, D.R. and Huffman, M.G. 1985. "Research specializations a factor in backcountry trail choice" in *Proceedings -- National Wilderness Research Conference: Current Research.* (Ogden, Utah: USDA Forest Service, Intermountain Research Station) 339-44.

Witt, P.A. and Goodale, T.L. 1981. "The relationship between barriers to leisure enjoyment and family stages" *Leisure Sciences.* 4, 29-49.

Wolfe, R.I. 1952. "Wasaga Beach -- the divorce from the geographic environment" *Canadian Geographer.* 2, 57-66.

_____. 1964a. "Perspective on outdoor recreation: A bibliographical survey" *Geographical Review.* 54, 203-38.

_____. 1964b. *A use classification of parks by analysis of extremes.* Research Report, No. 134. (Downsview: Ontario Department of Highways).

_____. 1966. *Parameters of recreational travel in Ontario: A progress report,* Report RB11. (Toronto: Ontario Department of Highways).

_____. 1977. "Summer cottages in Ontario: Purpose-built for an inessential purpose" in J.T. Coppock ed. *Second homes: Curse or blessing?* (Oxford: Pergamon) 17-33.

Wong, R.A.G. 1979. Recreational resource use conflict: Perceived conflict between cross-country skiers and snowmobilers. M.A. thesis, University of Alberta, Department of Geography.

World Tourism Organization. 1984. *Social and cultural impact of tourism movements.* (Madrid, Spain).

Yates, B. and Lee, J. 1984. *Defining the role of the public and private sector.* (Victoria: British Columbia Recreation and Sport Branch).

Young, G. 1973. *Tourism: Blessing or blight?* (Harmondsworth: Penguin).

Yu, J.M. 1980. "The empirical development of typology for describing leisure behavior on the basis of participation patterns" *Journal of Leisure Research.* 12, 309-20.

Zimmermann, E.W. 1964. *Introduction to world resources.* Ed. H.L. Hunker. (New York: Harper and Row).

Zube, E.H., Sell, J.L., and Taylor, J.G. 1982. "Landscape perception: Research, application and theory" *Landscape Planning.* 9, 1-33.

Zuzanek, J. 1978. "Social differences in leisure behavior: Measurement and interpretation" *Leisure Sciences.* 1, 271-93.

Index

250